Neoclassical and 19th Century Architecture/2

Robin Middleton / David Watkin

Neoclassical and 19th Century Architecture/2

The Diffusion and Development of Classicism and the Gothic Revival

Electa/RIZZOLI
NEW YORK

Photographs: Bruno Balestrini
Drawings: Studio Lodolo-Süss
Layout: Arturo Anzani

Library of Congress Cataloging-in-Publication Data
Middleton, Robin.
  Neoclassical and 19th century architecture.

  (History of world architecture)
  Translation of Architettura moderna.
  Bibliography: p.
  Includes index.
    Contents: v. 1. The enlightenment in France and
in England—v. 2. The diffusion and development
of classicism and the Gothic revival.
    1. Neoclassicism (Architecture) 2. Architecture,
Modern—17th-18th centuries. 3. Architecture,
Modern—19th century. I. Watkin, David, 1941—
II. Title. III. Title: Neoclassical and nineteenth
century architecture. IV series.
NA600.M513 1987 724 87-42631
ISBN 0-8478-0850-5 (pbk.: v. 1)
ISBN 0-8478-0851-3 (pbk.: v. 2)

Paperback edition first published
in the United States of America in 1987
by Rizzoli International Publications, Inc.
597 Fifth Avenue, New York, NY 10017

This volume is the redesigned paperback
of the original Italian edition published in 1977
by Electa S.p.A., Milan,
and the English edition published in 1980
by Harry N. Abrams, Inc., New York

Printed in Italy

TABLE OF CONTENTS

The chronological span of this book is 1750 to 1870. We have avoided reliance on the misleading descriptive term neoclassicism *and have emphasized the importance of both the rationalist theory developed in France and the Picturesque movement in England. The book is primarily a history of architecture and thus does not cover many of the important developments that took place during the years in question in town planning, transport, and engineering. We also felt it impossible, in a single volume, to give equal attention to each period and country. Thus, the reader will find less on England than on France, for English architecture has been examined by such historians as John Summerson, Henry-Russell Hitchcock, and Nikolaus Pevsner, whereas French architecture—particularly of the nineteenth century—has been much less extensively investigated. Architecture rests on intellectual as well as material foundations, and we hope that fresh light will be shed on the period by our emphasis on the theories and ideas that so often lay behind the new movements.*

Robin Middleton
David Watkin

Chapter Six
LATER CLASSICAL AND ITALIANATE ARCHITECTURE

FRANCE: *Percier and Fontaine to Garnier*

Building continued sporadically after the Revolution in France, but it was scarcely an auspicious time for architecture. There was little opportunity and a conspicuous lack of vigor in design. Arrangements and patterns evolved earlier in the eighteenth century were repeated to produce an array of neat, charming, and altogether well-planned and ornamented houses on the outskirts of Paris. But this was not the sort of activity to stimulate new talents. Architects turned to other occupations. Charles-Pierre-Joseph Normand (1765–1840) and Théodore Ollivier became engravers; others served as surveyors and military engineers in Napoleon's endless campaigns. Only Napoleon was able to act as a great patron, but not until after the coup d'état of 1799 that brought him finally to power. Most of the architects he employed on his larger projects had already made names for themselves before the Revolution. Rondelet restored once again the church of Ste.-Geneviève (now renamed the Panthéon). Chalgrin, who had started work on the Palais du Luxembourg in 1787, transformed its interior completely between 1803 and 1807 for the use of the Senate. The Salle du Sénat (disastrously redesigned in 1836 by Chalgrin's pupil Alphonse-Henri de Gisors) and the great extended stair with which Chalgrin replaced Rubens's gallery were unquestionably dramatic in a late eighteenth-century sort of way, but they were by then in the nature of established solutions. Chalgrin's Arc de Triomphe, the foundation stone of which was laid on August 18, 1806, was finer, though not as first conceived. He aimed, then, at the accepted grandeur of ancient Roman buildings, incorporating freestanding decorative columns, statues, and bas-relief panels. His projects of 1810, however, were more austere, and, as were all Chalgrin's works, faultless in proportion. Later Blouet was to complete the attic story of the Arc, destroying in the process the balance of Chalgrin's restrained classicism. Bélanger provided a design for an ambitious cast-iron dome for the court of the Halle aux Blés in 1805, two years after Legrand's and Molinos's timber dome burned down. He also began a very noble *abattoir* at Rochechouart in 1809, while Brongniart, as we have seen, started on the Bourse in the year before. Between 1806 and 1810 Gondoin, together with Jean-Baptiste Lepère (1761–1844), erected his most famous, if least enterprising, work, the Colonne Vendôme.

There were newcomers, though their architecture was even less precise and alive than that of the established practitioners. After much fuss and intrigue and no little competition, Ledoux's pupil Alexandre-Pierre Vignon (1763–1828) was commissioned in 1807 to build the Madeleine, incorporating some of the foundation of Contant d'Ivry's church. The result was a lifeless paraphrase of an antique Roman temple. The interior, in which the theme of the Roman Bath was developed with dogged determination and success of a kind, was the work of Jean-Jacques-Marie Huvé (1783–1852), who took over in 1828 and completed most of the building twelve years later, though decoration continued until 1845.

344. Jean-François-Thérèse Chalgrin, Palais du Luxembourg, Paris, Salle du Sénat, 1803–7

345. Jean-François-Thérèse Chalgrin, Palais du Luxembourg, Paris, grand staircase, 1803–7

211

On the same axis, on the opposite bank of the Seine, Bernard Poyet—the architect admired by Durand—added a giant Corinthian portico to the old Palais-Bourbon (now the Chambre des Députés), in 1808. This, once again, was intended to commemorate the architecture of ancient Rome, but it is patently a facade, lacking in all solid dignity. Two years later Jacques-Charles Bonnard (1765–1818), who had worked for the Abbé de Saint-Non in Italy, began the vast Ministère des Affaires Étrangères (afterward called the Cour des Comptes but now demolished) on the banks of the Seine. This was an Italianate building with round-arched windows, applied columns, and a lot more besides, of a sort that had been attempted by a French architect only once before—in 1776, by P.-A. Pâris for the Prince Bishop of Basel's palace at Porrentruy (never completed). But to the younger generation Bonnard's building was a revelation. They rioted in 1826 when the secretary of the Académie disparaged Bonnard's work in an oration. The Italianate mode, however, was not the creation of Bonnard. He had merely applied it with a greater degree of richness. The architects responsible for the new manner of the early nineteenth century were Charles Percier (1764–1838) and Pierre-François-Léonard Fontaine (1762–1853), whom we have already encountered as an emulator of Boullée and also as the notorious runner-up for the Prix de Rome in 1785. Both were pupils of Antoine-François Peyre (1739–1823), younger brother of Marie-Joseph Peyre. Percier, in fact, did win the Grand Prix in 1786. By the following year Percier and Fontaine were both in Rome, where they met Bonnard and together explored the celebrated antiquities and the ancient aqueducts. But they examined also Renaissance palaces, not only in Rome but in Florence as well, and the villas and farms of Tuscany. These were to be their hostages for the future. When they returned to France they studied French Renaissance architecture, and even the Gothic style, for their tastes were eclectic. With wonderful finesse and tact, they were able to subordinate these strains from the past within the system of forms and measures that they had inherited from the eighteenth century, to produce a new style of some distinction and novelty, yet one that was perfectly decorous. Together they became modish designers of interiors. One of these was so admired by the Empress Josephine that she commissioned them, in 1799, to rebuild her newly acquired house at Malmaison. They proposed a scheme that was Palladian in inspiration, but so enlarged and extended beyond sensible measure that it aroused Napoleon's rage; instead, they redecorated the existing house with marvelous flair, taking up details from Bélanger's Bagatelle and Pâris's designs for the Menus-Plaisirs, and thus fashioning the style that was later to be identified as Empire, the epitome of neoclassical taste. Absolutely, it was not new; what they had done was to rely on a greater sense of interval, and a hardness of outline and a crispness of detail, to effect the apparent change. Color was another aspect of their adaptation: They used more strong and acid tones than usual, chrome yellows, bottle greens, and azure blues, contrasting them with ebony or dark mahogany wood and bronze-gilt

347. Jean-François-Thérèse Chalgrin,
Arc de Triomphe, Paris, begun 1806,
completed 1836 by G.-A. Blouet

appliqués. Napoleon was much impressed. Before they quarreled with
Josephine as to the merits of a Picturesque garden, they had been made
Architects des Palais du Premier et Deuxième Consuls. Their official career began
in January 1801.

For Napoleon they worked exhaustively. They were ultimately responsible for the administration of his extensive proposals for the reorganization
of Paris—the introduction of new roads, markets, and fountains, and the
dispersal of the *abattoirs* and cemeteries to the periphery. They restored and
decorated for him the old royal palaces at St.-Cloud, Compiègne, Fontainebleau and Le Raincy, Eu and Rambouillet, and throughout Europe prepared
palaces for him and his nominees and family. Percier and Fontaine worked
for the whole Bonaparte tribe. But their best efforts were expended on the
Louvre and the Tuileries. They began in 1801 with the Tuileries,
introducing a magnificent array of apartments, in style representing a
continuation of the old Menus-Plaisirs, but wonderfully resourceful and
distinctive. These were all destroyed in 1870 with the demolition of the
Tuileries palace. In the same year they prepared designs for linking the
Tuileries with the Louvre; the Rue de Rivoli and the related Rue des
Pyramides are the results of these efforts. By 1808 they had started on the
interiors of the Louvre itself, where their crisp and inventive but altogether
static details may still be admired. Their greater ambitions were revealed
in 1811 when they designed a gigantic palace, larger even than Versailles,
on the heights of Chaillot for Napoleon's baby son, the Roi de Rome. This
was started, as was an equally gargantuan scheme on the opposite bank of
the Seine, in front of the École Militaire, for a series of four-square buildings
serving as a center of learning—an archive, a university, and an École des
Beaux-Arts. Here the dreams of Durand might have been realized. Percier
and Fontaine were his worthy followers, both as practitioners and as
teachers. They—or rather Percier—taught a whole generation of architects:
Augustin-Nicolas Caristié (1793–1862), François Debret (1777–1850),
A.-H. de Gisors (1796–1866), Huvé, Louis-Hippolyte Lebas (1782–1867),
Achille-François-Rene Leclère (1785–1853), Jean-Baptiste-Ciceron Lesueur
(1749–1883), and Louis-Tullius-Joachim Visconti (1791–1853) are only
some of their better-known pupils. But their teaching, though altogether
sensible and tolerant, as one might expect, was lax. Their followers had few
firm convictions, and even fewer ideas. They relied for inspiration on those
books that Percier and Fontaine published in successive years to enlarge the
French classical repertoire so that it would accommodate a mixed Italianate
style—the *Palais, maisons, et autres édifices modernes dessinés à Rome,* of 1798,
and the *Choix des plus célèbres maisons de plaisance de Rome et de ses environs,*
of 1809. Their own designs were illustrated in their *Recueil de décorations
intérieures,* of 1801, and their *Résidences de Souverains . . . de France, d'Allemagne,
de Suède, de Russie . . .,* written in 1833.

It is scarcely to be wondered at that architects felt without strong guidance
or convictions at the end of Napoleon's regime. Neither Louis XVIII nor

Charles X was much interested in architecture, and they made no attempt
to emulate Napoleon. "Il était un bon locataire", Louis XVIII remarked
of Napoleon, and decided to alter nothing at the Tuileries. Leadership in
architecture passed into the hands of the newly reestablished Académie des
Beaux-Arts and the closely related Conseil Général des Bâtiments Civils.
This, in effect, resulted in the dominance of one man, Antoine-Chrysostome
Quatremère de Quincy, *Secrétaire Perpétuel de l'Académie des Beaux-Arts* from
1816 to 1839. Quatremère de Quincy was an unsuccessful sculptor who
failed to win the Grand Prix but nonetheless traveled to Italy, where he
became friendly with such men as Jacques-Louis David, Antonio Canova,
and Sir William Hamilton. He was a great champion of Greek art, but this
was a distant ideal, and in practical matters he preferred to rely on his
knowledge of Roman antiquity. This was the model he upheld for French

348. Alexandre-Pierre Vignon, the
Madeleine, Paris, 1807–45

349. Jean-Jacques-Marie Huvé, the
Madeleine, Paris, interior, 1825–45

350. Charles Percier and Pierre-
François-Léonard Fontaine, Château
de Malmaison (Rueil-Malmaison),
library, 1799–1803

351. Charles Percier and Pierre-François-Léonard Fontaine, Château de Malmaison (Rueil-Malmaison), bedroom of the Empress Josephine, 1799–1803

352. Charles Percier and Pierre-François-Léonard Fontaine, Château de Malmaison (Rueil-Malmaison), music room, 1799–1803

architects. He determined that only those architects who had traveled to Italy and inspected its antique remains for themselves should be employed on official commissions. Naturally, he was not altogether successful in this. But through the years he did impose his doctrinaire ideals with extraordinary strictness. Hundreds, probably thousands, of uninspired and rigid buildings—churches, *mairies, palais de justice,* barracks, prisons, and hospitals—attest to his limited tastes. The epitome of this taste, perhaps, is the Palais de Justice in Lyons, by Louis-Pierre Baltard (1764–1846), with a facade made up of an unbroken line of twenty-four giant Corinthian columns—the prototype of that official architecture so favored in Washington, D.C., even today. The Salle des Pas Perdus, consisting of a succession of neatly defined, low-domed spaces, has just that added variety and interest that Quatremère de Quincy was to admire later in life. His early aims are represented by the works of Étienne-Hippolyte Godde (1781–1869), who did not win the Grand Prix, but nonetheless showed in such churches as St.-Pierre-du-Gros-Caillou (1822-30), Notre-Dame-de-Bonne-Nouvelle (1823–30), and St.-Denys-du-St.-Sacrement (1826-35), all in Paris, that a routine and lackluster classical spirit could be cultivated in France even more successfully than in Rome. Quatremère de Quincy could not but applaud. These are the embodiments of the architecture hinted at in the backgrounds of David's paintings. The Imperial Roman opulence of Huvé's interiors at the Madeleine, initiated in 1828, was not to Quatremère de Quincy's liking. Even less so were the rich decorations introduced in the following year into the Chambre des Députés by another pupil of Percier and Fontaine, Jules-Jean-Baptiste de Joly (1788–1865). His adjoining vestibule and related Salon du Roi, built by 1833, and the richly decorated and gilded library (both, incidentally, incorporating paintings done by Delacroix from 1838 to 1847) seemed to Quatremère de Quincy utterly vulgar. But he was not altogether opposed, as we have seen, to some liveliness of decoration or color in architecture. He always encouraged mural painting. His *Jupiter Olympien,* which was published in 1815, gave evidence of some ability to rethink conventions concerning the antique and would serve to stir the color controversy. Seven years later he organized a competition to provide a model for a new and marginally richer architecture than such men as Godde were able to offer. This was to be carefully controlled. The plan was to remain based on the established basilican pattern, but something of the old splendor of San Paolo fuori le Mura in Rome was introduced. The competition was won by a pupil of Percier and Fontaine, Louis-Hippolyte Lebas. Quatremère de Quincy was always distrustful of their students, and his misgivings in this instance were justified. Lebas built the church of Notre-Dame-de-Lorette during the next thirteen years, starting with a basilican plan, erecting on it a portico that was said to be proportioned on that of the Doric Temple of Hercules, at Cora in Italy, but that was endowed, nonetheless, with florid Corinthian columns. The interior was an extraordinary *pasticcio* of an Early Christian basilica, painted and gilded everywhere,

he passed it on to Hittorff. Hittorff added brightly painted porticos to his Rotonde des Panoramas (1838-39) and, as we have seen, to the Cirque National—both on the Champs-Élysées—and elaborately decorated the Cirque d'Hiver, Boulevard des Filles-du-Calvaire. However, his real opportunity to demonstrate how the studied and serious classical style of the early nineteenth century might be transformed, but in conformity with antique precedents, came with the completion of St.-Vincent-de-Paul, overlooking the Place Lafayette, Paris. This church was sketched first, in 1824, by Hittorff's father-in-law, Lepère, who had worked with Gondoin on the Colonne Vendôme. But building was not begun in earnest until 1830, by which time Hittorff had revised the design completely. It is the largest basilican church of the period, with two tiers of columns inside supporting an open, timber-trussed roof. Externally it is preceded by a large pedimented portico set against a flat masonry wall with a central projection, and is flanked by two square towers. The site and the setting lend some grandeur to the composition, but all feeling for mass is lacking and the detailing is disappointingly thin. Internally the same criticisms would apply were the interior not transformed into a riot of strong color: The columns are apricot; above, there are frescoes by a host of Ingres's pupils, including Jean-Hippolyte Flandrin; the roof trusses are brilliant blues and reds, all scattered with gold, in imitation of those at Monreale cathedral, which Hittorff saw as a latter-day expression of what he had imagined as the colorful architecture of Greek antiquity. Even today this interior is vibrant. For the outside Hittorff proposed something parallel. In 1846 he started to cover the wall of the portico with large, brightly colored enameled plaques, painted by Gros's pupil Jollivet. This panorama of biblical scenes was intended to extend over the entire surface. Seven of these were eventually put up, but the clergy was scandalized by the nudity of Adam and Eve—and everyone else by the blaze of color—and in 1861, at the clergy's behest, the plaques were taken down, though they still survive in a depot at Ivry-sur-Seine.

Hittorff built a great deal besides. Between 1836 and 1840 he flattened out Gabriel's Place Louis XV, by then renamed the Place de la Concorde, topped the pavilions with heavy statues, and added the obelisk, the fountains (of cast-iron), and the lamp standards. These were all originally gilt. He embellished the Champs-Élysées with an array of fountains, shelters, restaurants, and the circus and panorama already mentioned. Then in 1855 he designed the houses around the Place de l'Étoile and began what is now the Avenue Foch, leading to the Bois de Boulogne, where he began excavating the lakes. To the east of the Place de la Concorde he extended the Rue de Rivoli, designing the first of the large-scale *hôtels* in Paris on the American pattern, the Grand Hôtel des Chemins de Fer (now the Grands Magasins du Louvre). Opposite Perrault's Louvre facade he built the ungainly Mairie du 1er between 1855 and 1861, as a pendant to St.-Germain-l'Auxerrois, which he was forced to paraphrase. He found no

that was both fastidious and coarse. He employed a great many sculptors and painters, and the church became at once a focus of artistic attention—an attention, when related to the ideas put forward in the *Jupiter Olympien,* that was to undermine, if not destroy, much that Quatremère de Quincy had stood for.

Hittorff, the exponent of a highly colored image of Greek antiquity, was the agent of change. In 1834, ten years after his return from Italy, and at the height of the quarrel concerning the application of color in Greek architecture, he designed two side altars for Notre-Dame-de-Lorette, gilded, pedimented affairs that incorporated panels of vividly colored enamel. The commission had been offered first to Jean-Auguste-Dominique Ingres, but

*XXV. Charles Percier and Pierre
François-Léonard Fontaine, Château
de Malmaison (Rueil-Malmaison),
bedroom of the Empress Josephine
1799–1803*

XXVI. Charles Percier and Pierre
François-Léonard Fontaine, Château
de Malmaison (Rueil-Malmaison),
music room, 1799–1803

354. Charles Percier and Pierre-
François-Léonard Fontaine, Palais
Royal, Paris, Galerie d'Orléans,
1829

355. *Charles Percier and Pierre-François-Léonard Fontaine, Palais Royal, Paris, staircase in the Montpensier wing, 1829*

356. *Charles Percier and Pierre-François-Léonard Fontaine, Rue de Rivoli and Place des Pyramides, Paris, begun 1803*

enjoyment in this task, for he loathed the Gothic style. But he was no favorite of Baron Haussmann, the all-powerful *Préfet de la Seine,* who was intent to embarrass him. They were involved soon enough in bitter litigation about the works in the Bois de Boulogne and the payment of fees. Hittorff won, but Haussmann had his revenge. By changing the alignments of the streets he saw to it that Hittorff's greatest work, the Gare du Nord, designed in 1859 and started two years later, did not act as a terminal feature to a main boulevard.

The Gare du Nord was a fitting conclusion to Hittorff's career. It reflected faithfully the disparities of his approach to architecture. The planning was excellent and sufficiently flexible to allow for the gradual transformation from a mixed goods and passenger terminal to one for people alone. The construction of the sheds was simple, economical, daring, and successful— A.-R. Polonceau's newly developed gable trusses were used, and all the ironwork was made in Glasgow. But the architecture of the facade was an assorted medley of classical motifs, all of unrelated scale, used neither correctly nor with sufficient panache to transcend the lack of convention. Hittorff was not a creative architect. Not one of his buildings is resolved. He applied decoration, usually of a meager kind, in an attempt to disguise his failure to compose convincingly, but even here he appeared to be fiddling. He was, however, wonderfully adventurous in other respects, especially as a technical innovator. In 1828 he introduced safety curtains of iron into the Théâtre de l'Ambigu Comique (demolished 1966). For the roof of his Rotonde des Panoramas he adapted the principle of the suspension bridge; for that of the Cirque National he employed an extremely elegant lattice timber truss, and repeated this with an even greater refinement at the Cirque d'Hiver. His prowess in this respect was always acclaimed and was slowly emulated. And his archaeological theories, too, though they had little enough to do with archaeology, opened the eyes of a whole generation of architects in France to the possibility of breaking from the established classical routine and developing a new architecture. The use of applied color in architecture after 1830 was a sign of rebellion.

The rebels of the 1830s are usually accounted as Guillaume-Abel Blouet, Émile-Jacques Gilbert, Félix-Jacques Duban, Henri Labrouste, Louis-Joseph Duc, and Léon Vaudoyer. But their contributions to architecture were very different and quite distinct.

Blouet (1795–1853) and Gilbert (1793–1874) emerged first. Blouet trained with Delespine, Gilbert with Durand at the École Polytechnique and then with Vignon at the École des Beaux-Arts. They both won the Grand Prix, Blouet in 1821, Gilbert in the year following; they worked together in Rome and again, after their return, when Blouet was appointed architect to the Arc de Triomphe in 1831, with Gilbert as his *Inspecteur.* Blouet, a protégé of Quatremère de Quincy, had been sent on an official mission to Greece in 1828; when his restoration studies of the Doric temple on Aegina were published in 1838, the temple was revealed in bright color, primarily

blue and red. Gilbert made his attestation in the brilliantly colored interior of the chapel that forms the focus of his vast and very austere Asile d'Aliénés at Charenton, on the edge of Paris, built between 1838 and 1845. But Blouet's and Gilbert's idea of reform in architecture was based on nothing so superficial as the application of color.

They thought to enrich architecture by making moral and social aims determine its arrangement, as never before. Like many intellectuals of their generation, they were sustained by the humanitarian ideas of Saint-Simon and Charles Fourier. Saint-Simon was not at first much interested in architecture or even in art—"Il n'y a aujourd'hui d'hommes qui se vouent à la poésie que ceux qui ne peuvent pas réussir dans les travaux de l'intelligence," he wrote in 1813 in his *Mémoire sur la science de l'homme.* But by the year of his death, in 1825, when he wrote *Le nouveau christianisme,* he had reserved a place for architects among the leaders of society, alongside the engineers and the factory owners. He made no positive proposals himself, although his disciples, led by Émile Barrault, were to propound a doctrine at both the Saint-Simonist expositions of 1828 and 1830, and, especially, in the pamphlet *Aux artistes: du passé et de l'avenir des beaux-arts,* issued in 1830, which held that the history of the arts followed a succession of "organic" and "critical" periods, the organic being identified as pre-Periclean Greek and that of the Middle Ages, expressive both of a unity of religious belief and social aspiration. The early Greek temple and the Gothic cathedral were thus seen as embodiments of integrated societies. Victor Hugo's architectural ideas, contained, in particular, in the second edition of his *Notre-Dame de Paris,* of 1832, were a direct response to such propaganda. But the Saint-Simonists themselves did not pursue these ideas to any consequence, nor were they to interpret them with any resounding success. Under the leadership of Barthélemy-Prosper Enfantin, a group of Saint-Simon's followers did set out in 1834 to build a city for the workers digging the Suez Canal. The plan of the city was in the shape of a human figure, the buildings corresponding to the functions of the body, administrative buildings and scientific institutes at the head, academies and temples at the heart, and so on. But the disciples did not get far with their plans. They were decimated by cholera. Fourier, however, suggested an architectural form for his ideas, at first reluctantly, but by 1829, when he published *Le nouveau monde industriel et sociétaire,* he included a sketch plan for one of his communes, which he called a *phalange.* This appeared as a bird's-eye perspective on the title page of *Le phalanstère* in June 1832, the year in which an attempt was made to found such a commune at Condé-sur-Vesgre, near Rambouillet. Victor Considerant was to depict his *phalanstère* as a palace of Versailles in 1834 in *Considérations sociales sur l'architecture.* But the opportunity for building such a community was to be rare. Only one was built in France, André Godin's *familistère* at Guise, begun in 1859, still standing and still working. No architect was involved. Godin employed a former art student, E. André, to prepare the drawings. The type was to

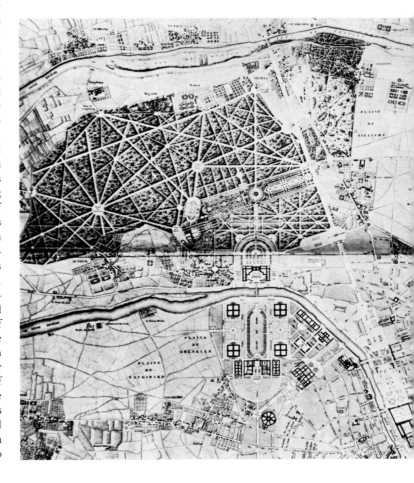

become familiar in America—where Godin himself financed a phalanstery in Texas in 1853—but in France such experiments were so isolated and of so specific a nature that they had only an indirect influence on architecture. Later low-cost houses for workers, notably those built by Émile Müller for the Société Mulhousienne des Cités Ouvrières, beginning in 1853, and even his pupil Émile Cacheux's minimal houses, put up in Auteuil (Villa Émile Meyer and Villa Dietz Monnin) and elsewhere in Paris in the 1880s, all aimed to provide single dwellings with gardens, not collectives. The workers were to buy their houses and to become respectable members of the propertied classes.

Gilbert's and Blouet's model was provided by C. B. Beccaria in Italy and John Howard in England, who in the late eighteenth century had initiated

362. Louis-Hippolyte Lebas, Notre-Dame-de-Lorette, Paris, 1823–36

363. Louis-Hippolyte Lebas, Notre-Dame-de-Lorette, Paris, interior, 1823–36

364. Étienne-Hippolyte Godde, St.-Pierre-du-Gros-Caillou, Paris, interior, 1822–30

365. Jacques-Ignace Hittorff and Jean-Baptiste Lepère, St.-Vincent-de-Paul, Paris, 1824, 1830–46

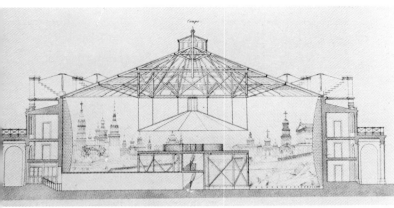

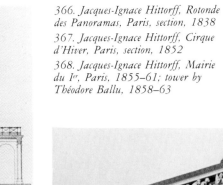

366. Jacques-Ignace Hittorff, Rotonde des Panoramas, Paris, section, 1838

367. Jacques-Ignace Hittorff, Cirque d'Hiver, Paris, section, 1852

368. Jacques-Ignace Hittorff, Mairie du Ier, Paris, 1855–61; tower by Théodore Ballu, 1858–63

369. Jacques-Ignace Hittorff and Jules Jollivet, project for the decoration of the portico of St.-Vincent-de-Paul with enameled panels, one of which was painted in 1846, with six more to follow in 1852, all being taken down in 1861

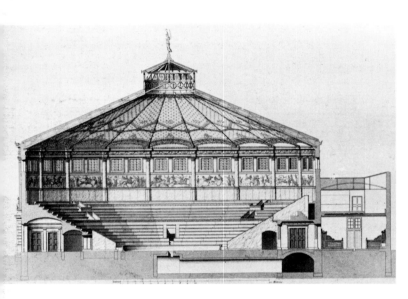

370. Jacques-Ignace Hittorff and
Jean-Baptiste Lepère, St.-Vincent-de-
Paul, Paris, interior, 1830–46

371. Jacques-Ignace Hittorff, Gare
du Nord, Paris, 1861–65
372. Jacques-Ignace Hittorff, Gare
du Nord, Paris, detail of the sheds,
1861–65

a series of penal reforms that resulted in the gradual separation of criminals from the sick and the insane. Criminals, in turn, were categorized according to sex, age, and the nature of their crimes, so that by degrees the only means of ensuring that they did not adversely influence one another was to provide each with an individual cell—a self-contained unit, fully serviced, that might ensure total isolation and thus opportunity for moral redemption. Many prisoners went mad under these conditions and regrouping began once again. The architectural image that embodied these ideals was Jeremy Bentham's Panopticon. Though never realized, this was reflected in the arrangement of the ill-fated penitentiary erected at Millbank in London, between 1812 and 1821. The aim was the continuous surveillance of all prisoners from a single observation post; the obvious expression of this was the radial plan. This was introduced into France in 1825, when Lebas, architect of Notre-Dame-de-Lorette, won a competition for a model prison on the site of La Roquette in Paris. Though he had visited Millbank, it is evident that he had not grasped its rationale. He produced a plan of giant formality, a hexagon with six wings linked to the center. There, he placed a chapel. Prison reformers soon realized that the building was unlikely to prove satisfactory. In 1830 a magistrate, G. de Beaumont, was sent with Alexis de Tocqueville to study prisons in America, where remarkably efficient systems of organization were being evolved, especially in Philadelphia. De Tocqueville spent too much time collecting material for *La démocratie en Amérique* (1835, 1840). By 1836 another tour of American prisons was needed; on this occasion the magistrate F. A. Demetz was provided with Blouet as his companion. At the same time Gilbert was appointed to design La Nouvelle Force at Mazas, together with Jean-François-Joseph Lecointe (1783–1858), an early associate of Hittorff. Work there started in 1843. The great period of prison reform had begun, and an architecture embodying the new humanitarian ideals was initiated.

Gilbert continued always to use the patterns of organization and the stylistic details that he had inherited from Durand, and so the change was not so much in any alteration of form or details as in a careful consideration of their use in relation to the function they were to perform. Nothing in Gilbert's architecture was done for effect. Everything had a straightforward raison d'être. His prison, which was opened in 1850, consisted of an administrative block linked to a domed rotunda—an observation post on one floor, a chapel on the next—from which radiated six wings at a forty-five-degree angle to one another, containing three floors of individual cells. Each cell was fully serviced with hot and cold water, a WC, and a heating and ventilation system. The organization of life in the prison determined the architecture in every way, as it had in that even more strictly utilitarian structure from which Gilbert derived many ideas, the Pentonville prison, put up in London between 1840 and 1842 by Major Joshua Jebb. But the prison at Mazas was not looked upon simply as a solution to some readily defined problem. "Le prison de Mazas," Adolphe Lance wrote in

373. Victor Considerant, project for a
phalanstère, 1834
374. André Godin and E. André,
familistère, Guise, begun 1859

375. André Godin and E. André,
familistère, Guise, interior court,
begun 1859

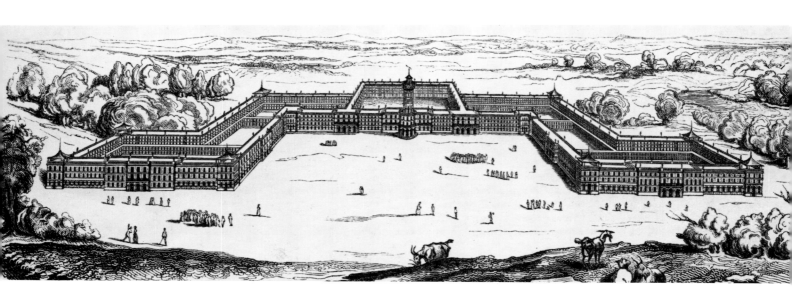

XXVIII. Félix-Jacques Duban,
Galerie d'Apollon, the Louvre, Paris,
1848–52

376. Louis-Hippolyte Lebas, house of
detention for juvenile offenders, Place
de la Roquette, Paris, plan, 1825

377. Guillaume-Abel Blouet, penal
farm colony, Mettray, near Tours,
plan, designed 1839

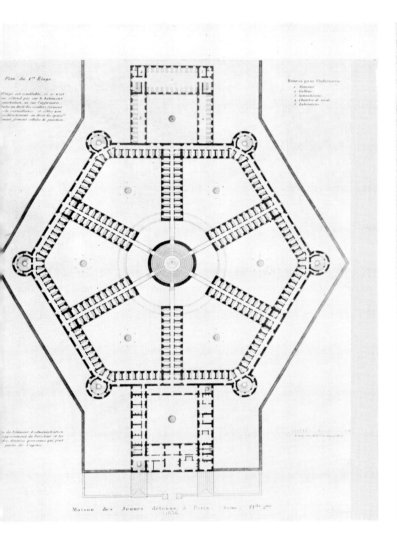

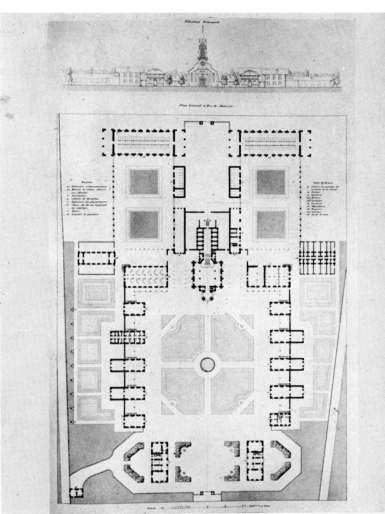

the *Encyclopédie d'architecture* in December 1853, "n'est pas exclusivement une bâtisse bien entendu et un instrument administratif, c'est une oeuvre d'art" (pp. 175–82).

Gilbert's other buildings were all expressions of humanitarian reform in administrative guise, often of the most repressive if well-meaning kind. The new theories on the treatment of the insane led to his appointment in 1838 as architect of the Asile d'Aliénés, built during the next seven years on the hillside at Charenton, to the east of Paris, in a series of long, terraced pavilions, linked by colonnades, with a chapel, as we have seen, forming the focus. The different types of madmen were isolated here within the individual pavilions, men to one side, women to the other. Police reforms resulted in Gilbert's Préfecture de la Police on the Île de la Cité in Paris, of 1862 to 1876. Hospital reforms produced his Hôtel-Dieu nearby, put up between 1864 and 1876 with the aid of his son-in-law, Arthur-Stanislas Diet (1827–1890), who also completed Gilbert's asylum and prefecture. By the time the Hôtel-Dieu was completed, the simple geometrical ideals of Durand had proved inadequate to such a building. Even before it was finished part was dismantled and much redesigned. The doctors were never to be satisfied. But the sheer regularity of the architecture, the elegance even of the colonnaded courts, are undeniably impressive. Gilbert's only other building was the morgue erected on the Pont St.-Michel, Paris, opposite the east end of Notre-Dame, from 1861 to 1863. This has long since been demolished.

Blouet pursued his utilitarian aims largely through teaching. In 1846, when L.-P. Baltard died, a change in approach was at last possible in the training at the École des Beaux-Arts, and Blouet was appointed to succeed him as *Professeur de Théorie de l'Architecture.* The following year he began publication of his *Supplément à la traité théorique et pratique de l'art de bâtir de Jean Rondelet,* which, as we have remarked, was largely a catalogue of early nineteenth-century engineering achievements. He was responsible for only one noteworthy work of architecture—a church at Fontainebleau and the attic story of the Arc de Triomphe apart—a penal farm colony at Mettray, near Tours, designed in 1839, finished a few years later. The architecture here consists of no more than a series of dull utilitarian dormitory pavilions set formally on either side of a nondescript church, mildly medieval in inspiration, with the farm buildings behind. Yet Michel Foucault has recognized the system of reform that was enacted within as the ultimate limit of coercion on humanitarian grounds. Blouet became thereby the accepted authority on prison architecture.

The remaining members of the group of reform, Duban, Labrouste, Duc, and Vaudoyer, were less doctrinaire in their attitudes: They upheld the ideals of Durand, Rondelet, and the Saint-Simonists but did not allow them full play in their architecture; they were more concerned to infuse them into a renewed classical tradition. All were Grand Prix winners, starting with Duban in 1823 and continuing to 1826, when Vaudoyer was awarded the

380. Émile-Jacques Gilbert and
Arthur-Stanislas Diet, Hôtel-Dieu,
Paris, 1864–76

381. Émile-Jacques Gilbert and
Arthur-Stanislas Diet, Hôtel-Dieu,
Paris, courtyard, 1864–76

prize. In Rome, Duban and Labrouste met Hittorff and Blouet; all of them met Gilbert, who served as their mentor. They formed a close-knit group and continued through life to collaborate and support one another. But their architecture revealed them as very different. Félix-Jacques Duban (1797–1870), who had trained under Percier, had a passion for intricate and lively surface decoration, though it is fair to note that he integrated it far more successfully into his compositions than did Hittorff. In 1832 he took over the building of the École des Beaux-Arts from his brother-in-law François Debres. The foundations were already laid, but the great building facing the court on the Rue Bonaparte is his. It is a compression of all his Italian learning. The triumphal arches of Rome, the Colosseum, and the Cancelleria are all hinted at in the facade; inside, the frescoes of Pompeii no less than those of Raphael are recalled. The glass-covered courtyard with its cast-iron columns was conceived and designed by Duban but put up only between 1871 and 1874 by Ernest-Georges Coquart. The court in front and at the side was equally an assemblage, of fragments of medieval and Renaissance buildings rescued by Alexander Lenoir for the Musée des Monuments Français. The whole was inordinately admired when it was completed, in particular the attic floor (for which Labrouste served as *Inspecteur*) and the treatment of the roof, which was regarded as something of a novelty. This was hipped with a prettily detailed iron ridgepiece. Duban's reputation was made. But he did not build much else of consequence, though his superb Italianate house at 7 Rue Tronchet, Paris, for the Swiss collector the Comte Pourtalès, is deserving of study. Duban was active largely as a restorer, starting with the Ste.-Chapelle in 1837, tackling then in turn the Château de Blois, that at Fontainebleau, and then the Louvre, where some richly modeled and gilded rooms survive to attest to his activity, together with some forlorn railings in the corners of the courtyard, for which he was ridiculed and therefore resigned. But in 1858 he did design a building of some nobility and largeness of scale, the extension to the École des Beaux-Arts on the Quai Malaquais. Curiously, critics who had spent years castigating him for the fussiness of his details thought this too bald and bold.

Pierre-François-Henri Labrouste (1801–1875) was an architect of greater consistency and refinement, and of far greater stature. The beginning of his active career, however, was to be long delayed. He was a student of Lebas and A.-L.-T. Vaudoyer but was not prepared to accept their academic ideals without the most painstaking independent investigation. In 1824 he won the Grand Prix with a design for a *tribunal de cassation.* In 1828 he sent, as his fourth-year *envoi* from Rome, a restoration study of the three Doric temples of Paestum. His meticulous measurements proved that C. M. Delagardette's *Ruines de Paestum,* of 1799, was altogether untrustworthy. This was an affront to academic dignity. Labrouste went further: He developed a theory on the history of the people who had built the temples and showed how their social aspirations were reflected in their architecture. One of the buildings, he argued, was not a temple, but a civic structure.

382. *Félix-Jacques Duban, Hôtel*
Pourtalès, Paris, 1836

383. *Félix-Jacques Duban, Hôtel*
Pourtalès, Paris, staircase, 1836

384. *Félix-Jacques Duban, École*
des Beaux-Arts, Paris, forecourt,
1832–40

385. Félix-Jacques Duban, École des
Beaux-Arts, Paris, façade on the Quai
Malaquais, 1858–62

386. Félix-Jacques Duban, Galerie
d'Apollon, the Louvre, Paris,
1848–52

He illustrated this, hip-roofed—decked with large paintings, trophies, and
inscriptions—as Jean Houel had done many years earlier, in 1787, in a
restoration study of one of the Doric temples of Agrigento, illustrated in
the fourth volume of his *Voyage pittoresque des îles de Sicile, de Malte, et de Lipari*.
But Labrouste went further; he added graffiti. He wished to penetrate to
the reality of the architecture, to present the buildings as they might really
have existed. Naturally, he applied color. Many of his assumptions were
wrong, but what roused the members of the Académie to fury was his
deliberate dismissal of the ideal. And he compounded this rude rejection
of established criteria in the following year, sending in as his fifth-year *envoi*
a design of a frontier bridge between Italy and France that was modeled
on a coarse Roman provincial work, the Flavian bridge at St.-Chamas, near
Marseilles. For almost ten years the members of the Académie saw to it that
he received no major commission. He became a student idol, and for
twenty-six years from 1830 directed the most austerely intellectual *atelier*
in Paris. Not one of his students won the Grand Prix. During this time he
entered and won a number of competitions for utilitarian buildings, a
Hospice d'Aliénés at Lausanne in 1837, a prison for Alessandria, Italy, in
1840, and an *abattoir* in Provins in 1841. None of these was built. His
opportunity came in October 1838, when he was appointed architect to the
new Bibliothèque Ste.-Geneviève, facing Soufflot's great church. There
were difficulties over the acquisition of the site, but in January 1840
Labrouste's initial scheme was approved in principle, though the revisions
were not settled for another two years and money not voted until 1843.
A final plan was approved in July 1844 after work on the foundation had
begun. The building, completed in December 1850, is very simple in
arrangement. It is a long rectangle, entered on the ground floor, with stack
rooms to the left, offices and rare books to the right. At the rear of the
building is a separate stair hall leading up to the reading room, which
occupies the whole of the upper level. This is a room of great dignity. The
effect is achieved by means of a completely independent system of cast-iron
columns and arches arranged to provide two long narrow naves, a spine
down the center, hinting at the "civic" temple at Paestum and also at the
medieval refectory at the former Abbaye de St.-Martin-des-Champs, Paris,
which his pupil Lassus had recently measured and which his friend Léon
Vaudoyer was about to turn into a library for the Conservatoire des Arts
et Métiers—an echo, one must assume, of Saint-Simonist theory. There is,
of course, nothing overtly Gothic about Labrouste's detailing. This, if
anything, recalls his visits to Pompeii. The exterior is even more noble and
purified. The arches inside are reflected in the arched openings of the upper
floor—windows above, infilling panels below, each of which is, in turn,
punctured by a small window to light the small workrooms arranged on the
perimeter within. The ground floor is pierced by a row of round-headed
windows and an equally reticent rounded doorway, decorated only with
lamps of learning. The division between the two floors was at first marked

387. Félix-Jacques Duban and
Ernest-Georges Coquart, École des
Beaux-Arts, Paris, covered interior
courtyard, designed 1863, built
1871–74

388. Pierre-François-Henri Labrouste,
Collège Ste.-Barbe, Bibliothèque
Ste.-Geneviève, and Keeper's house,
Paris, plans, 1840–50
389, 390. Pierre-François-Henri
Labrouste, Bibliothèque Ste.-Geneviève,
Paris, cross section and facade,
1842–50

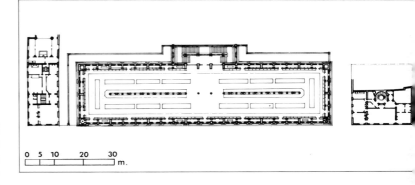

by no more than a strong horizontal molding, but the members of the *Conseil Général des Bâtiments Civils* thought this too sharp. When the stack rooms were raised nineteen centimeters (seven and one-half inches) Labrouste introduced the frieze of garlands, which echoes that on the Panthéon opposite and, more important, provides just that degree of movement required to render the facade less static. The silhouette is strong and square. On either side Labrouste designed two buildings that show how he could vary his arrangements to relate to their functions and yet ensure a unified whole. To the east are the staff quarters (1847–48); to the west the Collège Ste.-Barbe (1845–47), his old school, of which one of his brothers was head. Another brother, Théodore Labrouste (1799–1885), collaborated with him here as architect.

The facade of the Bibliothèque Ste.-Geneviève is altogether Labrouste's own—though it should be remarked how closely it relates to that of the École de Dessin, nearby, at 8 Rue Racine, designed and built between 1841 and 1844 by Simon-Claude Constant-Defeux (1801–1871), soon to be appointed *Professeur de Perspective* at the École des Beaux-Arts. Labrouste's facade, however, contains mnemonic references to many others that he had admired: Sir Christopher Wren's library at Cambridge; Leon Battista Alberti's Tempio Malatestiano in Rimini; Michelozzo's Banco Medaceo in Milan; and Jacopo Sansovino's Biblioteca Marciana in Venice. Even Egyptian temples are said to be embodied therein. This distillation of knowledge, which we have seen to lie also at the heart of Duban's work, was to be regarded as Labrouste's great contribution. From it, Neil Levin has suggested, was to spring that movement known somewhat inaccurately as the *néo-grec.* This flourished in France in the 1870s, though as late as 1911 the English architect A. E. Richardson was writing of it in the *Architectural Review* as the basis of renewal: "The true *néo-grec* style is the epitome of design, its interest a reflection of the tireless mind of the designer, who, having obtained a great many ideas on his subject, melts these very ideas in the crucible of his imagination, refining them again and again until the minted metal gleams refulgent. All material is the same to such a one. By these means and these alone, is original design possible" (July 1911, p. 28).

Labrouste did indeed succeed in restoring to nineteenth-century architecture some of the classic wholeness of that of the Greeks, but he aimed at a larger synthesis. He used his lifts, his heating and lighting systems, and his cast-iron columns not for utilitarian reasons alone, nor even to shock (though he did), but in order to relate his building organically to a nineteenth-century industrialized society, of which it was to be a noble expression. He intended it to represent the moment of achievement in a third organic period of architecture (the Saint-Simonists, as we have seen, had recognized two others, the Doric Greek and the Gothic). Neil Levine has recently shown that to make quite explicit his aim he decided in August 1848—just after the riots of July that marked the end of the July Monarchy, and just after the publication of the *Discours sur l'ensemble du positivisme* by

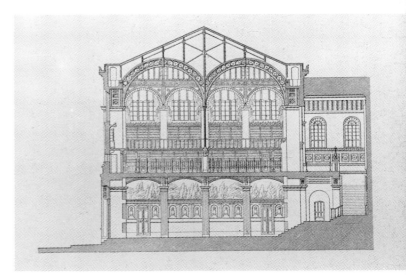

1859, he began work on the main reading room, filling part of the court for which Boullée had prepared his designs. This was Labrouste's second masterpiece. But magnificent as it is, it represents no more than an extension of ideas already worked out to perfection at the Bibliothèque Ste.-Geneviève. Only his stack room, tiered galleries of cast iron, built between 1862 and 1867, shows him grappling to renewed effect with his initiatory themes. This, to early twentieth-century eyes, was his greatest creation. Even his contemporaries admired it, and for much the same reasons. "Tout," Louis-Auguste Boileau wrote in 1871 in *Le fer*, "jusqu'au moindre boulon et rivet, devient un objet d'art de nouvelle création."

Labrouste's other works need not detain us: a handful of tombs; a farm colony at Mesnil-St.-Fermin (1845–48); a large and dull seminary at Rennes (1854–72; now the Faculté des Lettres), whose construction he did not supervise; a house for the banker Louis Fould (1856–58; now gone), another for M. Vilgruy (1860–65; still standing at 9 Rue François 1er, Paris), and the Hôtel Rouvenat (1861; now gone) at Neuilly-sur-Seine, all three disappointing pastiches of the architecture of Louis XIII's reign; a small boxlike villa for a jeweler, M. Thouret (1860; still standing, though altered, at 68 Boulevard Bourdon, Neuilly-sur-Seine); and the Hôtel de l'Administration du Chemin de Fer PLM, Paris (1861–63; 44 Rue Neuves-des-Mathurins), which he did not complete and which was torn down in part within a few years.

Louis-Joseph Duc (1802–1879) and Léon Vaudoyer (1803–1872) were, like Labrouste, to pour their energies into no more than one or two buildings. On his return from Rome in 1831, Duc became *Inspecteur* of the July Column, in the Place de la Bastille, under Jean-Antoine Alavoine (1778–1834). Soon he succeeded to the commission and at once started to apply decoration to Alavoine's sheer shaft. For the inauguration, in 1840, he designed some temporary pavilions, Greek in inspiration, brightly painted in yellow and red. In the same year he took over the work of completing the Palais de Justice in Paris. He did a great deal there, but the focus of all his effort was the Salle des Pas Perdus, referred to also as the Vestibule d'Assises, on the Rue de Harlay. This was started in 1857 and finished eleven years later, though much rebuilt and changed internally after damage suffered in 1870. Its hipped and heavily encrusted roof relates it at once to Duban's first building at the École des Beaux-Arts; its rhythmical bays, glazed above and filled in below with panels bearing inscriptions, link it to the Bibliothèque Ste.-Geneviève. But Duc wanted no fusion of structure, form, and expression. The structure—the arched vaulting within, the enclosing walls pierced with flattened arched openings—was to be seen and expressed as a humdrum working part of the architecture; the poetry, and all that mattered, were to arise from the artistic handling of an independent system of decoration, set in contradistinction to the rest. An array of columns derived from the Doric order, the highest form of expression in architecture, was thus set as a sculptural element in front of

Auguste Comte, Saint-Simon's renegade disciple—to inscribe the names of the authors whose works were contained within the library on the panels of the facade, arranging them in chronological order from Moses to Berzelius (a Swedish chemist much admired at the time, to whom Michel Eugène Chevreul, for instance, had dedicated his book on color theory), illustrating the progress of humanity from monotheism to scientism. The name of Psellus in the center just over the door, marking the meeting of east and west, the central stage in the history of metaphysics as outlined by Comte. The carving was completed in two months. The Bibliothèque Ste.-Geneviève thus became, demonstrably, a temple of all learning, a beginning of the new way. The letters were painted red.

Three years after completion, in 1853, Labrouste was appointed to succeed L.-T.-J. Visconti as architect at the Bibliothèque Nationale. He tidied up the existing conglomeration with skill and ruthlessness; then, in

ITZ
ZE
ON
TON
EURY
S CANTEMIR
ON

ISAAC DE BEAUSOBRE
J-ALB. FABRICIUS
BOERHAAVE
DOM EDM. MARTENE
MONTFAUCON
ROLLIN
J-B. ROUSSEAU
HALLEY

LESAGE
VAUVENARGUES
FRÉRET
MURATORI
D'AGUESSEAU
CORMONTAIGNE
HOLBERG
FIELDING

FONTENELLE
MONTESQUIEU
MOSHEIM
RÉAUMUR
RICHARDSON
CRÉBILLON
J-CHR. WOLFF
RAMEAU

TAYLOR
TROUIN

MASSILLON
VICO
POPE

LA CAILLE
CLAIRAUT
STERNE

393. Pierre-François-Henri Labrouste,
Bibliothèque Ste.-Geneviève, Paris,
reading room on the second floor,
1842–50

the wall. There was much more to Duc's composition—recollections of the Temple of Hathor in Egypt, details borrowed from the Temple of Athena Nike—but they need not be discussed. He aimed, clearly, to separate the practical and the expressive elements in architecture. And he was acclaimed. Viollet-le-Duc himself sat on the committee that awarded him the Prix de Cent Mille Francs in 1869 for the greatest work of art produced in France during the century.

Léon Vaudoyer made no such startling contribution to the development of architecture. He was closer to Labrouste, with whom he had been at school, and was said to be an intellectual, though we have little evidence of this. In 1838 he began work with his father, A.-L.-T. Vaudoyer, on the transformation of St.-Martin-des-Champs into the Conservatoire des Arts et Métiers. Work continued for years, right up to 1897, but it is of no great distinction or interest. The effects are contrived and awkward. But in 1845, the same year in which he took over from his father at St.-Martin-des-Champs, he prepared the first designs for his most important work, the cathedral at Marseilles. Its horizontal banding appeared on his drawings only in 1852, a year after John Ruskin had published the *Stones of Venice*. Ruskin's influence here would be unlikely, though the cathedral is an extraordinarily eclectic work. Vaudoyer's range of sources here was wider, and also more overt in expression, than that employed by his friends. The plan is thirteenth-century Gothic; the forms and many of the details are Byzantine. But the most notable influence of all is that of the Florence cathedral. Vaudoyer, less self-sure perhaps than Labrouste, aimed to provide an exemplar of a new architecture on the very threshold of an "organic period,"

at the end of an age of transition. He built on the basis of a Gothic plan because it was typically French. He selected Byzantine details because that style was a prelude to Gothic (he saw the pointed arch as a simple development of the arcade) and early Renaissance architecture because it marked the transition from an ecclesiastical authority to that of classical humanism. He had added, it seems, the Renaissance to the succession of "époques organiques" recognized by the Saint-Simonists. The result of all this thought and learning is not particularly impressive. Vaudoyer had insufficient feeling for the forms he was handling and assembled them without conviction. The building up of the docks alongside the cathedral has not enhanced its splendor, though in the interior something of the grand and thoughtfully—often brightly—colored architecture that he envisioned may still be experienced. The cathedral, finished only in 1893, was not much imitated in France, although echoes of it occur in the French colonies on the southern shores of the Mediterranean. And in Marseilles itself, Vaudoyer's pupil and assistant Henri-Jacques Espérandieu (1829–1874) took it as the point of departure for his first independent work of importance, the ungainly Notre-Dame-de-la-Garde (1853–64), which dominates the hill on the other side of the port. Vaudoyer's precepts, if we are to judge by Espérandieu's later buildings, all in Marseilles, were not of the stirring kind, nor were they sustaining. In 1858 Espérandieu started to design the Bibliothèque Municipale; four years later he began the flamboyant and highly ostentatious Palais de Longchamp, taking over ideas suggested a few years earlier by the sculptor Frédéric-Auguste Bartholdi. There was an ugly court case, but Espérandieu was exonerated. He went on, in 1862, to build the École des Beaux-Arts, which was a coarsened and undisciplined variant of Duban's; then followed the observatory and the *abattoir*. His works were florid and attractive only from afar; they give evidence of neither skill in design nor sustained intellectual effort.

Vaudoyer was no doubt aware of his inability to give convincing form to his ideas. He avoided building as long as he could—traveling at length in Germany, England, Spain, and Algeria, refusing many commissions—and was equally hesitant in expressing himself in writing. All his friends were agreed that he had thought long and hard about architecture, but he published no book on the subject, though he did contribute to such Romantic journals as the *Journal des artistes* and *Le magasin pittoresque* and, after its founding in 1840, to the *Revue générale de l'architecture et des travaux publics*. Indeed, his chief claim to fame is to have coined the term *architecture parlante* to describe the works of Ledoux, which he reviewed in *Le magasin pittoresque* in December 1852 (p. 388). He was intrigued, but did not approve. Ledoux's symbolism was to him too blatant by far.

The influence of the architects we have been considering was strongly felt in the second half of the century, in instigating both a more thoughtful eclecticism and a greater concern for precision in planning, engineering, and the design of details. Inevitably these became richer and, in the hands

399. Pierre-François-Henri Labrouste,
Hôtel Vilgruy, Paris, 1860–65

400. Louis-Joseph Duc, Palais de
Justice, Paris, façade on the Rue de
Harlay, 1857–68

401. Louis-Joseph Duc, Palais de
Justice, Paris, Salle des Pas Perdus,
1857–68

of the less strictly trained architects, were debased and vulgarized. Espérandieu is a case in point. However, the career of Charles-Auguste Questel (1807–1888), a pupil of both Blouet and Duban, who himself worked on the largest scale at Nîmes (where he first noticed Espérandieu), at Grenoble, and at Paris, may be adduced to show a contrary process at work. On the whole, however, the extent and the pace of building during the Second Empire served to degenerate architecture; the rational tradition was disastrously weakened. But a few—very few—architects were able to turn this to their advantage. It became in their hands a liberating stimulus.

The greatest period of activity in the history of French architecture was initiated on June 22, 1853, when Baron Georges-Eugène Haussmann (1809–1891) succeeded Amédée Berger as *Préfet de la Seine*. On June 29, seven days after his appointment, Haussmann was called to St.-Cloud and shown a plan with the emperor's personal proposals for the remaking of Paris marked down in blue, red, yellow, and green, according to their relative urgency. It was this plan that Haussmann carried out in the years that followed. Paris was to be "la capitale des capitales." The city was virtually rebuilt. Streets and boulevards were opened up and lined with regular facades. The destruction was terrible. At intersections and focal points great public buildings and churches were erected; within the first ten years of Haussmann's administration more than fifteen large churches had been begun, and ten more were to follow. Almost all the old bridges over the Seine were rebuilt and five new ones begun. Markets were erected, including the great Halles Centrales. The latter were started afresh as an iron construction in 1853 by the architects Victor Baltard (1805–1874) and Félix-Emmanuel Callet (1792–1854). The Bois de Boulogne (1853–58), the Bois de Vincennes (1858–60), the Parc Monceau (1860–62), the Parc des Buttes-Chaumont (1864–67), the Parc de Montsouris (1867–68), and no fewer than thirty new squares were laid out and embellished with pavilions, railings, and appropriate street furniture. The streets were lighted by gas and the drainage system extended. Water in quantity was brought into the city. By the end of the Second Empire there were sixty public fountains in Paris. Paris itself was extended. On January 1, 1860, Passy, Auteuil, Les Batignolles-Monceau, Montmartre, La Chapelle, La Villette, Belleville, Charonne, Bercy, Vaugirard, and Grenelle were formally incorporated within the city. A few years later the building of *mairies* in these new *arrondissements* was begun. But from all this ferment only one or two names of interest emerge.

Haussmann, like his patron Louis-Napoleon, was a man of much common sense but less than common sensibility. Moreover, he mistrusted architects. He chose as his collaborators Eugène Belgrand (1810–1878), Maillebiau, and Jean-Charles-Adolphe Alphand (1817–1891), members all of the École des Ponts et Chaussées. Baullet-Deschamps, the only trusted architect, acted as surveyor of roads. Victor Baltard, who had won the Grand Prix in 1833, was appointed *Architecte en Chef de la Ville de Paris* and in that capacity

redecorated and rebuilt a host of churches; but apart from the Halles Centrales and the church of St.-Augustin (1860–71), with cast-iron columns inside, he has little claim to architectural recognition. Hector-Martin Lefuel (1810–1880), a pupil of Jean-Nicolas Huyot (1780-1840), was employed to reconstruct the Louvre and to link it finally to the Tuileries. He started in 1854, modestly enough, executing the plan that Visconti had left, but within a few years was piling sculpture and ornament onto the building with an exuberance that would have shocked Visconti. Lefuel's work was hurried and ill considered, but much appreciated in court circles. In 1853 he was commissioned to build the theater at Fontainebleau—which he designed in the eighteenth-century style that he had already introduced into the Salle des États in the Louvre.

Haussmann appointed Antoine-Nicolas-Louis Bailly (1810–1892), a pupil of Debret and Duban, to design the Tribunal de Commerce (1858–64), adapted at the emperor's request from the town hall at Brescia. Bailly's other important building of the period, the Mairie du IVᵉ (1826–67), is no less pompous, if more prosaic. Théodore Ballu (1817–1885), a contractor's son and a disciple of Lebas, emerged also at this time. He completed Franz Christian Gau's Gothic pastiche Ste.-Clotilde, restored the Tour St.-Jacques, and, between Hittorff's Mairie du 1ᵉʳ and St.-Germain-l'Auxerrois, built that absurd tower that won for the ensemble the nickname of "porte-huilier." In 1861 he began work on La Trinité, a well-sited and richly adorned but not in the least impressive church. The Renaissance vaulting is all of *papier-mâché.* Bally built several other churches. But of all the new architects employed by Haussmann only one produced anything of more than marginal worth, Gabriel-Jean-Antoine Davioud (1823–1881). His buildings are well considered and possessed always of some straightforward merit, though they are undeniably dull. He studied for three years at the École de Dessin, perhaps under Viollet-le-Duc, then in 1841 entered the *atelier* of Vaudoyer. His studies completed, he began work with Victor Baltard on the Halles Centrales, and on his recommendation was made *Inspecteur des Promenades* and put in charge of the Service des Fontaines. For Alphand he put up a host of pavilions and lodges in the Bois de Boulogne between 1855 and 1859, all intentionally Picturesque in an English sort of way, with an admixture of the Swiss-chalet style (one chalet was brought direct from Berne). Equally ambitiously, he worked at the Bois de Vincennes, the Parc des Buttes-Chaumont, and the Parc Monceau, where his showy grilles, inspired by those of Emmanuel Héré at Nancy, are particularly deserving of praise. For the Champs-Élysées, in 1857, he designed a new circus and panorama, still standing, a building of less structural quality than Hittorff's. Then in the following year, he designed the first of his four great fountains, the Fontaine St.-Michel at the beginning of the Boulevard St.-Michel, a mass of metal and stone that was both praised and rudely dismissed. Charles Darcel remarked in the *Gazzette des beaux-arts* in 1860, "C'est une oeuvre banale, sans signification et sans caractère" (p.

44), but César-Denis Daly (1811–1893), influential editor of the *Revue générale de l'architecture,* thought far too much of it. Later came the Fontaine de Château d'Eau (1867–74); the Fontaine de l'Observatoire (1870–75), with figures by Jean-Baptiste Carpeaux; and the Fontaine de la Place du Théâtre-Français (1872–74). In 1860 Davioud started on two mammoth theaters, the Théâtre du Châtelet and the Théâtre Lyrique (now Théâtre de la Ville), both completed within two years. Darcel was as brutal in his comments as before; Daly published a magnificent monograph on the buildings. They are undeniably grand and were not uncomfortable, but as architecture they are altogether indigestible.

The Magasins Réunis, on the Place de la République, begun in April 1865 and completed in January 1867, are likewise adequate up to the point they reached and are distinguished by their planning and structural organization above much of the architecture of the time; but that is all. As such later works as the Mairie du XIXᵉ (1876–78) and the vast Palais du Trocadéro (1876–78) attest, Davioud was a thoughtful and extremely industrious architect who gave a great deal of attention to fine, finished detail. But he was incapable of communicating through architecture the feelings that had originally impelled him to take it up.

Many of Haussmann's architects were uninspired. Yet men such as Davioud were influential and widely imitated. And it would be a mistake to think that they achieved nothing in the field of architecture and landscape design. The Parc des Buttes-Chaumont is a wonderfully rich amalgam of the traditional Picturesque and the railway age. The train tracks running alongside the park are integrated with perfect fluency into the landscape design, as is the vast panorama of the industrialized city. The new vistas and spaces that Haussmann gave to Paris, moreover, demanded a new breadth of scale and a grandness of public performance that one architect at least was able to perceive and respond to. This man was Jean-Louis-Charles Garnier (1825–1898). He expressed both the ostentation and the power of the Second Empire with such intensity and candid freshness when he built the Opéra that it is almost impossible not to be enthralled by it. Certainly he changed thereby the direction of French architecture.

For two years Charles Rohault de Fleury worked under the emperor's personal direction on the design of the new opera house; then in 1860 he was suddenly dismissed, in order, it was widely thought, that the empress's favorite, Viollet-le-Duc, might be appointed architect. We may be thankful that Viollet-le-Duc proposed a competition instead. One hundred and seventy-one sentries were submitted, including one from the empress. Early in 1861 the winners in the first stage were announced. Paul-René-Léon Ginain was first; second came Botrel and Adolphe-Nicolas Crepinet, then Antoine-Martin Garnaud and Louis Duc. Garnier was fifth. In the second stage of the competition Garnier was unanimously acclaimed. Garnaud died soon after, of grief, it was said. Ginain never forgave Garnier. The empress was furious. When he went to the Tuileries to show her his project, she

408. *Victor Baltard, St.-Augustin,*
Paris, 1860–71

409, 410. *Victor Baltard,*
St.-Augustin, Paris, details of the
interior

411. Gabriel-Jean-Antoine Davioud,
Fontaine St.-Michel, Paris, 1858–60

exclaimed, "Qu'est cela, ce n'est pas un style; ce n'est ni du Louis XIV, ni du Louis XV, ni du Louis XVI." Garnier had his reply. "Madame," he said, "c'est du Napoléon III, et vous vous plaignez" (*Bulletin de la Société de l'Histoire de l'Art Français,* 1941–44, p. 83). Garnier thus gave a name to the style but, though the empress became reconciled, the building was not much admired by Louis-Napoleon, who visited it only once, in 1862, when he laid the foundation stone. The gala opening did not take place until January 5, 1875, more than four years after the battle of Sedan.

The most illuminating comments on the building were made by Garnier himself, first in *Le théâtre,* published in 1871, in which he outlined his aims, then in the texts to the two magnificently colored folios of *Le nouvel Opéra de Paris,* issued in 1878 and 1881, in which he judged of his success. He was clear and frank in all his explanations, sometimes facetious, never pretentious. He saw the Opéra as the embodiment of man's most primitive instincts: that of gathering together in ceremony around the campfire to share thoughts and dreams, to hear and to see and be seen. The spectacle was thus not to be enacted on the stage alone; theater involved all encounters, all actions. The spectators themselves were actors. And Garnier described in detail how he had fashioned his architecture with these ideas in mind. The Opéra was the entire society of the Second Empire. There were, of course, distinctions between different categories of people—those who paid more and those who paid less—and the part of each in the ritual was clearly assessed and defined. If one came by carriage or foot there was a sequence prepared, and also a place for intermingling—even though this might be at a distance. Even the act of queuing for tickets was considered a part of the ceremony. Care was lavished on every detail. In the main foyer there were mirrors set into the columns so the women might glance at themselves and make last minute adjustments to their dress or expressions before entering the great stair hall, a climax to the architecture. Here all excitement, all passion was stirred. Here society disported itself in its splendor; people saw and were seen as they passed in procession up the stairs—which were copied, Garnier happily admitted, from Victor Louis's at Bordeaux. The lesser members of society watched from on high. The spectacle, the stuffs, the scents, and the diamonds were no less part of the architecture than the marbles, the draperies, and the chandeliers. "La lumière qui étincelera," he wrote in *Le théâtre,* "les toilettes qui resplendiront, les figures qui seront animées et souriantes, les rencontres qui se produiront, les saluts qui s'échangeront, tout aura un air de fête et de plaisir, et sans se rendre compte de la part qui doit revenir à l'architecture dans ce effet magique, tout le monde en jouira et tout le monde rendra ainsi, par son impression heureuse, hommage à ce grand art, si puissant dans ses manifestations, si élevé dans ses résultats."

The flights of Garnier's stairs soar with perfect fluency through the stair hall, they are at once easy and satisfying, yet they provide just that degree of surprise and excitement needed in all artistic success. There is a tension

413. Antoine-Nicolas-Louis Bailly,
Tribunal de Commerce, Paris,
1858–64
414. Antoine-Nicolas-Louis Bailly,
Mairie du IVe, Paris, 1862–67

415. Gabriel-Jean-Antoine Davioud,
Théâtre du Châtelet, Paris, 1860–62
416. Gabriel-Jean-Antoine Davioud,
Théâtre Lyrique (now Théâtre de la
Ville), Paris, 1860–62

417. Jean-Charles-Adolphe Alphand
and Gabriel-Jean-Antoine Davioud,
Parc des Buttes-Chaumont, Paris,
1864–67

418. Jean-Charles-Adolphe Alphand
and Gabriel-Jean-Antoine Davioud,
Parc des Buttes-Chaumont, Paris,
suspension bridge

in every form. With their related corridors and foyers, the stairs seem to provide the best of all possible ceremonial approaches to the auditorium, itself, sadly, one of the least remarkable features of this remarkable building. Garnier agreed, but, as always, he had his explanation. The auditorium, he said, would seem to be the natural climax for the architecture, yet when it was most in use attention was necessarily directed at the spectacle on the stage. The auditorium was then in semidarkness. Only for relatively short periods was it brilliantly lit and vibrant, but the audience was then static, and when the people moved they moved inevitably to the foyers and stairs, where they could enact their communal ceremonies with greater freedom. The lobbies and corridors were thus made larger than ever before, with areas for sitting, and with smoking rooms for the men (with fire and sun motifs) and ice cream parlors for the women (with lunar motifs). The decoration throughout was sumptuous. There was color everywhere, inside and out. Salviati the glassmakers' fortune was soon made. "Alors," Garnier wrote in *Le nouvel Opéra,* "vous ferez vos maisons moins blanches . . ." (vol. 1, p. 18).

Garnier rejoiced in his achievement. It expressed, he said, as all good architecture should, his entire personality: "J'ai beau chercher en parcourant le grand vestibule du nouvel Opéra, si je verrai quelques défauts à signaler: ma recherche est vaine, et je ne trouve vraiment rien à regretter dans cette partie du monument" (*Le nouvel Opéra,* vol. 1, p. 215). This, like other such pronouncements by the architect, is no more than a statement of fact. Garnier well knew how to satisfy practical requirements: He dismissed the heating and ventilating engineers who had worked on the Châtelet theaters because they thought of the Opéra only as a duct, and designed all this part himself, as well as the stage machinery and structure; and he searched France until he found marble blocks large enough for the maximum possibilities of architecture. He knew exactly when to be extravagant with space, with form, or with decoration. There is nothing coarse or vulgar about his building, as some of his contemporaries thought and as many people since have declared who believe themselves to have good taste. Le Corbusier detested it. Garnier could play with consummate mastery and gusto with most of those sacrosanct essentials of architecture—mass, rhythm, texture, and outline—and achieve a splendidly unified character. The silhouette of the Opéra when viewed from the Avenue de l'Opéra is superb. Even Haussmann admired it to the extent of eliminating the trees that were planned to line the avenue. The facade itself, massive and heavily decorated and gilded, is yet monumental in the best possible sense of the word: it possesses, as Garnier himself remarked, a considered dignity. "C'est l'art qui y séjourne," he wrote in *Le nouvel Opéra,* "et l'art ne doit pas être entaché de pruderie; il faut seulement que la richesse soit quelque peu digne, parce que si l'art peut danser la gavotte ou le menuet, il doit se garder du cancan" (vol. 1, p. 23). He did not even object to bad taste if there was in it passion and warmth.

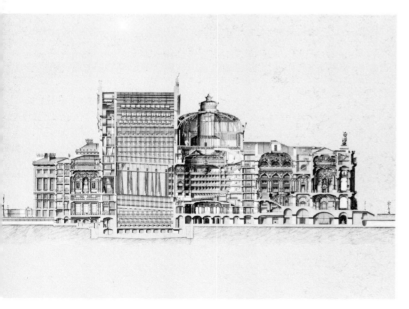

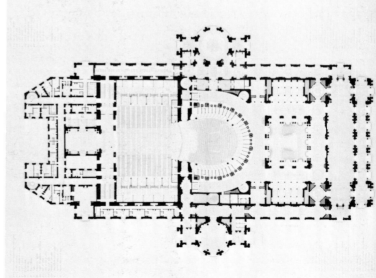

419. Jean-Louis-Charles Garnier,
the Opéra, Paris, 1862–75
420. Jean-Louis-Charles Garnier,
the Opéra, Paris, longitudinal section,
1862–75

421. Jean-Louis-Charles Garnier,
the Opéra, Paris, plan, 1862–75

422. Jean-Louis-Charles Garnier,
the Opéra, Paris, staircase, 1862–75

All that Garnier did and admired was conditioned by his classical training. As a young man, a pupil of Lebas, he had won the Grand Prix with a design for a Conservatoire des Arts et Métiers, similar in style to the buildings Questel was later to build at Grenoble. He had developed these quattrocento and cinquecento tastes in Florence itself, where the Académie de France had moved from Rome under threat of attack from Garibaldi's army. But he undertook Roman studies as well—Trajan's Column and the Temple of Vesta—and later traveled to Sicily with the Duc de Luynes. In 1852, at the end of a three-year stay in Italy, when still a young man of twenty-eight, he traveled to Greece with Théophile Gautier and with Edmond About, who was later to write his account of the journey in *La Grèce contemporaine.* In Greece, Garnier felt, he perceived for the first time the true quality of classical architecture. He saw that there was emotion and human life latent in it, and a harmony and meaning not present in mere building: "Plaine de l'Attique, rocher de Minerve," he wrote in 1869 in *À travers les arts,* "c'est en vous voyant que j'ai compris la puissance magique de l'art et la majesté de l'architecture antique . . ." (p. 268). But his vision of Greek architecture was not that of Winckelmann. His restoration study of the Temple of Jupiter Panhellenius at Aegina was vibrantly colored, the colomns in yellow, the walls of the cella and the architraves and friezes all bright red, with the metopes picked out in blue. There was, he admitted, no justification for this, other than that it pleased him. Between the columns were rich bronze grilles, once again no part of archaeological study.

Garnier always remained faithful to his Mediterranean inheritance; it was part of a world of smiling intelligence, unruffled by calculation and hardheaded need. In all his buildings he sought to stir this sense of buoyant ease and success. It is apparent in the Cercle de la Librairie (1878–79) at 117 Boulevard St.-Germain and, further along, in No. 195, the Maison Hachette (1882), a lavishly planned block of apartments; even more in those buildings he put up along the Riviera—a hotel, a school, a church, the Villa Bischoffsheim, and his own house at Bordighera; in the observatory at Nice; but most especially in the theater and casino at Monte Carlo, begun in 1878. This, before its gradual alteration, was another radiant masterpiece.

As a student, even before he entered the École des Beaux-Arts, Garnier had studied under Viollet-le-Duc at the École de Dessin (where he met Carpeau, who was to design *Les Danseuses* for the Opéra). Later he worked as an assistant to Viollet-le-Duc, but he came, as must be already evident, to reject all that Viollet-le-Duc stood for. He dismissed his architecture readily enough, together with that of all Viollet-le-Duc's followers: "On hésite dans l'appréciation de ses oeuvres plus personelles. Est-ce un souvenir du passé? Est-ce un essai de novation? Cela est difficile à dire" (*À travers les arts,* p. 48). And he went much further even in rejecting his theories: "Le raisonnement *a priori* est donc inutile, puis qu'il se produit inconsciemment. Il serait nuisible s'il voulait remplacer le sentiment et prendre la première place au detriment de la main qui opère et les yeux qui jugent.

425. Jean-Louis-Charles Garnier, the
Opéra, staircase, 1862–75

426. Jean-Louis-Charles Garnier,
Villa Garnier, Bordighera, 1872

427. Jean-Louis-Charles Garnier,
Panorama Français, Paris, 1881

C'est pour cela que je repousse instinctivement et volontairement l'école utilitaire qui, voulant remplacer l'école de l'impression, part du raisonnement seul et, mal guidée dans son choix, repoussant le contrôle du sentiment, tombe à tout instant dans le faux et produit sous le spécieux prétexte de logique, des oeuvres bâtardes et incohérentes'' (*Le théâtre*, p. 414). This was a theme he returned to again and again. He saw no future in an architecture based on rationalism, on science, on engineering, least of all on new materials: "Je le dis tout de suite, c'est là une erreur, et une grande erreur: le fer est un moyen, ce ne serait jamais une principe" (*À travers les arts*, p. 75). But if he was thus rejecting Viollet-le-Duc and his admirers, he was renouncing also that framework of reason, that particular thoughtfulness and concern, that had sustained the classical tradition in France. With Viollet-le-Duc were eliminated Durand, Rondelet, Gilbert, Blouet, and Labrouste. Certainly, Garnier did not expect that an artist should have moral or political convictions, or, if he had, that they should be allowed to inflect his work. One could not, he said, begin with fixed ideas, with any theory at all. The imagination must be allowed free play in works of creation. The rationale, if such was required, could be invented later.

If Garnier's works had not been so obviously successful, such statements would not have mattered. But the example of his easy mastery served, effectively, to destroy the thoughtful tradition of French architecture. His buildings were widely imitated, both inside and out. Opera houses all over the world commemorate his. An Italian, Squadrelli, conflated it with the Monte Carlo casino, throwing an admixture of Secessionist ironwork on top,

to provide the local casino for San Pellegrino at the turn of the century. The result, as may be expected, was dreadful. Very few men possessed Garnier's talents. In France careful and serious architects did make a determined attempt to restore to the classical tradition its measured dignity and its system of belief: among them, E.-G. Coquart (1831–1902), Henri-Adolphe-Auguste Deglane (1855–1931), P.-R.-L. Ginain (1825–1898), Charles-Louis Girault (1851–1932), Julien-Azaïs Guadet (1834–1908), Victor-Alexandre-Frédéric Laloux (1850–1937), Paul-Henri Nénot (1853–1934), and Jean-Louis Pascal (1837–1920). Guadet, Nénot, and Pascal, incidentally, trained at the Opéra. But they were no longer sustained by a faith, even of a specious sort. Architecture in France had for the moment lost its sap and its savor.

ENGLAND: *C.R. Cockerell to Barry*

It cannot be denied that in nineteenth-century England most of the finest minds and the most brilliant designers, with the exception of Cockerell, were drawn to the Gothic not the Classical Revival. There is simply no classical parallel to the astonishingly rich concatenation of Gothic Revivalists—A. W.N. Pugin, John Ruskin, William Morris, William Butterfield, George Edmund Street, and George Frederick Bodley. Harvey Lonsdale Elmes and George Basevi came close to matching them in achievement, but since they both died young, they appear as late Georgian rather than as Victorian architects. Sir James Pennethorne and Sir Charles Barry lacked imaginative

greatness, while Alexander ("Greek") Thomson, though a brilliantly individual exponent of the classical tradition, somehow remains a figure of Scottish rather than of European importance.

With Charles Robert Cockerell English classicism achieved a new level of scholarship and imagination. During his remarkable *grand tour* of 1810–17 he became not only one of the leading archaeologists in Europe but also a greater expert on antique architecture than any English architect before or since. Excavating the late Archaic Temple of Jupiter Panhellenius on the island of Aegina with a group of English and German colleagues in 1811, Cockerell was involved in the discovery of the pedimental sculpture now housed in the Glyptothek in Munich. In the same year he was responsible for discovering the sculptured frieze of the fifth-century Temple of Apollo Epicurius at Bassae, and in 1813 he helped conduct the arrangements by which this sculpture was purchased by the British government. He incorporated casts of it in several of his buildings, notably the Ashmolean Museum, Oxford; the highly independent Ionic order of the temple also recurs with powerful effect in a number of his works. Indeed, his discoveries in Greece gave him a sense of the sculptural basis of Greek design, which influenced the development of his own architecture by enabling him to see the weaknesses of the current Greek Revival. We can trace this process in his diaries of the 1820s, where he criticizes not only the work of his contemporaries but also his own. Of his Literary and Philosophical Institution at Bristol (1821), he noted that the portico, based on the Temple

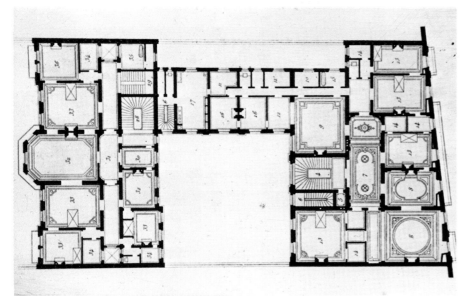

of Vesta at Tivoli but with Corinthian capitals that imitate the one he had discovered at Bassae, was "inharmoniously attached" to the main building. An even more revealing self-criticism is that of Lough Crew, a Greek Revival mansion that he built in Ireland from 1820 to 1825. In 1823 he already found it "very plain, too bald . . . its squareness left me an unpleasant impression . . . it would have been well to rusticate between the pilasters." Finding the Athenian Ionic capitals of the portico too minuscule to enliven a monumental building, he decided "never again [to] use Athenian order except in small scale."

One of the first buildings in which Cockerell began to realize his own stylistic ambitions was the Westminster Life and British Fire Office, in the Strand, London (1831; demolished 1908). Its Greek Doric order was not applied in the form of the usual attached portico but was deeply embedded in the facade. The depth and richness of articulation, the sense of layers within layers, are reminiscent of Italian Mannerism, particularly two buildings by Palladio: the Villa Barbaro at Maser (c. 1555–59) and the Loggia del Capitaniato at Vicenza (1571). Once formulated, this allusive style was soon used to create a series of highly independent yet highly classical masterpieces: Cambridge University Library (only partly executed), the Ashmolean Museum, Oxford, and the Royal Exchange, London (unexecuted), all of the late 1830s, and the branches of the Bank of England at Bristol, Manchester, and Liverpool, of 1844–45. Such a composition as his St. Giles's facade of the Ashmolean blends Greek, Roman, Renaissance,

and Baroque vocabulary into a language "the study of which," as one critic observed of the Liverpool Bank of England, "is a liberal education" (H. H. Statham, *A Short Critical History of Architecture*, 1912, p. 527). What immediately strikes the visitor to any building by Cockerell, whether it be a major public building like the Cambridge University Library or the lodge to a country house, as at Wynnstay, Denbighshire (1827), is the sheer largeness of scale of the parts and of the whole. We feel at once that we are in the presence of a man possessed of a profound intelligence, who thinks architecturally with a persuasive conviction and authority. Exactly the same impression is given by the work of C.-N. Ledoux—both large buildings, such as the Rotonde de la Villette, Paris, and smaller ones, such as the *grenier à sel* at Compiègne. We know that Cockerell was an admirer of Ledoux, in particular of his Hôtel de Thélusson in Paris (see D. J. Watkin, *The Life and Work of C. R. Cockerell, R. A.,* 1974, p. 124).

In the early 1850s Cockerell designed the interiors of St. George's Hall, Liverpool, following the premature death of the architect of the building, Harvey Lonsdale Elmes (1814–1847). Cockerell's exquisite Concert Hall, in which the fine calligraphy of his rich classical ornament is demonstrated at its best, is an admirable foil to the harder sobriety of Elmes's exterior. St. George's Hall, of which the final designs were settled by Elmes in 1841, is in plan a brilliant imaginative re-creation of the *tepidarium* of the Baths of Caracalla, which Elmes seems to have known from Blouet's *Restauration des thermes d'Antonin Caracalla à Rome* (1828). It is in no sense a mere

archaeological restoration and ranks as one of the finest neoclassical public buildings in Europe.

The death of the gifted young Elmes in 1847 was a tragedy for the classical tradition in England. So, too, was that two years earlier of the fifty-one-year-old George Basevi. The latter was a favorite pupil of Soane, and his masterpiece was the Fitzwilliam Museum, Cambridge, a commission he was awarded after an open competition held in 1834–35. Like St. George's Hall, this massive building was inspired by the public architecture of the Roman Empire, in this case the Capitolium at Brescia, dating from the third quarter of the first century A.D. From this source comes the method by which Basevi's monumental Corinthian portico is extended on each side so as to form a colonnade and thus integrated powerfully into the body of the building in a way that one is tempted to call Baroque, although Basevi's stylistic sympathies are shown to be different by his architectural use of casts from the Bassae and Parthenon friezes in the interior.

For a variety of reasons, some of which seem to be accidental, the Gothic Revival was particularly associated with a religious, architectural, and intellectual tradition centered in Oxford, Cambridge, London, and the south of England generally. The classical tradition, by contrast, tended to flourish in Scotland and in the north of England. Thus, the "hyper-Corinthian luxury" (H. S. Goodhart-Rendel's apt characterization) of the Fitzwilliam Museum was echoed in the magnificent Town Hall, of 1845, at Leeds, Yorkshire, by Cuthbert Brodrick (1822–1905) and in William Hill's Town Hall at Bolton, Lancashire, of 1866. Liverpool also reflected a classical bias, from 1823, when John Foster designed St. Andrew's Church of Scotland, Rodney Street, manifestly inspired by Cockerell's Hanover Chapel, Regent Street, London (1821), to 1875, when Cornelius Sherlock (d. 1888) designed the Picton Reading Room, with its spectacular semicircle of Corinthian columns. In Edinburgh, the "Athens of the North," a more sternly Greek note was retained, as can be seen in Thomas Hamilton's Royal College of Physicians (1844–46) and in W. H. Playfair's National Gallery of Scotland (1850–57). In Glasgow a more masterly architect, Alexander Thomson (1817–1875), provided an astonishingly rich and powerful interpretation of the late international neoclassicism of Schinkel and Cockerell. His Caledonia Road Free Church of 1856 is a characteristic example of his work, which, confined to Glasgow, exercised little or no influence on his contemporaries elsewhere.

In London the one architect who seemed capable of perpetuating the intellectual classicism of Cockerell was Sir James Pennethorne (1801–1871). He was a pupil of John Nash, who told him, when Pennethorne was setting out on his *grand tour* of France and Italy in 1824, to seek the advice of Cockerell. Pennethorne later noted that "by Cockerell's urgent advice I paid more attention to the palaces and modern architecture of Italy than to the works of ancient art." The significance of this can hardly be overemphasized.

Perhaps Pennethorne's most important work was his Museum of

437. Charles Robert Cockerell,
Ashmolean Museum, Oxford, view
from the southeast, 1839–41

438. Charles Robert Cockerell, Bank
of England, Bristol, 1844

439. Charles Robert Cockerell,
Concert Hall, St. George's Hall,
Liverpool, detail of a caryatid,
1851–54

440. Charles Robert Cockerell,
Concert Hall, St. George's Hall,
Liverpool, 1851–54

441. Harvey Lonsdale Elmes,
St. George's Hall, Liverpool, 1841
442. Harvey Londsdale Elmes,
St. George's Hall, Liverpool, plan,
1841

443. George Basevi, Fitzwilliam
Museum, Cambridge, 1834
444. Cuthbert Brodrick, Town Hall,
Leeds, 1853

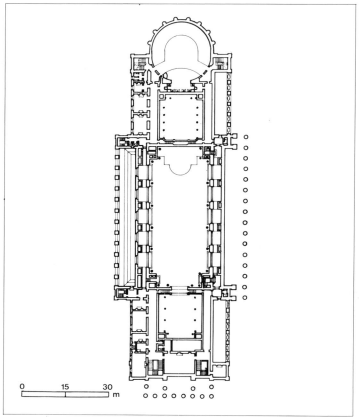

446. *Cornelius Sherlock, Picton Reading Room, Liverpool, 1875*
447. *Thomas Hamilton, Royal College of Physicians, Edinburgh, 1844–46*

448. *Alexander Thomson, Caledonia Road Free Church, Glasgow, 1856*

Economic (or Practical) Geology, in Piccadilly, London, designed between 1844 and 1846, the first cultural monument of the Victorian age to be sponsored by the state. A building of great earnestness, sobriety, and authority, it showed what architects in the classical tradition were capable of when, assured of that tradition's refinement, logic, and dignity, they did not feel obliged to compete with the more immediately eye-catching effects of the fashionable Gothic and Italianate revivals. The museum's monumental but undemonstrative facades, in cream Colchester brick and Ancaster stone, concealed a dense and subtle plan that exploited interlocking volumes with a sophistication lacking in many later Gothic Revival buildings. Along the second story ran the great top-lit exhibition gallery, forty-seven meters (one hundred fifty-five feet) long, with a large rectangular opening in the floor that illuminated the Doric Hall below. The gallery, in which the horizontal and the vertical supports were of cast iron, was a space both formed and frankly defined by its construction. In this it differed from the two other great contemporary buildings in London that employed cast-iron construction: Robert Smirke's British Museum (1824–47), where the presence of cast iron is completely hidden, and J. B. Bunning's Coal Exchange (1847), where it is boldly exposed. Pennethorne adopted the perhaps more attractive solution of revealing that cast and wrought iron helped determine the shape of the room but then moderating the disclosure by covering the surface of the metal with plasterwork.

Pennethorne's geological museum was demolished in 1935, and his important interiors at Buckingham Palace (1852–58) were mutilated in 1902. His somewhat grim but constructionally interesting Public Record Office (1851–66) survives, as does his west wing (1856) at Sir William Chambers's Somerset House, where he brilliantly and modestly adapted Chambers's style. As architect to the Office of Works, Pennethorne enjoyed the kind of settled civil-service position that some other architects of the period, including Schinkel, occupied. He was thus preserved from the embarrassment of entering the scandalously conducted architectural competitions of the nineteenth century, which so impeded Cockerell's career. One of the fruits of Pennethorne's official position was the commission for buildings for the University of London in Burlington Gardens in 1866. However, he became a pawn in the "Battle of the Styles," which was being played so absurdly between Liberal and Conservative politicians in the 1860s. He was thus obliged to present designs in both Gothic and Italianate modes in 1866–67, and the result is a dour piece of classicism with strongly French overtones. It is symptomatic of the failure of English architects to maintain the classical tradition in the face of competition from the Gothic and Italianate revivals.

The master of the Italianate Revival was Sir Charles Barry. Though comparatively of humble birth, he forged a career for himself that was one of the spectacular successes of the nineteenth century. His early work was varied, ranging stylistically from a Gothic manner reminiscent of Wyatt's

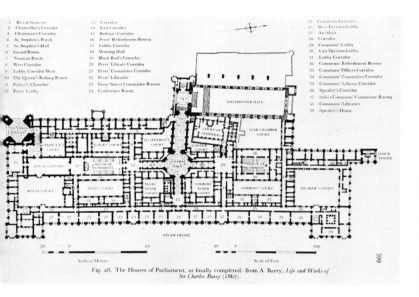

1	Royal Staircase	13	Corridor	25	Commons' Entrance
2	Chancellor's Corridor	14	East Corridor	26	West Division Lobby
3	Chairman's Corridor	15	Bishops' Corridor	27	Air Shaft
4	St. Stephen's Porch	16	Peers' Refreshment Rooms	28	Corridor
5	St. Stephen's Hall	17	Lobby Corridor	29	Commons' Lobby
6	Guard Room	18	Waiting Hall	30	East Divisions Lobby
7	Norman Porch	19	Black Rod's Corridor	31	Lobby Corridor
8	West Corridor	20	Peers' Library Corridor	32	Commons' Refreshment Rooms
9	Lobby Corridor West	21	Peers' Committee Corridor	33	Commons' Offices Corridor
10	The Queen's Robing Room	22	Peers' Libraries	34	Commons' Committee Corridor
11	Prince's Chamber	23	Peers' Select Committee Rooms	35	Commons' Library Corridor
12	Peers' Lobby	24	Conference Room	36	Speaker's Corridor
				37	Select Commons' Committee Rooms
				38	Commons' Libraries
				39	Speaker's House

Fig. 28. The Houses of Parliament, as finally completed: from A. Barry, *Life and Works of Sir Charles Barry* (1867).

Fonthill Abbey (St. Peter, Brighton, 1823–28), via the Schinkelesque trabeation of his Royal Institution, Manchester (1823), and Nos. 16–17 Pall Mall, London (1833–34; demolished 1913), to the early Italian Renaissance manner of Brunswick Chapel, Hove, Sussex, (1827) and two important buildings of 1829, the Attree Villa, Brighton, and the Travellers' Club in Pall Mall. He shot to fame in 1836 when he had the extraordinarily good fortune to be selected as architect of the New Palace of Westminster. The terms of the competition, in keeping with the sentimental and literary romanticism of an increasingly nationalist age, called for a "Gothic or Elizabethan" style in order to emphasize the supposed medieval roots of English government. Barry's complex masterpiece, with its essentially classical disposition (despite the elaborate Gothic detail provided by A. W. B. Pugin), was a curiosity that exercised no significant architectural influence but that has undoubtedly continued to color, up to the present day, the Englishman's notion of the political framework within which he expects his country to be governed.

Barry's choice of a Cinquecento Palazzo style for the Travellers' Club was fraught with consequences for the nineteenth century. It suggested that the Palladian Revival of early eighteenth-century England had returned, though the architects and styles that had come to be admired were not those that had appealed to Lord Burlington and his circle. Burlington had been interested in Palladio as an exemplar of order, harmony, and the antique, not as a representative of Italian culture; the Victorians were interested in the warmth and color of the Renaissance as an Italian phenomenon. The Travellers' Club was in some sense the culmination of Englishmen's obsession with the *grand tour,* an institution that had persisted without interruption from at least the time of the foundation of the Society of Dilettanti. The club members were anxious to build a noble mansion in which those who had made the *grand tour* could meet each other and return hospitality to the foreign gentlemen who had entertained them on their travels. It was not, therefore, inappropriate that its architecture should be a tangible memorial of this *entente cordiale.* Barry chose as his model Raphael's Palazzo Pandolfini in Florence, though in execution he abandoned the elaborate rusticated surrounds to the ground-floor windows that had appeared in his first proposals for the Pall Mall facade. For the much larger Reform Club of 1837, farther along the same street, Barry chose as his model the grander Palazzo Farnese by Antonio da Sangallo and Michelangelo. But neither of Barry's clubs was in any sense a copy. The planning of both was extremely novel, particulary at the Reform Club, whose great central *cortile* became a recurrent theme in different Victorian building types. In tribute to the classical impetus that gave rise to these buildings, the Morning Room of the Reform Club was adorned with a cast of the Parthenon frieze, the Library of the Travellers' with a cast of the Bassae frieze (the latter doubtless on the recommendation of Cockerell, who was a founder-member).

Barry developed his Italianate style in a series of spectacular country

houses: for example, Trentham, Staffordshire (1833 onward), Shrubland
Park, Suffolk (1849–50), and Cliveden House, Buckinghamshire (1850).
Others were quick to follow his lead. Thomas Cubitt provided mansions
in this style during the 1840s for George Hudson, the railway king, at Albert
Gate, London, and for Queen Victoria and Prince Albert at Osborne House
on the Isle of Wight. Far more distinguished that anything by Cubitt and
much by Barry was Dorchester House, Park Lane, London (1850–63), by
Lewis Vulliamy (1791–1871). It was designed in close collaboration with
its owner, R. S. Holford, the art collector and shipping magnate, who was
evidently trying to rival Barry's Bridgewater House of 1846–51 for Lord
Ellesmere. Based on Baldassare Peruzzi's Villa Farnesina, Rome (1509–11),
Vulliamy's Dorchester House was one of the great buildings of the
nineteenth century, and its destruction in 1929 was a major loss to British
architecture. It expressed the culmination of those opulent, aristocratic
Mediterranean sympathies that had developed in the 1830s and 1840s at
the end of the long Georgian and Whig heyday. The sumptuously decorated
interior reached a climax in the second-floor ballroom, or saloon, which,
by a brilliant theatrical stroke, opened through three archways directly into
the upper spaces of the stair hall. The whole house thus became alive with
sound and movement on evenings when great balls and receptions were
held. The dining room was designed by Alfred George Stevens (1817–
1875), a pupil of Bertel Thorvaldsen and undoubtedly the finest of the
Victorian sculptors. He was in deep sympathy with the cinquecento,
particularly with Michelangelo, and was, of all nineteenth-century designers,
the closest in temperament and talent to Cockerell. His Willington
Monument in St. Paul's cathedral (1856), a great triumphal arch of marble,
is one of the noblest memorials to the nineteenth-century Italianate Revival.
His magnificent chimneypiece in the dining room at Dorchester House took
ten years to design and construct (1859–69). Its incredible cost of 1,778
pounds shocked even the millionaire Holford.

To remind us of what we have lost at Dorchester House is a building in
the same vein, though perhaps of even greater quality and originality: the
Free Trade Hall, Manchester (1853), by Edward Walters (1808–1872),
who had worked in the offices of both Cubitt and Vulliamy. William Bruce
Gingell (1819–1900) was another talented architect in the Italianate
manner. His West of England and South Wales District (now Lloyds) Bank
at Bristol (1854) is a stylish variation on the theme of Pietro Sansovino's
Libreria Vecchia, Venice. Samuel Angell (1800–1866) had also made a
special study of cinquecento architecture; he lectured on Giacomo da
Vignola at the Royal Institute of British Architects in 1850, and in 1856
produced the sumptuous Clothworkers' Hall, Mincing Lane, London
(destroyed 1940). An interesting offshoot of the taste for things Italian was
the vogue in the 1840s for the "round-arch style" in church architecture,
which included every kind of variant from Early Christian and Byzantine
to Italian Romanesque and Norman. The most elaborate example of this

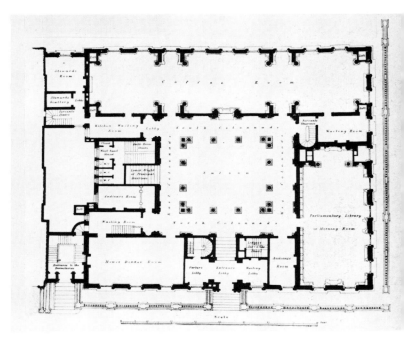

taste is afforded by the church of St. Mary and St. Nicholas at Wilton, Wiltshire (1840–46), by Thomas Henry (1807–1880) and David Brandon. In a rich Italian Romanesque style, with a campanile over thirty meters (one hundred feet) high, it contains ancient Roman columns of black marble from the Temple of Venus at Porto Venere. A building of rare quality in the round-arch style is the museum of Trinity College, Dublin, of 1852–57, by Sir Thomas Newenham Deane (1828–1899) and Benjamin Woodward (1815–1861). Though organized around a central glazed courtyard, rather like Barry's Reform Club, the building has naturalistically carved capitals inspired by Ruskin and details in a Venetian early-Renaissance mode.

The Palazzo style was agreed upon as appropriate, for a variety of practical and associational reasons, for commercial premises and private clubs, but when it came to the style in which a great building of national and symbolic importance should be built, the latent battle between the exponents of the classical and the Gothic came with some violence to the surface. The particular victim of the strife was Sir George Gilbert Scott (1811–1878), who between 1856 and 1861 was forced more than once to remodel his Gothic design for the Foreign Office to suit the Renaissance tastes of the Prime Minister, Lord Palmerston. Ironically, the result was one of Scott's best buildings, though it must be said that he had much help from Matthew Digby Wyatt (1820–1877).

After the 1860s the classical tradition lost impetus and the best architects worked in other veins. It was revived, together with an interest in Cockerell, between 1890 and 1910 with some surprisingly impressive results.

GERMANY

There were many similarities between the development of German and English architecture between 1790 and 1840; thus, a number of the major designs and buildings by Gilly, Schinkel, and Klenze have already been mentioned in the course of our discussion of the Greek Revival and the Picturesque. Certainly the intensely eclectic work of the greatest German architect of these years, Karl Friedrich Schinkel, reminds us immediately not of France or Italy but of England. Schinkel also developed a "functional" interpretation of classicism, which was successfully revived in Germany between 1900 and 1940 as a reaction against both the Wilhelmine Baroque and Bauhaus bleakness. Schinkel particularly appealed to his countrymen during the first half of the twentieth century in part because of what they saw as his essential "Germanness." As head of the Public Works Department, Schinkel became identified with the creation of the new Germany between the Napoleonic Wars and the foundation of the empire in 1871. Indeed, so much was he seen as part of its reforging that the royal family walked behind his coffin in his funeral procession.

He provided the center of Berlin with a number of striking monuments in different styles: Greek Revival for the Royal Guardhouse (1816–18),

457. *Lewis Vulliamy, Dorchester House, London, west facade, on Park Lane, 1850–63*

458. *Lewis Vulliamy, Dorchester House, London, stair hall and corridor on the second floor, 1850–63*

459. *Lewis Vulliamy, Dorchester House, London, south (entrance) front, 1850–63*

460. *Lewis Vulliamy, Dorchester House, London, stair hall, 1850–63*

462. Alfred George Stevens, Wellington Monument, St. Paul's cathedral, London, 1856

463. Sir Thomas Newenham Deane and Benjamin Woodward, Trinity College Museum, Dublin, stair hall, 1852–57

464. Sir Thomas Newenham Deane and Benjamin Woodward, Trinity College Museum, Dublin, 1852–57

465. Samuel Angell, Clothworkers' Hall, London, 1856

466. Thomas Henry Wyatt and
David Brandon, St. Mary and St.
Nicholas, Wilton, Wiltshire,
1840–46

467. Sir George Gilbert Scott and Sir
Matthew Digby Wyatt, Foreign
Office, London, 1856–73

State Theater (1818–21), and Altes Museum (1822–28); Gothic for the grim brick Friedrich-Werdersche church (1821–30) and the cast-iron Kreuzberg War Memorial (1818); and a cross between Functional and North Italian quattrocento for the School of Architecture (1831–36). Despite the claims that have been made for his ability as a town planner (H. G. Pundt, *Schinkel's Berlin: A Study in Environmental Planning*, 1972), it must be confessed that, unlike John Nash in London, he was not able to make a coherent impact on the city of Berlin, which remained dominated by its Baroque and eighteenth-century planning and monuments.

One of the most prolific and eclectic architects of all time, Schinkel is difficult to sum up, to generalize about, to fit into a pattern. It is possible that his important study-tour of England in 1826 influenced the development of his "functional" style, with its prominent use of iron. He was both appalled and attracted by the architecture of the Industrial Revolution in England, and it seems that it was after observing the giant cotton mills that he conceived the idea of a fireproof architecture whose gridlike brick skin would wrap around an iron frame. The various explorations he made of this after his return from England include two unexecuted proposals—a bazaar for Unter den Linden (1827) and a State Library (1832–39) nearby—the Royal Customs Warehouses (1829), the School of Architecture, and the spectacular cast-iron staircases in two of the palaces in the Wilhelmstrasse that he remodeled for the king's sons, Prince Karl (1827) and Prince Albrecht (1829–33).

We have touched elsewhere on Schinkel's work in a Picturesque vein that, too, has English overtones: Schloss Glienicke, Schloss Charlottenhof, and Schloss Babelsberg. It culminated later in the 1830s in two unexecuted fantasies: a palace on the Acropolis for the king of Greece (Otto von Wittelsbach of Bavaria) and a palace at Orianda, in the Crimea, for the empress of Russia, who was a daughter of King Friedrich-Wilhelm III of Prussia. Both display a rich polychromy inspired by the researches of Hittorff, a great admirer of Schinkel; both are examples of Schinkel's special gift for distributing symmetrical Grecian forms in an asymmetrically landscaped composition; and both give the impression of sumptuous film sets. The palace on the Acropolis, which turned the Parthenon into a kind of glorified garden ornament, is the apotheosis of what some scholars have called Romantic classicism.

Leo von Klenze (1784–1864), like Schinkel, was a North German who turned to architecture after meeting the visionary and influential young Friedrich Gilly. He studied in Paris in the opening years of the nineteenth century under Percier and Fontaine and also under J.-N.-L. Durand at the École Polytechnique. After working from 1808 to 1813 as court architect to Napoleon's youngest brother, Jérôme, who had been elevated to the throne of Westphalia, Klenze met Crown Prince Ludwig of Bavaria, in 1814. The young prince, who had purchased the Aegina Marbles in 1811, shared Klenze's passion for antiquity and in 1816 persuaded his father, Maximilian

470. *Karl Friedrich Schinkel, Altes Museum, Berlin, 1822–23*
471. *Karl Friedrich Schinkel, Altes Museum, Berlin, hall, 1822–23*

472. *Karl Friedrich Schinkel, School of Architecture, Berlin, 1831–36*

473, 474. *Karl Friedrich Schinkel, project for a palace, Orianda, Crimea, atrium and courtyard, 1838*

XXXVI. Karl Friederich Schinkel, project for a palace, Orianda, Crime atrium, 1838

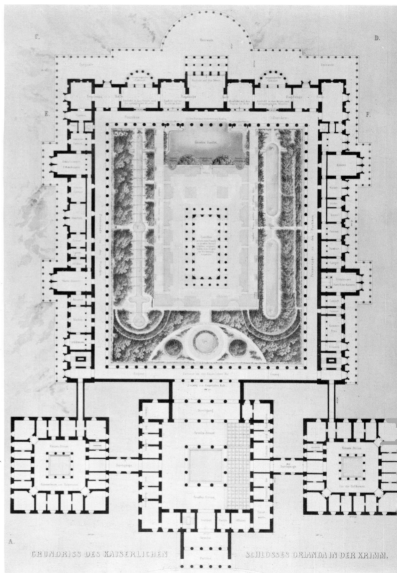

I, to appoint Klenze as supervisor of court buildings in Munich. This royal
support in architectural endeavor finds a close parallel in the relationship
between Schinkel and the crown prince in Berlin, between Percier and
Fontaine and Napoleon in Paris, and between Nash and the Prince Regent
in England. Klenze and the crown prince made the same kind of sweeping
impact on Munich that Nash did on London, though the German architect
and his patron worked in a style rather different from Nash's. Their principal
contributions were the great Ludwigstrasse, running north from the royal
Residenz, and the Königsplatz, which lay to the west of the Ludwigstrasse
on the route into the city from the royal palace of Nymphenburg.

In 1816 Klenze designed two major buildings that reflect the influence
of his French masters. The Glyptothek in the Königsplatz is notable as the
first public sculpture gallery ever erected. It was commissioned by the crown
prince, who wished to house the Aegina Marbles suitably. In contained
Roman as well as Greek antiquities, and its Grecian portico is flanked by
Roman aedicules. From the same year dates the very different Leuchtenberg
Palace, off the Ludwigstrasse, designed for Napoleon's stepson, Eugène de
Beauharnais, who had married the crown prince's sister. Perhaps the first
major monument of the Renaissance Revival, it was inspired, like Barry's
Reform Club of twenty-one years later, by the Palazzo Farnese. Klenze
doubtless knew the engravings of Italian domestic architecture of the
fifteenth and sixteenth centuries that Percier and Fontaine had published
in their *Palais, maisons, et autres édifices modernes dessinés à Rome* (1798). The
fifteenth-century Florentine style chosen by the crown prince for much of
Klenze's street architecture in Munich may also owe something to the plates
in *Architecture toscane,* published in 1815 by Auguste Grandjean de
Montigny, Klenze's predecessor as architect to King Jérome. Klenze's
Pinakothek, or Picture Gallery, in Munich (designed 1822–25; built
1826–36) antedates both Smirke's British Museum and Schinkel's Altes
Museum and, unlike either of these, reflects a neo-Renaissance vocabulary.
In 1823–24 Klenze visited Sicily and Paestum with the crown prince, and
there he made detailed drawings of the Greek temples while the prince fell
in love with the Palatine Chapel at Palermo. In 1824 he became director

of the Building Authorities for Bavaria, and his position was further
consolidated in the following year when the crown prince succeeded his
father, as Ludwig I. Between 1826 and 1843 Klenze remodeled the Munich
Residenz for Ludwig in a variety of styles ranging from that of the Königsbau
(based on the Pitti Palace) to that of the Allerheiligen Hofkirche (based
on the Palatine Chapel at Palermo).

Klenze's great monuments in the neo-antique, as opposed to the
neo-Renaissance, tradition are the Walhalla (1830–42) near Regensburg,
the Befreiungshalle (1842), near Kelheim, and, in Munich, the Ruhmeshalle (1843) and Propylaeon (1843) and Propylaeon (1846–60; conceived in
1817). We have already described the Walhalla and the Propylaeon as the
culmination of the neoclassical obsession with the Parthenon and the
Athenian Propylaea, which, in nineteenth-century Germany, was colored
by a growing nationalism. The Ruhmeshalle (Hall of Fame) is a bald Greek
Doric stoa, whereas the Befreiungshalle (Hall of Liberation) is a vast, bizarre
rotunda erected to commemorate the War of Liberation against Napoleon
of 1813–15. Conceived by the architect Friedrich von Gärtner (1792–
1847), the Befreiungshalle was completely remodeled after his death by
Klenze, in whose hands it emerged as a stark, brutal, militaristic fortress.

The third member of the great trio of German nineteenth-century
architects is Gottfried Semper (1803–1879), a generation younger than
Schinkel and Klenze. Like them he was trained in both Germany and France:
His masters were Gärtner, Gau, and Hittorff. From Hittorff he derived an
interest in antique polychromy, which he studied in Italy and Greece from
1830 to 1833, and he published some of the results of his research in
Verläufige Bemerkungen über bemalte Architektur und Plastik bei den Alten (1834).
Unlike Hittorff and Klenze, he never worked in a neo-Greek mode but
immediately opted for the Renaissance when he began to design major
works in Dresden: the Opera House (1837–41), the Villa Rosa (1839), the
Oppenheim Palace (1845), and the Königliche Gemäldegalerie (1845–48).
Some of his best buildings in this vein were designed during his lengthy
residence in Switzerland: the Town Hall at Winterthur (1863–67), the Fierz
Commercial Building at Zurich (1864–65), and his project for the Zurich
railroad station (1860). He later turned to the neo-Baroque, when, in the
1870s, he rebuilt the Dresden Opera House after a fire and designed major
public museums in Vienna. However, it is not his buildings that principally
concern us but his ideas on ornament and functionalism published in *Der
Stil in den technischen und tektonischen Künstern* (2 vols., 1860-63; 2d ed.,
1878–79), which we will discuss in a later chapter.

RUSSIA

From the time of its foundation by Peter the Great in 1703, St. Petersburg
(Leningrad) was intended to be a port of entry for Western influence. The
astonishing mélange of work done there by Italian, French, British, German,

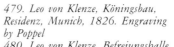
479. Leo von Klenze, Köningsbau, Residenz, Munich, 1826. Engraving by Poppel

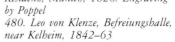
480. Leo von Klenze, Befreiungshalle, near Kelheim, 1842–63

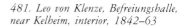
481. Leo von Klenze, Befreiungshalle, near Kelheim, interior, 1842–63

and Russian architects during the next century and a half realized as nowhere else Quatremère de Quincy's vision of a classical "communauté d'instruction et de connaissance, une certaine égalité du goût et du savoir . . . entre toutes les contrées de l'Europe." The fashion during the reign of the Empress Elizabeth (1741–62) was for rococo, and it was in that style that the palace of Tsarskoe Selo (1749–56), about fifteen miles from St. Petersburg, and the Winter Palace (1754–62), in the city itself, were executed, both by the Italian Count Bartolommeo Francesco Rastrelli (1700–1771). Catherine the Great (who reigned from 1762 to 1796) reacted against her aunt's tastes and adopted a neoclassical style that entered St. Petersburg in two buildings by the French architect Jean-Baptiste-Michel Vallin de la Mothe (1729–1800): the Old Hermitage (1764–67) and the Academy of Fine Arts (1765), which was based on a restrained design by his cousin, J.-F. Blondel. Ivan Yegorovich Starov, a Russian architect trained in Paris under de Wailly, continued to develop the new style in his church and belfry at Nikolskoe (1774–76; destroyed 1941) and in the Tauride Palace in St. Petersburg, whose impressive Catherine Hall is flanked on each side by eighteen pairs of Ionic columns. Giacomo Antonio Domenico Quarenghi (1744–1817), who traveled to Russia from Italy in 1779–80, introduced a monumental Palladianism at the English Palace in the English Park at Peterhof (1781–89) and at the Hermitage Theater (1782–87).

The most remarkable foreign importation was probably the mysterious Scottish architect Charles Cameron (c. 1743–1812), who was in Rome in the 1760s, published the *Description of the Baths of the Romans* in 1772, and was working for Catherine at Tsarskoe Selo in 1779. Her first choice had been Clérisseau, whom she invited in 1773 to design a house in the "antique" style to be built on the grounds of Tsarskoe Selo; however, she was annoyed by Clérisseau's proposals for a vast Roman palace combining elements from the Baths of Caracalla and Hadrian's Villa at Tivoli. Nevertheless, in 1780 she asked him for designs for a triumphal arch to be built in Russia by Cameron, and in the following year she bought more than a thousand of his drawings in Paris. Clérisseau's surviving model and drawings make it clear that the arch would have been of exceptional scale and originality, with the central round-headed opening flanked by square-headed openings with Doric columns. The commission for the additions to Tsarskoe Selo fell to Cameron, who, using some of Clérisseau's drawings, produced a breathtakingly lovely series of apartments in a glittering Adam style in 1779–84, and went on to add the Cameron Gallery and Agate Pavilion to Rastrelli's palace in 1782–85. The great open colonnades on the second floor of the Cameron Gallery are curiously similar to those on the south front of West Wycombe Park, Buckinghamshire (c. 1755), attributed to John Donowell. Because of the steeply sloping site, the gallery has at its south end a superb open staircase leading down to the lake in two widely curving arms that terminate in a single straight flight.

Cameron's other principal work was the palace at Pavlovsk, built for

485. Charles Cameron, Palace of
Grand Duke Paul, Pavlovsk,
principal facade, 1781–85

486. Charles Cameron, Palace of
Grand Duke Paul, Pavlovsk, Grecian
Hall, 1781–85

487. Charles Cameron, Cameron
Gallery, Tsarskoe Selo (Pushkin),
1782–85

488. Adrian Dimitrievich Zakharov,
Admiralty, Leningrad, 1806–15

489. Adrian Dimitrievich Zakharov, Admiralty, Leningrad, detail, 1806–15

490. Karl Ivanovich Rossi, Arch of the Winter Palace (now General Staff Arch), Leningrad, 1819–29

491. Karl Ivanovich Rossi, Senate and Synod, Leningrad, 1829–34

Grand Duke Paul between 1781 and 1785. Again, influence from Clérisseau and Adam is apparent, particularly in the magnificent Grecian Hall, inspired by Adam's great hall at Kedleston, Derbyshire (c. 1761 onward), and in the Italian Hall, the rotunda in the center of the palace, which is an echo of the saloon at Kedleston. In the park Cameron erected the circular Temple of Friendship in 1780 (demolished), the first building of the Greek Doric style in Russia.

Nineteenth-century classical architecture in Russia began spectacularly in 1804 with the St. Petersburg Exchange by the French architect Thomas de Thomon (1754–1813). This monumental templar building, combining elements taken from Boullé and from the temples at Paestum (which de Thomon had visited), was part of the major redevelopment of the imperial capital carried out by Alexander I (reigned 1801–25) and his brother Nicholas I (reigned 1825–55) in emulation of the achievement of Catherine the Great and with the deliberate aim of making it a city unrivaled in the splendor of its public buildings. The Exchange was swiftly followed by perhaps the largest neoclassical building in the world, the Admiralty (1806–15), by Adrian Dimitrievich Zakharov (1761–1811), a Russian-born architect who had been trained under Chalgrin in Paris in 1782–86. The lateral facades of this brilliant and varied building provide reflections of Zakharov's stay in Paris, for they were inspired by Pierre Rousseau's archway at the Hôtel de Salm, under construction in 1782–85. Similarly, de Thomon's theater (destroyed 1813) was based on Peyre's and de Wailly's Théâtre-Français, in Paris. The French architect Auguste Ricard de Montferrand (1786–1858), a pupil of Percier, built St. Isaac's cathedral (1817–57) to a not very coherent design based on Soufflot's Ste.-Geneviève; nevertheless, it boasts an important iron-framed dome, whose exterior was inspired by Wren's dome at St. Paul's cathedral. The Academy of Mines at St. Petersburg (1806–11), by Andrei Nikiforovich Voronikhin (1760–1814), a pupil of de Wailly, has a giant twelve-columned Paestum-Doric portico, but the more important architect Karl Ivanovich Rossi (1775–1849) moved away from the néo-grec toward a style more Italianate and more festive. Italian-born but Russian-trained, he became the principal architect and town planner in St. Petersburg after 1816. Rossi's grand and rich style can be appreciated in the New Michael Palace (1819–23; now the Russian Museum), the General Staff Arch and flanking office buildings (1819–29) in front of the Winter Palace, the Alexandra Theater (1827–32), and the Senate and Synod (1829–34).

Though less striking than that of St. Petersburg, the transformation of Moscow into a city of great classical architecture during the late eighteenth and early nineteenth centuries bespeaks the vitality and adaptability both of Russian architects and of the classical style. The extent and quality of the work—which included public buildings, palaces, and mansions—are still little appreciated. Vasili Ivanovich Bazhenov, another pupil of de Wailly, conceived a remarkable scheme for rebuilding the Kremlin about 1772, but

492. *Matvei Feodorovich Kazakov,*
Senate Building, Kremlin, Moscow,
1771–85

493. *Giacomo Antonio Domenico*
Quarenghi, Matvei Feodorovich
Kazakov, and Ivan Petrovich
Argunov, Sheremetev Palace,
Ostankino, near Moscow, 1791–98

it was not executed. His highly ornamental Pashkov Palace (now the Lenin Library) of 1784–86 maintained links with the Baroque. The work of his assistant Matvei Feodorovich Kazakov (1733–1812), more than that of any other architect, gave the new Moscow its classical character. Kazakov's mighty triangular Senate Building in the Kremlin (now the Council of the Ministers of the USSR), of 1771–85, was a fulfillment of Bazhenov's Kremlin project. Its great Doric rotunda is flanked internally with impressive freestanding Corinthian columns, as is his Hall of the Noblemen's Assembly of 1784–86 (now the Hall of Columns, House of the Trade Unions). Kazakov, who had traveled in France and Italy, was an admirer of Palladio, as can be seen in both his public buildings (Golitsyn Hospital, 1796–1801) and his private palaces (Demidov House, 1789–91; and Batashev House, 1798–1802). He was also interested in reviving ancient Russian forms and mingling them with Gothic details, as he did with bizarre effect in the Petrovsky Palace (1775–82; altered 1840). Like Bazhenov's church of Our Lady of All Sorrows, Kazakov's Moscow churches of the 1780s and 1790s—SS. Cosmas and Damian, St. Philip the Metropolitan, Ascension, and St. Martin the Confessor—are asymmetrical in composition. The familiar Russian rotunda and tall campanile create a staccato effect oddly reminiscent of E.-M. Gauthey's church at Givry-sur-Saône (1770–91) and George Steuart's New St. Chad, Shrewsbury (1790).

A number of Moscow buildings of the turn of the century are associated with Quarenghi. He remodeled the Catherine (Golovin) Palace, incorporating a Tuscan colonnaded hall, and added a startling hemicycle of Tuscan columns to the facade by Yelezvoi Nazarov of the Sheremetev Pilgrims' Refuge. One of the grandest private palaces of the period was built at Ostankino in 1791–98 for Count Sheremetev by Quarenghi, Kazakov, and Ivan Petrovich Argunov. With its superbly ornamented theater and, on the grounds, the Italian and so-called Egyptian pavilions, Ostankino has something of the quality of Cameron's work for Catherine the Great at Tsarskoe Selo.

In the early nineteenth century the principal Muscovite architects who followed Kazakov were the Italian-born Domenico Gilardi (1788–1845), Afanasy Grigoryev (1782–1868), and Osip Beauvais (1784–1834). By Grigoryev and Adam Menelaws is the Razumovsky House (1801–3). Its powerful facade is based on the motif by now familiar to us in the work of Kent, Adam, and Ledoux: an open screen of columns in front of a coffered apse. Gilardi's Khrushchev House (1814) and Lopukhin House (1817–22) are Palladian in theme, enlivened with crisp Empire decoration. Gilardi, however, did inject a more astringent note into Muscovite classicism, and his influence was, in some ways, comparable to the impact of Gilly in Germany. Strikingly reminiscent of Gilly are his adaptation of Kazakov's Music Pavilion of the Equerry on the Kuzminki estate (1819) and his completion in the late 1820s of Quarenghi's and Kazakov's Suburban Palace (begun 1788). Between 1809 and 1818, with his father, Giacomo, Gilardi

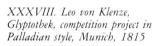

XL. *Johann Carl Ludwig Engel,*
Senate, Helsinki, 1818–22

XLI. *Johann Carl Ludwig Engel,*
University Library, Helsinki, reading
room, 1836–45

494. *Giacomo Antonio Domenico Quarenghi, Matvei Feodorovich Kazakov, and Ivan Petrovich Argunov, Sheremetev Palace, Ostantkino, near Moscow, view of the park, 1791–98*

495, 496. *Giacomo Antonio Domenico Quarenghi, Matvei Feodorovich Kasakov, and Ivan Petrovich Argunov, Sheremetev Palace, Ostankino, near Moscow, views of the interior, 1791–98*

built the Widows' House, and from 1823 to 1826 the Guardianship Council Building. The former is notable for a great octostyle portico of unfluted Greek Doric columns, the latter for a similar portico of Greek Ionic columns and a superb vaulted stair hall with two tiers of unfluted marble columns. His most impressive private house is the Lunin House (1818–23), on Nikitsky Boulevard, but his major work was the reconstruction, in 1817–19, of Kazakov's Moscow University of 1786–93. For Kazakov's elegant Ionic order on the entrance portico he substituted a powerful Greek Doric and also reworked the side pavilions in a harder, chunkier style. In a similar fashion, Menelaws remodeled the English Club (now the Museum of the Revolution of the USSR) with a Greek Doric portico. Greek Doric also are Osip Beauvais's squat, truncated columns set in a rusticated arch in the grotto of the Alexandrovsky Garden.

Beauvais's name is particularly associated with the planning in Moscow carried out after the disastrous fire of 1812, for he was director of the commission for rebuilding the city. In front of his Bolshoi Theater (1821–24) the Theater (now Sverdlov) Square merges with the Resurrection (now Revolution) Square. At the Tverskaya Zastava he built a splendid triumphal arch (1827–34), based on the Arch of Titus in Rome, to mark the spot where the victorious army had returned to Moscow from the Napoleonic Wars. It has now, unfortunately, been moved to the Mozhaiskoye Highway.

During the 1830s German influence penetrated where French and Italian had for so long held sway. In 1838, following the fire at the old Winter Palace in St. Petersburg in December 1837, Leo von Klenze was called from Munich by Nicholas I to design the New Hermitage Museum. Klenze's vast building on the banks of the Neva next to the Hermitage Theater is an impressive amalgam of French, Russian, and German classicism: The monumental porch supported by giant *atlantes* carved by Alexander Ivanovitch Terebenev has a Russian grandiosity; the principal staircase echoes the one of 1803–7 by Chalgrin at the Palais du Luxembourg; the restrained Grecian trabeation of the facades was inspired by Schinkel, as was the careful layout of the galleries, with pictures hung on low side screens and with rooms allotted to the different schools of painting.

In Moscow the classical tradition came to an end in two great buildings by the German-born architect Konstantin Andreevich Ton (1794–1881): the Great Kremlin Palace (1838–49) and the huge church of the Redeemer (1839–83), whose odd, half-Byzantine, half-classical style points forward to the nationalistic Slav Revival of the later nineteenth century.

SCANDINAVIA

In the early nineteenth century the capital cities of Scandinavia—Copenhagen, Helsinki, and Christian (Oslo)—produced a rich harvest of public buildings in the classical style that had been developed since the mid-

497. Caspar Frederik Harsdorff, mortuary chapel for Frederik V, cathedral, Roskilde, 1768–78; completed by Christian Frederik Hansen, 1821–25

498. Christian Frederik Hansen, Vor Fruc Kirke, Copenhagen, 1811–29

499. Christian Frederik Hansen, courthouse and prison, Copenhagen, 1803–16

500. Christian Frederik Hansen, Vor Fruc Kirke, Copenhagen, interior, 1811–29

501. M. Gottlieb Bindesbøll, Thorvaldsen Museum, Copenhagen, courtyard, 1837–48

eighteenth century in France, England, and Italy and that was to be so strikingly codified by Schinkel in Germany. Indeed, there is a strong German flavor to Scandinavian classicism in these years. However, the new style had been imported very early from France by two French architects, Nicolas-Henry Jardin (1720–1799), who lived in Denmark from 1755 to 1771, and Jean-Louis Desprez (1743–1804), who was employed by Gustavus III of Sweden beginning in 1784. Jardin's dining room of 1755–57 for Count A. G. Moltke in what is now the Amalienborg Palace in Copenhagen has been described as "the earliest surviving room decorated entirely in the Neo-Classical taste by a French architect" (S. Eriksen, *Early Neo-Classicism in France,* 1974, p. 57). Caspar Frederik Harsdorff (1735–1799), first a pupil of Jardin at the Royal Academy in Copenhagen, later studied under Blondel in Paris. His mortuary chapel for Frederick V in the cathedral at Roskilde, built in the 1770s, is a cool and beautiful blend of Blondel's and Adam's styles. Desprez, who was principally a stage designer, built the Botanicum at Uppsala in 1788 with a long, low portico of eight Greek Doric columns. This Greek enthusiasm had already been expressed in the designs of the Swedish-born Carl August Ehrensvärd (1745–1800), whose visit to Paestum in 1780–82 had resulted in his primitivist Doric project of 1785 for a dockyard gate at Karlskrona. The most important Scandinavian architect to emerge in these years was Christian Frederick Hansen (1756–1845). In his architectural group composed of town hall, courthouse, and prison, with its attendant archways (1803–16), he brought to Copenhagen the Franco-Prussian style that Gilly had developed out of the work of Ledoux. Hansen's principal achievement is the cathedral at Copenhagen, the Vor Fruc Kirke (designed 1808–10; built 1811–29), with its Doric colonnades supporting an immense coffered barrel vault reminiscent of Boullée's celebrated project for the new hall of the Bibliothèque Nationale. Hansen's pupil M. Gottlieb Bindesboll (1800–1856) produced the memorable Thorvaldsen Museum in Copenhagen (1837–48), an idiosyncratic blend of styles borrowed from Egypt, Greece, and Schinkel. In his other works Bindesboll tended toward the Rundborgenstil ("round-arch" style), as did his follower J. D. Herholdt (1818–1902), for example, in the Copenhagen University Library (1855–61).

The foundation of a new capital in Norway after that country's separation from Denmark in 1814 created great opportunities for the architect Christian Heinrich Grosch (1801–1865), a pupil of Hansen. At Christiania he built the Exchange (1826–52), using a baseless Tuscan order *in antis,* the Norwegian Bank (1828), and, most important, the University (1841–52), which has a markedly Schinkelesque trabeation. Here, a Greek Ionic portico leads into a fine Greek Doric hall.

Perhaps the most attractive project of the period in Scandinavia was the development of Helsinki after the city became a Russian gran duchy in 1809. The plan of the newly chosen capital of Finland is the work of the architect Johan Albrekt Ehrenström (1762–1847), but all the major public buildings

505. *Johann Carl Ludwig Engel, hospital, Helsinki, 1826*

506. *Johann Carl Ludwig Engel, University Library, Helsinki, staircase, 1836–45*

507. *Alessandro Pompei, Museo Lapidario Maffeiano, Verona, elevation and plan, 1739–c. 1746*

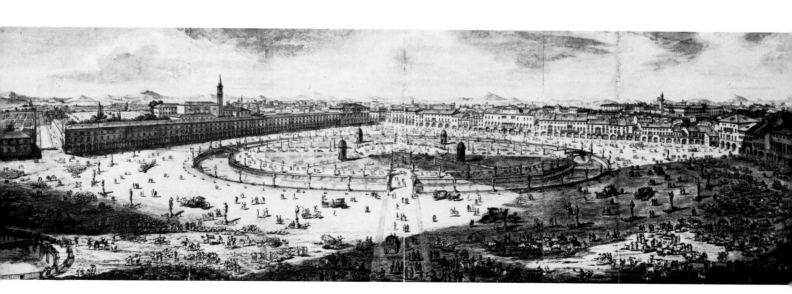

508. *Antonio Visentini, Palazzo Smith (now Argentine Consulate), Venice, 1751. Enlarged by Giannantonio Selva in 1784*
509. *Tommaso Temanza, S. Maria Maddalena, Venice, 1760, 1763–78*

510. *Andrea Memmo and Domenico Cerato, Prato della Valle, Padua, 1775–90. Engraving by Piranesi*

511. *Giannantonio Selva, Teatro La Fenice, Venice, 1790–92*
512. *Giannantonio Selva, S. Maurizio, Venice, begun 1806*

and many private houses are by the German-born Johann Carl Ludwig Engel (1778–1840). He created the superb Senate Square, dominated by his cathedral (designed from 1818 onward; built 1830–51) at the top of a great flight of steps, and flanked by his University (1828–32) and Senate (1818–22). The University Library, with its magnificent colonnaded reading rooms, was designed in 1833 and later, and built from 1836 to 1845. Perhaps the most striking features of Engel's work are his Doric staircases: The massive, freestanding Paestum-Doric columns of the Senate staircase unexpectedly carry groin-vaulted ceilings, whereas two stories of fluted and unfluted columns create a complex web of trabeation in the staircase at the University Library.

ITALY

Italy was partially unified under the French from 1796 to the fall of Napoleon in 1814, but not until the late nineteenth century was it formally united under a single ruler, Victor Emmanuel II. For most of the period under consideration it was thus a conglomeration of odd and often opposing states, controlled for the most part by outside powers. Piedmont was completely oriented to France until the Treaty of Aix-la-Chapelle in 1748. Lombardy was a province of Austria until the arrival of Napoleon. Parma remained an outpost of French culture after 1748, when Louis XV's daughter married the Bourbon duke. Venice maintained a staunch independence until Napoleon dismissed the last doge. Trieste owed allegiance to Austria but became a free port in 1719, which inevitably changed things. And so one might continue. There was no common culture. From the middle years of the eighteenth century there was, in addition, very little money. Circumstances were not auspicious for architecture.

Early in the eighteenth century there was, indeed, a short but brilliant flowering of the late Baroque. In Piedmost Filippo Juvarra and Bernardo Antonio Vittone were busy; in Roma those monuments that still give pleasure without alloy—the Spanish Steps (1723–25), the Piazza S. Ignazio (1727–28), and the Fontana di Trevi (1732–62)—were being built. But in the middle years of the century this heady architectural splurge suddenly ceased. Activity continued in the south, where the Bourbon had taken over in 1738. Charles III summoned Ferdinando Fuga (1699–1782) and Luigi Vanvitelli (1700–1773) to Naples in 1751, and there they began some of the largest schemes ever devised for the Bourbons—Fuga's Albergo de' Poveri and the granary, Vanvitelli's royal palace at Caserta and the barracks. But inspiration was weak, and architecture in Italy entered the doldrums.

Even in Venice and on the nearby mainland, where building continued and the fiery Lodoli, as we have seen, was preaching his radical doctrines, little of interest was being done. Lodoli and his circle of intellectuals did not much influence the course of architecture, though Scipione Maffei's Museo Lapidario at Verona, completed about 1746 by Alessandro Pompei

513. *Raffaello Stern,*
Braccio Nuovo, Vatican Museum,
Rome, 1817–22

(1705–1772), must be regarded as a harbinger of neoclassicism, and Andrea Memmo's public-spirited works in Padua, the Prato della Valle and the hospital, both begun in 1775 by the local professor of architecture Domenico Cerato (1720–1792), were clearly intended to illustrate Lodoli's ideas. But architecture in the Veneto continued to be dominated by the influence of Palladio. Architects as diverse as the exuberant Giorgio Massari (1687–1766) and the over-fastidious Antonio Visentini (1688–1782), designer of the Palazzo Smith (now the Argentine Consulate), of 1751, and the Palazzo Coletti-Giusti, of 1766, both on the Grand Canal, used the elements and the compositional devices that Palladio had established. Ottavio Bertotti-Scamozzi, working in Vicenza on this same basis, was able to evolve an architecture of some power and conviction, but there was no fresh impulse. Yet a significant line of architectural descent can be traced in Venice, beginning with Massari's master, Andrea Tirali (1657–1737), and his nephew Giovanni Antonio Scalfarotto (1690–1764), designers, respectively, of the giant portico of S. Nicolò da Tolentino (1706–14) and of SS. Simeone e Giuda (1718–38), a high-domed, circular church, also fronted with a pedimented portico. Scalfarotto's nephew and disciple was Tommaso Temanza (1705–1789), architect of the small but robustly designed circular church S. Maria Maddalena (1760, 1763–78), but remembered chiefly as a stern teacher and propagandist, and especially as author of the *Vita dei più celebri architetti e scultori veneziani*, of 1778. Francesco Milizia was to derive much of his information from Temanza. Lodoli loathed him as an insufferable pedant. They were bitterly opposed, possibly in connection with the building of Temanza's first work, the Cappella dei Sagredo, in S. Francesco della Vigna, also in Venice. But Temanza was to attain success through his pupil Giannantonio Selva (1754–1819), who traveled to Rome, Paris, London, and, later, Constantinople, before he settled down to design a number of well-proportioned and clear-cut buildings based on one or two themes and no more, but so competently handled that they are of more than provincial interest: the Teatro La Fenice, Venice, built rapidly between 1790 and 1792, and much reorganized by G.B. Meduna after a fire in 1836, but still today resplendent; the Palazzo Dotti-Vigodarzere, in the Via Rudena, Padua, of 1796; and the two Venetian churches S. Maurizio, begun in 1806, and S. Nome di Gesù, of nine years later, both completed by Selva's assistant Antonio Diedo (1772–1847). With Diedo, Selva also designed the dull facade of the duomo at Cologna Veneta (1810–17) and that most famous and even more boring work associated with his name, the great mausoleum for Antonio Canova at Possagno, of 1819 to 1833 (however, credit—or the reverse—for this conflation of the Parthenon and the Pantheon has not yet been fixed). Selva's most celebrated pupil was Giuseppe Jappelli (1783–1852), the first of these Venetian architects to win international recognition—largely, it must be admitted, for that hydra-headed work, the Caffè Pedrocchi and the Pedrocchino in Padua—part Egyptian, part classical, begun in 1826, part

516. *Giannantonio Selva and Antonio Diedo (attributed), mausoleum of Antonio Canova, Possagno, 1819–33*

517. *Giuseppe Jappelli, Caffè Pedrocchi, Padua, 1826–31*

518. *Giambattista Piranesi, S. Maria del Priorato, Rome, begun 1764*

519. *Lorenzo Santi, Caffè (now Air Terminal), Venice, 1815–38*

520. Matteo Pertsch, Palazzo
Carciotti, Trieste, 1799–1806

521. Matteo Pertsch, Palazzo
Carciotti, Trieste 1799–1806 (right).
The Canal Grande and S. Antonio
Grande are in the background

522. Pietro di Nobile, S. Antonio
Nuovo, Trieste, 1825–49

523. Antonio Asprucci, Temple of
Aesculapius, Villa Borghese, Rome,
1787

524. *Francesco Gurrieri Pasquale Poccianti and Giuseppe Cacialli, Villa del Poggio Imperiale, Florence, begun 1806*

525. *Francesco Gurrieri Pasquale Poccianti, Sala d'Elci, Biblioteca Laurenziana, Florence, 1816–41*

Picturesque Gothic, begun in 1838, all completed by 1842. But Jappelli was also responsible for other equally arresting works, including the stern Doric meat market (1819–24), now the Scuola Pietro Selvatico, and the Villa Treves de' Bonfili, with its *giardino inglese* (now a public park), both in Padua; outside Padua, at Saonara, the far better preserved villa and garden of the Conti Cittadella Vigodarzere (begun 1816); the Villa Gera on the Via F. Benini at Conegliano (1827); and the Villa Manzoni at Patt di Sedico (1837), probably the largest in the province of Belluno. Altogether, Jappelli evolved a firm and competent style, one that impinges on international neoclassicism, even if it did not influence it.

When Napoleon reached Venice in 1807, he at once thought to make an impression by ordering large-scale works. Selva built the public garden at Castello for him, now greatly altered, and also the cemetery, also modified; but most of the major commissions went to outsiders. Giuseppe Maria Soli (1747–1823), from Vignola (though he had trained in Bologna under Malvasia), began the west side of the Piazza S. Marco in 1810. Lorenzo Santi (1783–1839), from Siena, also a pupil of Selva, designed the great stair and the ballroom inside Soli's Ala Napoleonica in 1822. Then he undertook that lively yet Doric-decked Caffè (1815–38), at the far end of the old Giardinetto Reale, now used as an air terminal, and finally the Palazzo Patriarcale tucked in at the side of the duomo (1837–50). There is nothing much to tell of architecture in Venice after this date.

In Rome, where the turmoil and intrigue occasioned by foreign visitors largely conditioned the form of international neoclassicism, there was even less sustained architectural activity. Piranesi, who arrived there from Venice in 1740, produced only the disappointing, if most intriguing, church of S. Maria del Priorato, high on the Aventine, begun in 1764. Quarenghi, who went in 1763 from Bergamo to Rome, where he met and studied with Selva, stayed long enough to rebuild the church of S. Scolastica at Subiaco (1771–77) before he was packed off to Russia in 1779 by Baron Friedrich Grimm. Carlo Francesco Giacomo Marchionni (1702–1786) was born in Rome but spent his early years in his family's native town of Montecelio, in the Marches. He was trained in Rome, under Filippo Barigioni, and in 1728 won first prize in the Concorso Clementino, at the Accademia di San Luca. By 1751 he had begun work on the Villa Albani, soon to become the mecca of Winckelmann and Mengs. This famous villa, heavily articulated both inside and out, with decorative details evidently influenced by Piranesi, was more or less complete by the end of 1762, though work in the interior continued until 1764, and on the terraces and garden buildings until 1767. It was a tour de force, but not one that had much influence. Nor indeed did Marchionni's other important work, the new sacristy of St. Peter's, erected between 1776 and 1784. This was viciously attacked by the only Italian critic of any acumen, Francesco Milizia (1725–1798), who had come from Otranto, via Naples, to Rome. He was hounded out of town for such effrontery. But his reputation had already been made with the publication

in 1768 of the first edition of the *Vita degli architetti più celebri,* to be followed four years after by *Del teatro* and in 1781 by the *Principii di architettura civile.* These were all to be translated abroad.

Neoclassicism came to Rome only after the death of Winckelmann in 1768. He was succeeded as *Commissario dei Musei e Soprintendente alle Antichità* by the archaeologist Giovanni Battista Visconti, who at once initiated the transformation of Innocent VIII's casina in the Vatican as a museum. The alterations to the octagonal court were begun by Alessandro Dori, but in 1772 Michelangelo Simonetti (1724–1781) took up the work, which was to be continued with real enthusiasm only after the election of Pius VI in 1775, when Simonetti was joined by Pietro Camporese (1726–1781). The Sala delle Muse, the Sala a Croce Greca, and the new access stairs are all theirs, while the Braccio Nuovo, built between 1817 and 1822, is by Raffaello Stern (1774–1820); together, these rooms make up a sequence of varied spaces, each based on an antique precedent, with the details also of unusual archaeological correctness. The result is indeed neoclassical, and most impressive, but not readily applicable to smaller-scale works.

A confident, easily imitated neoclassical style appeared in Rome only with the arrival of the French. Giuseppe Valadier (1762–1839), who had worked long and hard in the Papal States, and in particular at Urbino, where he had rebuilt the duomo, presented an initial project for the planning and development of the Piazza del Popolo and the Pincio in 1793. This ambitious scheme, with its ramps and carriageways climbing the hill, was at once taken up by the French. Alexandre-Jean-Baptiste-Guy de Gisors (1762–1835) and Louis-Martin Berthault were sent from France to supervise both it and the superb Casina at the top. The final project was not approved, however, until April 1813, and when Pius VII assumed control in 1816 further modifications were made, so that the full splendor of the whole was not to be experienced before 1820. By then Valadier had done several other works of a neoclassical kind: restorations to the Arch of Titus (1819–20) and the Colosseum (1820), but mostly large and pretentious villas. The grandest to be built at this time, the Villa Torlonia, on the Via Nomentana, was begun early in the nineteenth century to the designs of Valadier, who was succeeded within a few years by Giovanni Battista Caretti (1803–1878). He laid out the gardens and the first pavilions, but the later ones and the ruins were built from 1840 to 1846 by Jappelli, Antonio Sarti, and others.

In Rome there was little succession to these works, though Valadier's pupil Lorenzo Nottolini (1785–1851) set up in Lucca, where he designed a noble stairway and sculpture gallery for the Palazzo Ducale in 1818 and, in 1826, proposed a grand layout for the Prato del Marchese not unrelated to Memmo's town-planning venture in Padua. During these years he built a succession of bridges and aqueducts, town houses, and, in particular, the Specola (Observatory) and Rotonda, at Marlia nearby, that conferred something of cosmopolitan sophistication on this provincial outpost.

301

528. Leopoldo Laperuta, Antonio de Simone, and Pietro Bianchi, S. Francesco di Paola, begun 1809, redesigned 1817, finished 1831

529. Giuseppe Venanzio Marvuglia with Giuseppe Patricola, La Favorita (or Palazzina Cinese), Palermo, 1799–1802

530. Ennemond-Alexandre Petitot, La Venezia, Colorno, 1753–55

Clearly, the development of architecture in Venice and Rome was, at first, sluggish, and when the pace quickened it was owing largely to outside influence. Selva was probably more indebted to the English example than to the French (though in his obituary Diedo described Selva's early work as in the "gusto francese"), but most architects took their cue from Paris. This is not, of course, to suggest that the Italians themselves had nothing to offer, but rather to indicate that the style of 1800 was one the French had first fashioned and used—exploited, even—long before the Italians took it up and gave it their own particular twist. The French provided not only the ideas and the examples but also the authority and power. They were invaders intent to make their presence felt and seen. They were great builders. The same, to a lesser extent, was true of the Austrians. Throughout Italy the impetus for change came from outside.

In Trieste, Germanic influences were strong, starting with Matteo Pertsch, who had trained under Giuseppe Piermarini in Milan and adapted his master's La Scala for his first works of importance, the Teatro Grande (now Verdi), in 1798–1806. His mature works, too, relate to Milanese classicism: the vast Palazzo Carciotti (1799–1806), conspicuously and rather ridiculously domed; nearby, also on the Riva 3 Novembre, the front of S. Nicolò dei Greci (1818–19); and—still within the new quarter of the town then being developed—the Rotonda dei Pancera (c. 1818). The second and far more able architect active in Trieste was Pietro Nobile (1774–1854), from the Ticino area of Switzerland, who trained from 1803 to 1805 in Rome. But he was soon established in Trieste, where he designed the Fontana House in 1813–16 (built only in 1827–30) and the Accademia di Commercio e Nautica (now the Biblioteca Civica Hortis), of 1817. His major work was S. Antonio Nuovo (1825–49), a noble church, beautifully sited at the head of the Canal Grande, and of more spatial interest than anything else of the period. His Costanzi House, of 1840, trim and unadorned, is in a style that was by then long out of fashion in the rest of Europe. In 1817 he was called to Vienna, where he was to build the Theseus Temple in the Volksgarten, of 1822, and the nearby Burgtor, of 1821 to 1824, in a heavy classical style still coherent and strong.

In Genoa the spark was kindled by de Wailly. Work on his salon for the Palazzo Spinola, commissioned in 1772, was supervised by Emanuele Andrea Tagliafichi (1729–1811), who traveled two years later to Paris, where he was made a corresponding member of the Académie. His original contribution came in the stair hall and salon of the Palazzo Durazzo-Pallavicini, in the Via Balbi, begun in 1780. But the only Genoan architect of consequence was Carlo Francesco Barabino (1768–1835), designer of the Teatro Carlo Felice and the related Palazzo dell'Accademia (1825–28; badly damaged in 1944) and of the first project for the cemetery of Staglieno (1835, 1844–51). He had trained in Rome with Giuseppe Barberi.

In Florence, activity was stirred by the work of redecorating the Palazzo Pitti, from 1796 onward, by Gaspare Maria Paoletti (1727–1813). He was

responsible for the first design for the ballroom, while his pupils Giuseppe Cacialli (1778–1828) and Francesco Gurrieri Pasquale Poccianti (1774–1858) designed the highly articulated stairway in the garden wing. All were involved also in the rebuilding of the Villa del Poggio Imperiale, outside Florence, for Queen Marie Louise, whose kingdom of Etruria existed from 1801 to 1808. The powerful facade there was designed by Poccianti in 1806, but he left the work to Cacialli, to return to Florence, to the Pitti and to design the Sala d'Elci (1817–41) adjoining Michelangelo's Biblioteca Laurenziana. He also took up the system of aqueducts, filters, and cisterns in and around Livorno, which were to culminate in his Cisternone (1829–42), a not unworthy successor to Ledoux's gateway at Arc-et-Senans and certainly the most successful attempt in Italy, if not in all Europe, to realize the dreams of French visionaries. Giovanni Antonio Antolini, it seems, offered his advice, but Poccianti kept him at bay in Bologna by sending him his favorite salamis. The Cisternino, which came later, between 1837 and 1848, is powerful, too, but without dramatic impact.

Poccianti's facade for the Villa del Poggio Imperiale must have impressed deeply the young Antonio Niccolini (1772–1850), the stage designer, who worked there and also at Livorno. He reached Naples in 1808 (two years after the arrival of the French) and was commissioned one year later to design a new facade for G.A. Medrano's Teatro S. Carlo; the result was a tough Florentine (and French) leviathan, at odds with the sloppy Baroque architecture that the Bourbons had cultivated until then, *pace* the Vanvitellis. The facade was largely built in 1810. Six years later the old theater burned down and Niccolini was employed with Antonio de Simone to erect a new one behind it. For the Bourbons, who returned in 1815, he built extensively: On the Vomero he put up the Villa Floridiana (1817–19) and the adjoining Villa Lucia (1818) for Ferdinand I and his morganatic wife, Lucia Partanna; in the Piazza dei Martiri he refaced and decorated the Palazzo Partanna. Most of his energy was spent on designs for the reordering of the royal palace itself, but he saw none of this built.

Outside Naples his chief works were in Bari: the Teatro Piccini (now part of the Villa Comunale) and the church of S. Ferdinando, both projects supervised by his son Fausto.

The second altogether surprising and successful building begun at Naples under the French was the church of S. Francesco di Paola, enclosing the Piazza Plebiscito with curved colonnades. The Foro Murat, as it was first called, was established by a decree of February 1808; demolition was begun at once but Leopoldo Laperuta's design was chosen only later in the year. The colonnades were built and the church started with the assistance of Antonio de Simone, but when the Bourbons returned they decided that it should become a dynastic chapel, dominating the square, now named the Foro Ferdinando. A competition for a new church was held. Eventually, after much intrigue and trickery, Pietro Bianchi (1787-1849), a pupil of Luigi Cagnola from the Ticino area, was commissioned to build it in 1817. It was

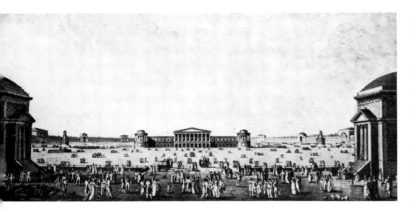

539. Giovanni Antonio Antolini,
project for the Foro Buonaparte,
Milan, 1801
540. Luigi Canonica, Arena, Milan,
aerial view, 1805–24

completed by 1831, the most carefully detailed and richly finished of all new churches in Italy.

Related to, but distinct from, the activity in Naples was that in Sicily, in Palermo, where the break from the late Baroque was occasioned by the Frenchman Léon Dufourny. He spent six years there, and between 1789 and 1792 built the Villa Giulia, a botanical institute, stiff and four-square, clearly inspired by the Doric temples of the island. This was soon extended by two pavilions in an even more consciously primitive style by Giuseppe Venanzio Marvuglia (1729–1814). He had studied under Vanvitelli in Roma and had pursued an active if undistinguished career in Palermo until, inspired by Dufourny, he began La Favorita, or Palazzina Cinese, in 1799, a curious but captivating confection, part classical, part Chinese. In the garden he built the Fontana dell'Ercole, a monstrous Doric column supporting a tiny statue of Hercules. His other late work, the Villa Belmonte, of 1801, high on the slopes of Monte Pellegrino, was less engaging and far more restrained. In 1805 he was elected a corresponding member of the Institut National des Sciences et des Arts (later the Académie des Beaux-Arts) in Paris.

Architectural activity, though fervid during the Napoleonic interlude, was, on the whole, sporadic. Only in Lombardy was it sustained and consistent over a long period. The *locus classicus* for reform, however, was not in Milan but in Parma, where an academy was established in 1752, to which, on the Comte de Caylus's suggestion, Soufflot's pupil Ennemond-Alexandre Petitot was invited in the following year. He introduced and cultivated the French tradition both in his teaching and by his example. As court architect he huilt the new facade of S. Pietro (1761) and the Palazzo di Riserva (1764), both painted yellow; he drew up plans for La Pilotta (1766), an extended palace that was not to be built but that served nonetheless as a point of reference for his pupils; and he altered and enlarged the Palazzo Ducale (1767 onward), known also as the Palazzo del Giardino. Neraby, in Colorno, he built La Veneria (1753–55) and S. Liborio (1775–91), both of which were thought to be very French: La Veneria on account of its round-headed windows, the church because of the freestanding columns inside, which were more in evidence in the initial scheme than in the one executed. Petitot's style was scarcely advanced, despite the evidence of his student projects. However, he was able to handle the elements of A.-J. Gabriel's style whith sufficient competence and confidence, and his academy became famous. When Catherine the Great decided to set up one of her own, she wrote to Petitot for advice. His pupils were legion: Agostino Gerli, Simone Cantoni, Carlo Felice Soave, Giocondo Albertolli, Carlo Antonio Aspari, and Faustino Rodi (1751–1835) among them. Gerli, who worked also in Paris, perhaps with Honoré Guibert, is often thought to have marked the beginnings of late eighteenth-century classicism in Lombardy with his decorations for the main salons of the Villa Longhi at Vialba, begun in 1769. But there was more to the new style than decoration.

Power in Milan was long the Austrian prerogative, but after 1796 it passed several times into the hands of the French, causing upheavals and changes in personnel. Both administrations, however, were efficient and ambitious, and their aims were not dissimilar. The pattern of architectural development, if not the personalities involved, continued throughout almost uninterrupted.

When Caylus visited Milan in the first half of the century he found it a miserable city, but with the building of canals in the Lombardy plain and the consequent spectacular expansion of agriculture, landowners became richer and thought to build both town and country houses. The Austrians, moreover, were able to collect taxes with greater success than ever before. Milan was slowly rebuilt. Roads were constructed and new areas opened up on the sites of the monastic establishments that had been suppressed—twenty-six were closed down in 1782 alone. In 1790 the old gates were torn down and the city limits increased. The building of houses continued apace. Under Napoleon's administration even larger planning proposals were instigated and much was built. The nature of the city was not, however, to be greatly changed until the middle of the nineteenth century, when silk and cotton mills were opened up and industrialization began. This is part of a later history.

Under the Austrians architecture in Milan was dominated by Giuseppe Piermarini (1734–1808), who had worked for twelve years in Rome and Caserta with Vanvitelli and was brought by him to Milan in 1769, when he was invited to rebuild the Palazzo Ducale. Soon after, Piermarini took the project over and was made *Architetto di Stato,* a position he held until he fled from the French in 1796. For twenty-five years he controlled all building; nothing was erected of which he did not approve. He also ensured a continuance of his tastes by presiding over the Brera Academy, founded in 1776. His first independent work was the Accademia Virgiliana in Mantua, designed in 1770, built between 1773 and 1775. This is uninspiring, with an uneasy relationship between plan and elevation indicative of Piermarini's weakness as an architect. Not that this seems to have affected his career. He began in Milan with the vast Palazzo Belgioioso (1772–81) on the piazza of the same name, with a facade that is heavily articulated, though each element, even the individual rustications, retains a curious isolation. Other houses followed, the best of which are the Palazzo Greppi (1772–78); the Palazzo Moriggia (c. 1775), in the Via Borgonuovo; and the Casnedi House (c. 1776), with facades made up, as it were, of thin layers of rectangular panels. They are, for the rest, unadorned: "Ces indignes façades à la Piermarini," Stendhal wrote in his guide to Rome, Naples, and Florence. But the major work of this period was the Palazzo Ducale, which he took up in 1773 and continued until 1778. Here he introduced for the first time the most famous of the seven Albertollis, Giocondo (1742–1839), who had taught design at Parma for ten years, before moving in 1772 to Rome and then to Naples to work with Vanvitelli. By 1774 he was in

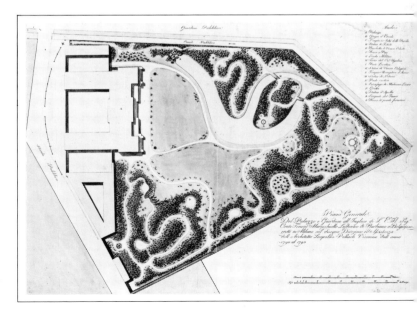

543. Luigi Cagnola, Porta Ticinese, Milan, 1801–14

Florence, cooperating with Paoletti on the Sala della Niobe in the Uffizi, and also at the Villa del Poggio Imperiale, to which he later returned. Late in 1774 Piermarini invited Albertolli to Milan, where he began on the interiors of the Palazzo Ducale—"il primo esempio," he said, "di buon gusto"—now sadly charred. He soon took over all the decorative work in Piermarini's buildings and began teaching also at the Brera Academy. He showed his students how to isolate forms and motifs and then assemble them in geometrical patterns. His pupils were numerous; it has even been suggested that Percier and Fontaine are to be numbered among them. Selva certainly was. Albertolli's publications, the *Ornamenti diversi inventati* (1782), *Alcune decorazioni di nobili sale ed altri ornamenti* (1787), and *Miscellanea per i giovani studiosi del disegno* (1796), made his style even more readily available. This was of the heavy sort, not unlike that of Jean-Louis Prieur and of

Neufforge. His only important independent building was the Villa Melzi (1805–15), at Bellagio, overlooking Lake Como. The facade, as in Piermarini's houses, is curiously flat.

Outside Milan, at Monza, Piermarini built the Villa Ducale (1776–80), once again decorated by Albertolli, though the chapel, still intact, was all to Piermarini's design. At Cassano d'Adda he erected a smaller variant in the extension to the Villa Borromeo (1780–85). Both these buildings are made up of cubic masses, the surfaces smooth and flattened, altogether without strength, as indeed was his last major work in Milan, the Teatro alla Scala (1776–78). The detail here is too lightweight. The interior has been many times altered. Yet within a year of laying the foundation stone Piermarini was busy on another theater in Milan, the Canobbiana (for those members of the aristocracy who had failed to get a box at La Scala), and was soon at work on others at Novara (1777), Monza (c. 1778), Mantua (1782–83), Crema (1783–85) and Matelica (designed 1803; built 1805–12). Those for whom he did not build imitated him: at Trieste, as we have seen; at Piacenza; and even as far afield as Lisbon, where J. Costa y Silva built the new opera house in 1792. Selva, who had been replaced as architect to the theater at Trieste by Piermarini's pupil Pertsch, disliked La Scala; it was, he noted, far too French. But there is really nothing particularly French about Piermarini's work. His contemporary Simone Cantoni (1739–1818), who had also worked for Vanvitelli but had trained between 1767 and 1768 in Parma and then with Tagliafichi in Genoa, was more French-inspired. Piermarini saw to it that he received no official commissions, but he built a great number of town and country houses and one public building, the Palazzo Ducale (1778–83) in Genoa. Milizia inspected the salon there and, even before its completion, conferred his approval. But the two works that reveal Cantoni at his most Gallic are the Palazzo Serbelloni (designed 1775; much revised and built 1779–94), 16 Corso Venezia, Milan, where Napoleon was received in 1796—though the grand salon was not complete until 1814—and the Palazzo Pertusati (1789–91), on the canal in Milan, now destroyed. The likes of these had not been seen in Italy. The first building has two attenuated Ionic columns set *in antis* within a central feature, topped by a steep pediment, screening a continuous bas-relief panel, a combination of motifs first used by Bélanger. The second was even more closely modeled on a Parisian *hôtel*, of the type of the Hôtel d'Argenson. But Cantoni was a wayward architect. For the Serbellonis he also built SS. Protasio e Gervasio at Gorgonzola (where in 1775 he had already designed the cemetery), a bold but broken composition consisting of a central portico linked by low arcades to two pavilions with great arched openings breaking into the pediments above. Behind the facade other features were piled up, topped by a lantern. The church, which shows Cantoni at his most idiosyncratic, was begun in 1802 and finished in 1842, when the campanile was completed by Giacomo Moraglia. Between these works came a long series of villas, starting with the Villa Olmo at Borgovico (1782–94), and

308

including the Villa Giovio at Brescia (1790–95) and the Villa Gallarati-Scotti at Oreno (1790–93). Together they present an extraordinary medley of styles, seme traditional, some more advanced, but having in common only Cantoni's consistent fondness for *atlantes* supported on attenuated pedestals in the attic story.

Piermarini's pupils Leopoldo Pollack (1751–1806) and Luigi Canonica (1764–1844) set the tone of a revised architecture more effectively. Pollack was trained in Vienna with his father, a builder, as was his younger brother Michael Johann, who was to become the most active architect in Budapest. In 1775 Pollack moved to Milan, where Piermarini at once set him to work on the Palazzo Ducale. Canonica, born in the Ticino, was trained by Piermarini at the Brera Academy and inherited thus his administrative skills. When the French arrived in 1796 and Piermarini fled to his native Foligno, Canonica assumed the title of *Architetto di Stato,* for which he was not forgiven: "Capace," Piermarini said of him, "della più nera ingratitudine." Canonica was trusted by the French, though, who invited him to Paris in 1805, and also by the Austrians, for he retained his position until 1807, when it was thought more democratic to set up a commission of five (the Commissione d'Ornato) to control building activity in Milan. Canonica was judicious and competent always. He laid out much of Milan and erected many public and administrative buildings, in particular, the enlargement of the Collegio Elvetico for the senate. Tact was one of his great qualities. This is evident in his own works, which merge into the street pattern: the Palazzo Brentani-Greppi (1829–31), in the Via Manzoni, for example, with its recessed roundels above the windows of the *piano nobile;* on the same street, the Palazzo Anguissola-Traversi (1829–30), with fluted Corinthian pilasters and a rich frieze. Behind, in the Via Morone, is the Anguissola House (1775–78), by Carlo Felice Soave (1740–1803), another Ticinese taught at Parma; its detailing is very much more lively and well thought out, especially on the garden front and in the interiors. Together, these buildings reveal the extraordinary homogeneity of the style developed in Milan at this period. Canonica designed only one building that stands out—and it can hardly have done otherwise—the vast Arena in the park, laid out between 1805 and 1807 and completed in 1824, with a triumphal gateway of 1813. This is very simple, but of a size and scale that lend it grandeur. The inspiration was not Canonica's alone but derives in part from the perfervid activity in Milan of both Giuseppe Pistocchi (1744–1841), who came from Faenza, and Giovanni Antonio Antolini (1753–1841), who came also from Faenza after a long stay in Rome, in 1800. In Milan they indulged themselves in a series of public-spirited projects for the area around the Castello Sforzesco, which, in effect, meant mammoth projects, of which Canonica's Arena was the only built result.

Pollack was a less dutiful follower of Piermarini; he had a style of his own. This was evident from the first, when he took over from Piermarini the building of the University of Pavia: In 1785 came the anatomy theater (Aula Scarpa); in 1786 he began the third court; and by 1787 the physics theater (Aula Volta) was complete, all three in a fashionable French manner. The main stair, not greatly different, was built much later, in 1828, by Giuseppe Marchese. Petitot approved what he saw there: "Bon, bon," was his laconic comment. But Pollack's reputation was made, rather, by the Villa Belgioioso (later Reale), of 1790–96, in Milan. This hints, once again, at French sources, but has, in addition, that tight-packed quality of Piermarini's facades at the Palazzo Belgioioso. The rich interiors provide an odd setting today for the Galleria d'Arte Moderna. The garden, to which Selva and Carlo Amati also contributed, is one of the earliest in the city in a full-fledged Picturesque style, preceding by almost a decade the publication in 1801 of Ercole Silva's pioneering study *Dell'arte dei giardini inglesi,* though not, of course, antedating Silva's own garden at the Villa Ghirlanda Silva in

Cinisello Balsamo. Pollack's most distinguished works followed soon after, the Villa Casati at Muggiò and the Villa Villani Rocca-Saporini, known as La Rotonda, at Borgovico, in both of which the central oval salon plays a dominant part, though in neither instance is it an effective part of the planning arrangements. Pollack, like Piermarini and Canonica, was an indifferent planner. And, again like Canonica, his work in seen to best advantage in the context of contemporary architecture. This may still be done at Borgovico, on the western side of Lake Como, starting with the Villa Carminati (Resta Pallavicino), by Soave, arriving halfway along at La Rotonda, and ending at Cantoni's Villa Olmo and, down a side street, Soave's Villa Salazar. This architectural panorama is wonderfully varied, yet unified.

Only one architect of note succeeded these men, Luigi Cagnola (1762-1833). He represents the climax in the development from Piermarini, a development from a desiccated planar geometry applied to facades to a robust and very solid geometry of form. Cagnola had intended to be a diplomat and began his career in 1795 in Vienna. There he first dabbled actively in architecture, designing a gateway. His initial work in Italy was the Villa Zurla (Vimercati-Sanseverino) at Vaiano Cremasco, almost complete in 1802, when it was damaged by earth tremors. This low, colonnaded building was the outcome of a few years of study at the Academy in Venice and also of a particularly close inspection of the works of Palladio—not that Cagnola's borrowings were ever to be much in evidence. He was a rabid nationalist, which he thought the correct attitude for one of aristocratic descent at that time of unrest, and he turned thus to Italian sources for inspiration: to Palladio, to the Florentine Renaissance, and to ancient Rome. These sources conditioned even his earliest works. In Milan he built the Porta Ticinese (or Marengo), of 1801-14, a simple pedimented portico, and the Arco del Sempione (or della Pace), of 1806–38. Other gates built there in those years were the Porta Nuova (1810–13) by Giuseppe Zanoia (1752–1817);the Porta Comasina (now Porta Garibaldi), of 1826, by Giacomo Moraglia (1791–1860); and, best of all, the Porta Venezia (1827–33) by Rodolfo Vantini (1791–1856). Of these, Cagnola's Arco del Sempione was the one most deliberately based on ancient Roman precedents and executed with the richest of materials and sculptural details. The finest panels were carved by Pompeo Marchesi, Cagnola was to prepare a design for Malmaison after the dismissal of Percier and Fontaine, but his next executed work was his own house. Begun a year or two before 1816, when he married his cousin Francesa del Marchesi d'Adda, it was continued for seventeen years after that date. This was his masterpiece. It is a great inflated piece of architecture set high on a hill overlooking Inverigo, all columns and pedimented porticos approached up giant stairways on one side, all rustications pierced with round-headed openings on the others. In the center is a flattened dome covering a circular hall. A small portico halfway up the hill has giant *atlantes* by Pompeo Marchesi. Formal geometry is the

550. *Giuseppe Mengoni, Galleria Vittorio Emmanuele II, Milan, 1865–77*

determining factor throughout. The internal planning and spatial organization are altogether inept. But having found his style, Cagnola stuck to it: at the Villa Cagnola at Verdello (c. 1820), which has surprisingly pretty floral frescoes in the rooms and romantic ruins in the garden; and the colonnaded church of Concorezzo (1818–58) and that mammoth Pantheon-like one at Ghisalba (1822–33). For neither of these churches did he design the campanile, though he was responsible for the very stylish one at Urgnano (1824–29), near Ghisalba, and another at Chiari (1832), further to the southeast. He built very little in the last years of his life, but he was long held in awe, both by his students and by architects throughout Italy and even abroad. He designed a mausoleum for Metternich and an imperial palace for Vienna, neither of which was built. He was, in fact, a very limited architect, but he appeared to provide a focus in Italy for a style that was based on national precedents demonstrably large in scale, and strong. His appeal to all those architects who prepared vast designs in 1813 for the Monumento alla Riconoscenza al Moncenisio—Selva, Cantoni, and Pistocchi among them—must have been hard to resist. His ability is at once apparent when his work is compared with that of such a follower as Carlo Amati (1776–1852), architect of S. Carlo al Corso in Milan, built, despite well-founded alarms as to its structural stability, between 1839 and 1847. This overscaled church brings to a close the classical movement in Milan, if not in Italy. The rest is gutless niceties. The next phase, beyond the scope of this book, is represented by the Galleria Vittorio Emmanuele II, built by English entrepreneurs with English capital, between 1865 and 1877, to the designs of Giuseppe Mengoni (1829–1877). This is an aspect of the late nineteenth-century process of industrialization and large-scale replanning in Italy, the most disastrous result of which was the destruction of the heart of Florence in 1888.

In all this history there has not been much evidence offered of intellectual endeavor. Much of what there was came during the eighteenth century from France. Milizia's debt has already been mentioned; other authors could be adduced: Paolo Frisi, whose *Saggio sopra l'architettura gotica* was published in Livorno in 1766, or Ermenegildo Pini, author of *Dell'Architettura. Dialoghi,* of 1770. But these are of no great moment. They offered compilations of French thought.

During the nineteenth century the intrusion of new ideas was owing to the activities of the Gothic Revivalists—as it was throughout most of Europe. The Gothic Revival came late to Italy; it began in the early nineteenth century as a foreign import, largely from England, and largely connected with garden decoration. The first structure of any significance was La Margheria at Racconigi, near Turin, of 1834–39, designed by Pelagio Palagi (1775–1860). On the other side of Italy, in Padua, Giuseppe Jappelli had completed his Gothic wing at the Caffè Pedrocchi by 1842. But these were essentially lighthearted, frivolous structures. Gradually, with the growth of Italian nationalism, an interest was stimulated in Italy's own Gothic past;

551. Camillo Boito, Palazzo delle
Debite Padua, 1872–74

552. Camillo Boito, Museo Civico,
Padua, 1879

553. Pelagio Palagi, La Margheria,
Racconigi, 1834–39

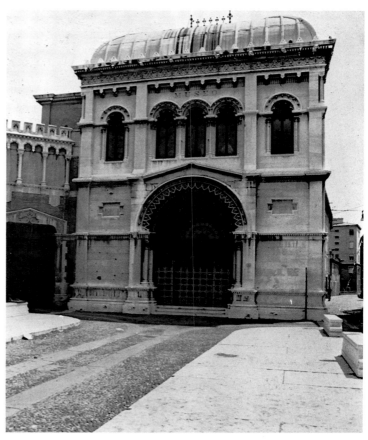

554. Hans Christian Hansen and Theophilos Eduard Hansen, National Library, University, and Academy, Athens, 1839–91

555. Aerial view of Athens in 1932, showing the town as laid out in 1836 by Friedrich von Gärtner, with the principal neoclassical buildings: top right, the Royal Palace; grouped together on the left, The National Library, University and arcade

a serious revival was planned. The most influential exponents were Pietro Estense Selvatico (1803–1880) and Camillo Boito (1836–1914). Selvatico, from the Veneto, was no great revolutionary. He adopted ideas from Pugin, Ruskin, and Viollet-le-Duc, but added a few of his own. He did not build much of interest. However, he trained Boito. Boito, though born in Rome, was taught at the Brera Academy in Milan under Friedrich von Schmidt (1825–1891), who was there from 1857 to 1859 but resigned when Milan was finally lost to the Austrians. He devoted much of his later life to the completion of the cathedral at Cologne. It was from neither Selvatico nor Schmidt, however, that Boito borrowed his ideas; these came from the writings of Viollet-le-Duc, whom he may possibly have met when they acted as judges together at the competition for the facade of Florence cathedral. Boito taught in succession to Schmidt at the Brera Academy for no less than forty-eight years. He was thus of some influence in establishing a new and invigorated doctrine on the lines suggested by Viollet-le-Duc. Among his pupils were Giuseppe Brentano, Luca Beltrami, Gaetano Moretti, and Giuseppe Sommaruga. His own buildings, in a stripped, flattened, and very Italianate medieval style, are of more distinction than any others of this sort in Italy—though they are not in the least engaging. At Gallarate, north of Milan, are two of his early works, a cemetery built in 1865, when he was twenty-nine, and a hospital six years later. These are comparatively restrained, but Boito's Gothic was already becoming more flamboyant and Venetian. At Padua, between 1872 and 1874, he built the Palazzo delle Debite and, five years later, the local museum. But the climax to his career was in Milan, the Casa Verdi, of 1899–1913, on the Piazza Buonarroti, complete with Verdi's colorful tomb chamber. Verdi's librettist, the composer Arrigo Boito, was Camillo's brother.

There are a number of buildings of this sort in Italy, though few were so carefully detailed; for the most part they are funerary chapels. The real energies of the Gothic Revivalists went rather into the completion or rebuilding of the facades of medieval churches. Throughout Italy there were competitions, revisions, disputes, and finally long-drawn-out building programs to finish off the churches of the Middle Ages. There was also a handful of staggering Gothic houses built late in the century: Ernesto Pirovano's Villa Crespi at Capriate d'Adda, of 1890, and Gino Coppedè's Castello Mackenzie at Genoa, of a few years later; and there are many more, even in Sardinia. It was not these stylish extravaganzas, however, that were to be influential in the future but rather the writings and teachings of Boito. He encouraged architects to use a wide variety of materials chosen not for their visual interest alone but also for their appropriateness to the particular role they were to perform. Brick was very popular; sometimes it was plastered, though this was not considered to be "honest." Stone was chosen to trim window surrounds to give added stength to the openings. Only colored plaques and tiles were allowed a purely decorative role. Each element was to be made distinct and expressive. Though the buildings might

556. François-Louis-Florimond Boulanger and Theophilos Eduard Hansen, Zappeion, Athens, circular court, begun 1874

557. Charles Bulfinch, Massachusetts State House, Boston, 1795–98

558. Thomas Jefferson, University of Virginia, Charlottesville, Pavilion IX, designed 1804–17

559. Benjamin Latrobe, Supreme
Court Chamber, Capitol, Washington,
D.C., 1815–17

be complete, the thinking behind them was direct and comparatively simple—simplistic, one might say. But Boito did provide the basis for the acceptance in Italy of Arts-and-Crafts ideas and, ultimately, of the Stile Florale—and thus of Futurism.

GREECE

Athens had shrunk to a settlement of less than ten thousand people by the end of the third decade of the nineteenth century. The revival of architecture, classical architecture in particular, was to start late; indeed, the movement was consolidated there only when it was already out of fashion in the rest of Europe. The style, paradoxical as it may seem, was a foreign import. It arrived in 1833 with the new monarch, Otto von Wittelsbach of Bavaria, likewise an import. The first plan for the renewed capital of Athens was drawn up by Stamatios Kleanthes—who had been trained by Schinkel in Berlin—together with Édouard Schaubert. But this plan was not accepted, nor was that sent to Greece to straighten things out by Otto's father, Ludwig I of Bavaria. Von Klenze proposed a vast palace in the Kerameikos district, not far from the Temple of Hephaestus. In the same year Schinkel, spurred by knowledge of this grand enterprise, proposed a royal palace on the Acropolis itself. It was a marvelous, Picturesque cluster of classic forms, mingled with the ancient temples. The interiors were to be richly colored. But Schinkel did not visit Greece and could not press his claims. The new town plan and the royal palace were finally undertaken in 1836 to the designs of a less ambitious and more practical man, Friedrich von Gärtner. These German architects, though they built little (and, indeed, von Klenze's only building in Athens, the Roman Catholic church of Aghios Dionysios, built between 1858 and 1887, was in Renaissance style), set the tone and the pattern for all major building to follow. Neoclassicism was adopted as the official style. This group of architects was succeeded, like the Bavarian dynasty, by Danes: Hans Christian Hansen (1803–1883) and his brother Theophilos Eduard Hansen (1831–1891). These men established neoclassicism in Greece, and set up an array of the most rigid, but also elegant and pristine, monuments to the style to be seen anywhere in the world today. Three of these are ranged together, the University (H. C. Hansen, 1839–49), the Academy (T. E. Hansen, 1859–87), and the National Library (T. E. Hansen, 1859, 1885, 1888–91). But they built a great deal more besides, and so did their pupil Ernst Ziller (1837–1923), who arrived in Athens in 1861, and their rivals and emulators, the Frenchmen François-Louis-Florimond Boulanger (1807–1875) and E. Troumpe and the Greek architects Panayotis Kalkos (1800–1870), Stamatios Kleanthes (1802–1862), and Lysandros Kaftanzoglu (1812–1885). Kaftanzoglu was trained in both Paris and Rome. These men were naturally active mainly in Athens, creating such extravaganzas as the circular court of the Zappeion (F. L.-F. Boulanger began this in 1874, but it was taken over by T. E. Hansen) and

Ilion Melathron, the house of no less a personality than Heinrich Schliemann (now the Supreme Court) by Ziller, of 1890. But major neoclassical buildings were put up also in Piraeus and scattered as far afield as Patras and the remoter islands. Their crisp, rigid forms and details were copied throughout Greece, transforming even the humblest of houses into models of classical rectitude. As late as 1920 the style survived, virtually unaltered and altogether intact. Now many of the lesser buildings are being destroyed. Others have been drastically altered, as was the Dimetrion House (1842–43) on Syntagma Square, by T. E. Hanse, which became the Hotel Grande Bretagne and survived as such until 1958, when it was demolished and rebuilt, only the ironwork being incorporated into the new hotel. Certainly this extraordinary postscript to the neoclassical movement has been much underestimated, by foreigners no less than by the Greeks themselves.

THE UNITED STATES OF AMERICA

The enthusiast for full-scale Greek Revival architecture will find no country so satisfying as North America. Here in the first half of the nineteenth century flowered prolifically, if sometimes coarsely, the seeds planted by James Stuart in his Doric temple at Hagley in 1758. Thomas Jefferson (1743–1826) and Benjamin Henry Latrobe (1764–1820) were the most interesting architects in late eighteenth-century America. Though many others were anxious to emulate their example during the Greek Revival of the nineteenth century, none possessed quite the quality of Latrobe. For another classical architect of comparable imagination, America had to wait for the emergence, in the 1870s, of Charles Follen McKim (1847–1909), trained in Paris.

The architect Charles Bulfinch (1763–1844) reflects the uncertain impact on America of the classicism of Chambers and Adam. His domed and colonnaded Massachusetts State House, Boston (1795–98), is a gross and inflated version of the work of Perrault, Chambers, and Adam, but it set the pattern for much official building in the nineteenth century. In the meantime, the more subtle Jefferson was working on the ever-changing designs for his own house, Monticello, at Charlottesville, Virginia. It was conceived in 1771 on a plan taken from Robert Morris's *Select Architecture* (1755) and adapted to a facade from Palladio's *Quattro libri*. The construction of this carefully thought-out, but not, by English standards, especially remarkable, building was carried out between 1771 and 1782. Work was resumed in 1793, and by 1809 the building had been completely transformed into a much more interesting and complex, though basically one-storied, house. With its varied and original planning, its Picturesque parkland setting, and its superb views of mountain scenery, Monticello realized Jefferson's dream of re-creating the Roman villas described by Pliny, admired by Lord Burlington and the English Palladians, and recorded

318

in Robert Castell's *Villas of the Ancients Illustrated* (1728).

In 1785-89 Jefferson designed the Virginia State Capitol, at Richmond, with a vast and rather vapid Ionic portico supposedly inspired by the Corinthian-columned Maison Carrée at Nîmes, which he had seen and admired a year or so earlier. In 1790 the site of the new federal city of Washington was selected and plans were drawn up by the Frenchman Pierre-Charles L'Enfant (1754–1825). On Jefferson's suggestion, competitions were held in 1792 for the president's house and the Capitol. The Irishman James Hoban (c. 1762-1831) won the competition for the former with an old-fashioned design copied from James Gibb's *Book of Architecture* (1728). The competition for the Capitol was inconclusive, and the rather pedestrian pile executed between 1792 and 1828 was the outcome of an uneasy alliance between the Frenchman Stephen Hallet and three English-born architects, Dr. William Thornton (1758–1828), George Hadfield (c. 1763–1826), and Benjamin Latrobe. The side wings and commanding dome with its cast-iron frame were added in 1851–65 by Thomas U. Walter (1804–1887).

It is a relief to turn from the Capitol to the novelty and charm of Jefferson's University of Virginia, at Charlottesville. The idea of an "academical village" consisting of small, linked buildings surrounded by grass and trees had been growing in Jefferson's mind between 1804 and 1810, but it was not until 1817 that the final plans were drawn up and the foundation stone laid. The captivating arrangement, with its two groups of five Palladian pavilions linked by colonnades and facing each other across a great lawn, seems to have been inspired (ironically, given the libertarian views of Jefferson) by the most remarkable monument of French absolutism, Louis XIV's Château de Marly, which Jefferson had visited with Maria Cosway when in Paris. In fact, Jefferson was anticipated by Soane, whose unexecuted designs of 1809 for the Royal Academical Institution in Belfast, Ireland, had also been inspired by the pavilion layout of Marly. With its low, detached buildings grouped around a huge lawn, William Wilkin's Downing College, Cambridge, England (designed 1804-6; executed 1807–20), was also a precedent for the University of Virginia. Each of Jefferson's ten pavilions, containing lecture rooms and living accommodations for ten professors, was differently designed than the others. Most contained references to such ancient Roman structures as the Ionic order of the Temple of Fortuna Virilis (Pavilion II) and the Doric order of the Baths of Diocletian (Pavilion I). Pavilion IX, with its central exedra, may have been inspired by Ledoux's Hôtel de Guimard (1770) or by Soane's project for Shotesham Park, Norfolk (1785). On Benjamin Latrobe's recommendation, Jefferson placed at the head of the whole composition a great Pantheon or Rotunda (executed 1823–27) containing a suite of three oval rooms and a superb circular library.

Latrobe arrived in Virginia in 1796, having been trained in England by the original if eccentric architect Samuel Pepys Cockerell. Latrobe's first

563. *William Strickland, Second Bank of the United States (later Custom House), Philadelphia, plan, 1818*
564. *Thomas U. Walter, Andalusia, near Philadelphia, 1835–36*
565. *Thomas U. Walter, Girard College, Philadelphia, main building, 1833–47*
566. *Henry Walter, Ohio State Capitol, Columbus, designed 1838, built 1848 onward*

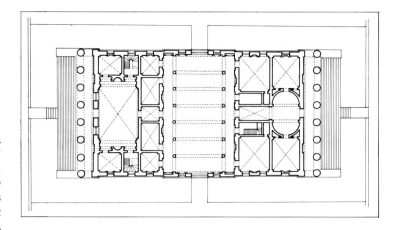

important work in America was his State Penitentiary at Richmond, Virginia (1797–98), whose powerful arched entrance gate is in Soane's "primitivist" style. Latrobe was soon attracted northward to Philadelphia, the national capital from 1790 to 1800, and the largest city in America. In 1798 he received the commission for the Bank of Pennsylvania there. Latrobe's austere templar building, a simple rectangle with a Greek Ionic portico at each end, culminated in a central, circular domed space articulated with a logic and purity evidently derived from the doctrines of Laugier; the top-lit dome recalled Soane's Stock Office of 1792 at the Bank of England. The demolition of Latrobe's building in the 1860s was a major loss for America. His next endeavor was the Philadelphia Waterworks (1798–1801; demolished 1827); here a rotunda rose from a rectangular base articulated with a radical Greek Doric order, and the whole seems to have echoed Ledoux's Rotonde de la Villette.

In 1803 Latrobe became Surveyor of the Public Buildings of the United States, a post that called for completing Thornton's Capitol Building in Washington, D. C. Latrobe's first House of Representatives was an oval colonnaded space with capitals derived from the Choragic Monument of Lysicrates in Athens. His Soane-like vestibule, with American maize-leaf capitals, built in the east basement in 1809, was rebuilt by him after the fire of 1814. Like Soane at the Bank of England and the Law Courts, Latrobe responded imaginatively to the task of working in cramped existing structures. After the fire he also rebuilt the Senate and House of Representatives on an improved plan incorporating a small rotunda with tobacco-leaf capitals of his own invention. Based on plans Latrobe had made as early as 1806–7, his Supreme Court Chamber, of 1815–17, beneath the Senate Chamber, is one of the most imaginative American classical spaces. Its trio of arches supported on stunted Greek Doric sandstone columns and its floating half-dome, strangely lobed, owe much to Ledoux and Soane.

Latrobe's best-known building is the Roman Catholic cathedral in Baltimore. With its low segmental dome and emphatically segmental arches, the interior recalls Soane's Bank of England, though the whole is unlike any church Soane ever designed. A masterpiece of sobriety and refinement, the building was designed in 1804–8 and executed in 1809–18; the onion-shaped tops to the belfry towers were added in 1832—but not to Latrobe's designs; his Ionic portico was not completed until 1863, and in 1890 the choir was tactfully lengthened.

Latrobe's pupils Robert Mills (1781–1855) and William Strickland (1788–1854) dominated the architectural scene until the 1840s. Mills worked in Latrobe's office from 1803 to 1808; his early works were centrally planned churches in Philadelphia and in Richmond, Virginia. In his octagonal Monumental Church in Richmond (1812), Mills interpreted the Greek Revival with a characteristically aggressive but thoughtful originality that established him as the heir of such architects as Bonomi and Gentz. In a similar vein was his Country Records Office of 1822 at Charleston, South

Carolina, designed in an unfluted Doric style and known, because of the manner of its construction, as the "Fireproof Building." His reputation was made with the Washington Monument at Baltimore (1814–29), a giant unfluted Doric column. After its completion, Mills moved to the city of Washington. He quickly set his mark on the capital with such large public buildings as the Treasury, the Patent Office, and the Washington Monument—all designed in 1836—and the Post Office of 1839. Bacause of their giant porticos and colonnades and, in the case of the Washington Monument, huge height, they created a more powerful and effective national image than the comparable though slightly earlier buildings in England by Wilkins and Smirke.

William Strickland rose to prominence with his remarkable Second Bank of the United States (later Custom House; 1818–24) in Philadelphia, the first American public building to be based on the Parthenon. His United States Mint (1829–33), in Washington, is an unremarkable classical block, but in 1832–34 came his most imaginative contribution to the Greek Revival, the Philadelphia Merchants' Exchange. The circular Corinthian colonnade of the Exchange, crowned by a tall lantern based on the Lysicrates Monument, has an impressive drama lacking in his last major work, the Tennessee State Capitol, at Nashville (1845–49), where the Lysicratean lantern is less happily related to the building below.

At least as successful as Strickland were his pupils Thomas U. Walter and Alexander Jackson Davis (1803–1892), who formed a partnership in 1829 with Ithiel Town (1784–1844). Town's templar State Capitol for Connecticut, at Hartford (1827), was a worthy successor to Strickland's Second Bank in Philadelphia and led to commissions for similar capitol buildings. The Parthenon was also the model chosen by Davis and Town for their impressive United States Custom House, New York City (now the Sub-Treasury), of 1833–42, and then by Ammi B. Young (1800–1874) for his domed, colonnaded, granite-built Custom House in Boston, Massachusetts (1837–47). Ithiel Town's Bowers House, Northampton, Massachusetts (1825–26), with its giant Ionic portico, is characteristic of countless temple-like houses of the first half of the nineteenth century; James Coles Bruce's Berry Hill, Virginia (1835–40), in the Greek Doric style, stands even closer to the paradigm: Wilkins's Grange Park of 1809. Yet another dramatically archaeological house worthy of comparison with Grange Park is Andalusia, north of Philadelphia, designed in 1835–36 by Thomas U. Walter. His patron was the influential Nicholas Biddle, who, unusual in his generation of Americans, had investigated Greek remains at first hand, in 1806. From Biddle also came the inspiration for Walter's singularly beautiful Girard College in Philadelphia (1833–47), whose centrally placed, Corinthian peripheral temple "contains an ingeniously planned three-story complex of groin-vaulted spaces, entirely of the latest (Millsian) fireproof construction" (W. H. Pierson, *American Buildings and Their Architects,* vol. 1, 1970, p. 437). The central temple is flanked on each side by a pair of templar dormitory buildings, the whole suggesting a highly colored version of the theme Wilkins had essayed at Downing College, Cambridge. For the giant portico of his Hibernian Hall in Charleston, South Carolina (1835), Thomas U. Walter adopted the Greek Ionic of the Erechtheum, but Henry Walter's Ohio State Capitol, Columbus (designed 1838 with the assistance of A. J. Davis; built from 1848 on by William Russell West and Nathan B. Kelly), is conceived on an altogether more heroic scale. Its vast octostyle Doric portico *in antis* builds up to a cylindrical cupola in a truly monumental composition. Uniting the styles of Ledoux and Schinkel, Walter here realized the fantastic unexecuted scheme of 1834 by Thomas Rickman and Edward Hussey for the Fitzwilliam Museum, in Cambridge, England.

This fecund classical tradition, gradually failing in quality if not in quantity, dominated American architecture until the 1860s. The return from Paris to Boston in 1865 of Henry Hobson Richardson (1838–1886) opened a new phase in the history of American architecture. Though he had been trained at the École des Beaux-Arts in Paris (1859–62) and had subsequently worked under Labrouste and Hittorff, Richardson did not import French classicism to America. His early works, including the Grace Episcopal Church, Medford, Massachusetts (1867–69), and the B. H. Crowninshield House, Marlborough Street, Boston (1868–69), owe something to contemporary Gothic Revival buildings in England. But in the 1870s, Richardson developed a rock-faced Romanesque—for example, the Brattle Square (now First Baptist) Church and Trinity Church in Boston, of 1870–72 and 1873–77—which owed more to France, and particularly to J.-A.-E. Vaudremer. Perhaps Richardson's finest works were such private houses of the 1870s and 1880s as the William Watts Sherman House, Newport, Rhode Island (1874–75), and Stoughton House, Cambridge, Massachusetts (1882–83), in a tile-hung Manorial style, with spreading plans recalling the work of Richard Norman Shaw.

Thus, Richardson has no real part in the present chapter. It was Charles Follen McKim, also a student at the École des Beaux-Arts (1867–70), and an assistant of Richardson, who instituted an academic classical revival in America. With his two partners, William Rutherford Mead and Stanford White, he produced a series of superlative classical masterpieces with a Roman rather than a French flavor. Despite the brilliance of their Boston Public Library (1887) and of their extensive work in New York City—the Villard houses (1882), Columbia University (1893), the University Club (1899), the Pierpont Morgan Library (1903), and the Pennsylvania Railroad Station (1904–10)—the determinist bias of recent architectural historians has prevented the firm of McKim, Mead & White from receiving the critical attention it deserves.

ENGLAND: *Walpole to Rickman*

By 1750 the Gothic Revival already had a long history in England. One of the most striking and earliest examples of the style is the library of St. John's College, Cambridge, of 1623–24. Justifying the elaborately Gothic design of its windows, a contemporary wrote to the master of the college: "Some men of judgement liked the best the old fashion of church window, holding it most meet for such a building." This justification of Gothic on grounds of environmental propriety was to be echoed for the next hundred years. Its most striking monuments are Sir Christopher Wren's Tom Tower at Christ Church, Oxford (1681), and Nicholas Hawksmoor's additions to All Souls' College, Oxford (1715–34), and his western towers at Westminster Abbey, London (1735–45). One of the first architects to imply that Gothic might have a romance and a quality in its own right was Sir John Vanbrugh, although he never employed the Gothic arch. However, his narrow, tall battlemented house at Greenwich, begun in 1717, is undoubtedly "emotionally Gothic" (J. Summerson, *Architecture in Britain, 1530–1830,* 5th ed., 1969, p. 237). He also argued keenly for the preservation of the "Holbein" Gate at Whitehall and, as we saw in Chapter 2, for the ruins of old Woodstock Manor in the park at Blenheim. If Vanbrugh provided a new emotional stimulus, William Kent created the new language of form that became known as "Georgian Gothic." Kent's innovatory role is thus of immense stylistic significance, but it is to be noted that the following list of his principal Gothic works contains not one that is anything more than an addition to an existing medieval or Tudor building: Esher Place, Surrey (1729–33); the gateway at Hampton Court, Middlesex (1732); the Courts of Chancery and of King's Bench, Westminster Hall (1739); and the pulpit at York Minster and choir-screen at Gloucester cathedral (both 1741). Kent's lighthearted, medievalizing style was basically an inaccurately Gothic treatment of the classical orders and, as such, proved easy to imitate. Batty Langley (1696–1751) developed Kent's hints and codified their details in his book confidently entitled *Gothic Architecture Improved by Rules and Proportions* (1747), though he evidently had some firsthand knowledge of medieval work.

The fruits of all this, in the later 1740s and 1750s, are particularly associated with the name of the Warwickshire squire and amateur architect Sanderson Miller (1717–1780). In addition to erecting sham castles at Edgehill, Warwickshire (1745–47), Hagley Park, Worcestershire (1747–48), and Wimpole Hall, Cambridgeshire (1750), Miller was one of a number of architects responsible for remodeling Arbury Hall, Warwickshire, from 1750 onward for Sir Roger Newdigate. Arbury was a Tudor house with pre-Reformation monastic origins, so the choice of Gothic could be justified on associational grounds. Its dramatic and beautiful Gothicization, which extended throughout the second half of the eighteenth century, is largely the work of the architect Henry Keene (1726–1776), and, though it contains a number of references to medieval sources, the overall

impression is entirely of the eighteenth century. At Lacock Abbey, Wiltshire, Sanderson Miller added a delightful Gothic gateway and great hall in 1754–55 intended to be in keeping with the existing monastic structures. But his most surprising Gothic building is one for which no claims to what we have called "environmental propriety" could possibly justify the choice of style. This is the astonishing Pomfret House built in Arlington Street, London, in 1760 for the widowed Countess of Pomfret. It was as though James Gibbs's Gothic temple at Stowe (1741) had been transferred from a rural to an urban setting.

The choice of Gothic as a style to be admired in its own right, not simply for associational reasons, had been anticipated by Horace Walpole at Strawberry Hill from 1749 to the 1790s. His selection of the Gothic style as a matter of taste is one of the three most important features of the house, the development of which has been so often told it scarcely need be repeated here. The two other points of importance are its asymmetrical growth, in which fortuitous development was emphasized, and the increasing archaeological knowledge that lies behind its stylistic details. With numerous borrowings from an astonishing variety of medieval sources, including tombs at Westminster Abbey and Canterbury, Salisbury, Ely, and Worcester cathedrals, as well as motifs taken from Old St. Paul's, Henry VII's Chapel at Westminster Abbey, and Rouen cathedral, Strawberry Hill was equally the product of collective endeavor as far as a "design team" was concerned. Between the 1750 and 1790s the learned amateurs Richard Bentley, John Chute, Thomas Pitt, and James Essex were assisted by a number of professional architects, including William Robinson, Robert Adam, James Wyatt, and the master mason at Westminster Abbey, Thomas Gayfere. Chute and Gayfere collaborated on the design of the Chapel in the Woods in 1772–74. With a facade based on Bishop Audley's chantry tomb at Salisbury cathedral, it was the most solid and convincing piece of Gothic at Strawberry Hill, for everywhere else the mood was one of rococo gaiety. Indeed, the house that Walpole had bought from the proprietress of a successful London toy shop always retained the aura of a plaything. Walpole's own attitude to it is captured both in a description of the staircase given to a friend in 1753—"[It is] so pretty and so small that I am inclined to wrap it up and send it to you in my letter"—and also in his comment, eight years later, "My buildings are paper, like my writings." Strawberry Hill, though visually so gay, was indeed a kind of paper architecture since many of its details were copied not directly from medieval buildings but from engravings of them in books in Walpole's library, notably Sir William Dugdale's *Warwickshire* (1656) and *St. Paul's* (1658) and John Dart's *Westminster* (1723) and *Canterbury* (1726). Paradoxically, the closest parallel to this Picturesque archaeology is the process by which the park at Shugborough, Staffordshire, was adorned by James Stuart during the 1760s with miniature versions of the Athenian buildings he was publishing with Revett in the *Antiquities of Athens.*

569. *James Wyatt, Fonthill Abbey,*
Wiltshire, plan, 1796–1807

570. *James Wyatt, Fonthill Abbey,*
Wiltshire, view from the southwest,
1796–1807

571. *James Wyatt, Fonthill Abbey,*
Wiltshire, view through St. Michael's
Gallery and the central octagon to
King Edward's Gallery, 1796–1807

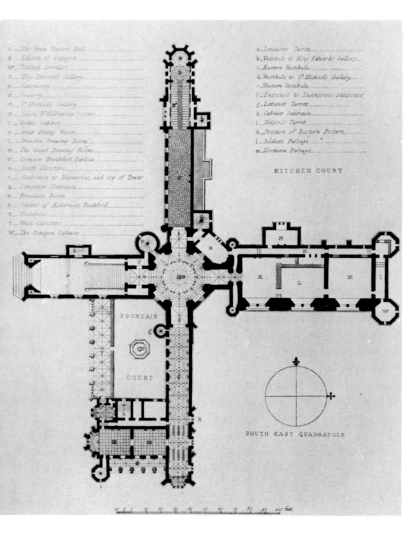

The product of a similar antiquarianism, of which Walpole highly approved, was the house of his friend Thomas Barrett, at Lee Priory, Kent (1783–90). Here James Wyatt, who had possibly been recommended by Walpole to Barrett, devised an extravaganza that was a little more archaeologically correct in some of its details than Strawberry Hill and yet, at the same time, almost more fanciful in its provision of an octagonal tower and spire. There were no medieval or monastic associations at Lee ("Priory" being a spurious addition by Barrett) so the choice of Gothic was purely aesthetic. Indeed, Wyatt prepared both classical and Gothic designs for Barrett to choose between. What particularly attracted Barrett and Walpole was Wyatt's ability to suggest growth and change in a building whose owner intended to create the impression of a small convent adapted for domestic use, presumably after the Reformation. In a letter of 1785 Walpole admired the make-believe that led one to "consider the whole as Gothic modernized in parts, not as what it is—the reverse." Its extreme irregularity of plan and outline also gave great pleasure to the eye nurtured on Picturesque principles. The domed octagonal library that forms the striking centerpiece of the whole composition may owe something to the fourteenth-century lantern over the crossing at Ely cathedral.

Ely, or possibly the plates in J. Bentham's *History and Antiquities of Ely* (1771), is also the source of the staggering central tower of Fonthill Abbey, Wiltshire, which Wyatt built for William Beckford between 1796 and 1807. But from Wyat's imagination alone came the brilliant cruciform plan with its breathtaking vista, more than ninety meters (three hundred feet) long, from the oriel at the end of St. Michael's Gallery, through the central octagon, to the oratory at the north end of King Edward's Gallery. Beckford's original idea, analogous to Barrett's for Lee Priory, was to create

326

572. Augustus Welby Northmore
Pugin, St. Marie's Grange, Wiltshire,
1835
573. Richard Norman Shaw, Adcote,
Shropshire, designed 1875
574. Edward Hussey, Anthony
Salvin, and William Sawrey Gilpin,
view toward Scotney Old Castle, Kent,
1835–43

572. Augustus Welby Northmore
Pugin, St. Marie's Grange, Wiltshire,
1835

573. Richard Norman Shaw, Adcote,
Shropshire, designed 1875

574. Edward Hussey, Anthony
Salvin, and William Sawrey Gilpin,
view toward Scotney Old Castle, Kent,
1835–43

a building resembling a convent, partly ruinous and partly converted to
domestic use, which he could use for occasional picnics or supper parties.
His obsession with the place grew until in 1805 he finally decided to live
in it permanently. The grounds were landscaped and planted in such an
appropriately sublime and exotic manner that house and setting eventually
became the high-water mark of Picturesque Gothic.

So far, we have seen the Gothic Revival as an aspect of the Picturesque
theory that developed from Vanbrugh, through Strawberry Hill and Payne
Knight's Downton Castle, to Fonthill Abbey and Nash's brilliant asymmetrical Irish castles Killymoon, near Cookstown (1803), Shanbally, County
Tipperary (1812), and Lough Cutra, County Galway (c. 1817)—not
forgetting, of course, Nash's own country seat, East Cowes Castle, Isle of
Wight (c. 1798; now demolished). We must investigate two other
traditions, associated respectively with castle and with church, which owe
rather less to the Picturesque. At Clearwell Castle, Gloucestershire (1727),
and Inveraray Castle, Argyllshire (begun 1745), Roger Morris (1695–
1749) echoed the formal, symmetrical castles of the Middle Ages, which
had already been revived in the Elizabethan and Jacobean periods at Mount
Edgecumbe, Cornwall, Lulworth Castle, Dorset, and Ruperra Castle,
Glamorganshire. From here it was but a step to James Wyatt's Kew Palace,
Surrey (1802–11), and Ashridge Park, Hertfordshire (begun 1808); to
Robert Smirke's Lowther Castle, Westmorland (1806); and to Eastnor
Castle, Herefordshire (1812), and Taymouth Castle, Perthshire (1806–10),
by Archibald and James Elliott (1760–1823; 1770–1810).

Church- far more than castle-building in the Gothic style seems almost
to have had a momentum of its own. The numerous Gothic churches erected
between the time, say, of the younger Wing's church at King's Norton,

575. *Augustus Welby Northmore Pugin, Alton Castle, Staffordshire, 1847–51*

576. *William Butterfield, vicarage, Coalpit Heath, Gloucestershire, 1844*

577. *Augustus Welby Northmore Pugin, Scarisbrick Hall, Lancashire, 1837–45*

578. William Butterfield, group
of cottages, Baldersby, Yorkshire,
1855–57

579. George Edmund Street, church
vicarage, and school, Boyne Hill,
Maidenhead, Berkshire, 1854

Leicestershire (1760–75), and of Charles Barry's St. Peter, Brighton (1823–28), do not reveal any substantial development in the understanding of medieval construction, although in his St. Luke, Chelsea (1819–25), James Savage introduced for the first time a masonry rather than a plaster vault. At the church of the Holy Trinity, Theale, Berkshire (1820–28), Edward Garbett and John Buckler (1770–1851) provided a strikingly complete and serious recreation of the lancet mode of Salisbury cathedral. Since Perpendicular was the mode usually adopted in eighteenth- and early nineteenth-century churches, Theale represents a significant attempt to enlarge historical understanding of medieval architecture. By basing the design of the tower on the demolished campanile of Salisbury cathedral, Garbett and Buckler delivered a sharp rebuke to eighteenth- century Gothicists, for the destruction carried out at Salisbury was attributed, not altogether fairly, to James Wyatt.

But the new and more serious phase of the Gothic Revival—of which the design of Holy Trinity, Theale, is a harbinger—was ushered in not so much by architects as by antiquarians and publishers in what J. M. Crook has called the "bibliographical revolution" (C. L. Eastlake, *A History of the Gothic Revival,* 1872; rev. ed., 1970, ed. J. M. Crook). Between the 1790s and the 1830s John Carter (1748–1817) and John Britton (1771–1857) produced a series of influential books on medieval architecture, which combined scholarship with topography and, like Stuart's and Revett's *Antiquities of Athens,* provided architects with an authentic new vocabulary. Carter's publications included the books *Views of Ancient Buildings in England* (1786–93), *Ancient Architecture of England* (1795 and 1807), as well as numerous articles in the *Gentleman's Magazine* attacking the ill-treatment and ignorant restoration of medieval buildings. Britton's principal works were *The Architectural Antiquities of Great Britain* (1804–14) and, more important, the superbly illustrated, fourteen-volume *Cathedral Antiquities of Great Britain* (1814–35). Thomas Rickman's *An Attempt to Discriminate the Styles of English Architecture* (1817) provided a vocabulary of identification—"Early English," "Decorated," and "Perpendicular"—that was a reassuring parallel to the familiar "Doric," "Ionic," and "Corinthian" of classical architecture, and that had the similar advantage of being easily memorized and applied. Finally, Augustus Charles Pugin's *Specimens of Gothic Architecture* (1821–23) spelled out the language of Gothic detail in technical drawings for the benefit of craftsmen and draftsmen. The scene was now set for the arrival of the hero, and, at the risk of writing determinist or progressivist history, it cannot be denied that Pugin's celebrated son, Augustus Welby Northmore Pugin, seemed destined in every way to fulfill that very role.

ENGLAND: *Pugin and His Impact*

A. W. N. Pugin (1812–1852) has probably exercised as much influence over English architecture and architectural theory as any other architect of

580. Augustus Welby Northmore
Pugin, St. Giles, Cheadle,
Staffordshire, 1839–44

581. Augustus Welby Northmore
Pugin, St. Giles, Cheadle,
Staffordshire, interior 1839–44

582. Augustus Welby Northmore
Pugin, St. Augustine, Ramsgate,
Kent, choir, 1845–50

583. John Loughborough Pearson, St. Mary, Dalton Holme, Yorkshire, 1858–61

any period. In a series of compelling books, by turns amusing, polemical, and scholarly—*Contrasts* (1836), *The True Principles of Pointed or Christian Architecture* (1841), *The Present State of Ecclesiastical Architecture in England* (1843), and *An Apology for the Revival of Christian Architecture in England* (1843)—Pugin made a case for the adoption of Gothic, not as one of a number of styles chosen on grounds of beauty or association but as *the* style, indeed, as "truth." Gothic was the truthful expression of true construction and function, of true religion (i.e., Roman Catholicism), and of the true genius of the English people. Thus, Pugin could claim that what he was defending was "not a style but a principle" (*An Apology,* p. 44). In so doing, he laid the foundations of Victorian architecture and—by implying the special merit of a building that reveals its construction—of modern architecture as well. Whatever our feeling about his conclusions, it cannot be denied that Pugin was one of the few Englishmen who have theorized coherently about architecture; however, to say that he was English is not strictly true. A. C. Pugin was a French emigré, and it is to the intellectual tradition of French theorists from Perrault to Laugier and beyond that his son belonged. Pugin's first book, *Contrasts,* upheld the Gothic cause by an entertaining attack on the Reformation as the begetter of a false religion and a false (i.e., classical) architecture; however, five years later, guessing perhaps that an English Protestant audience might require a wider variety of argument, Pugin justified his passionate adherence to Gothic by echoing the language of eighteenth-century neoclassical rationalism. The equation of architectural beauty with structural honesty was familiar in France and Italy through the writings of such men as Cordemoy, Laugier, and Lodoli, but it had made little impact in England. The rational and academic analysis of Gothic structure as a basis for a modern architecture initiated by Cordemoy was brought to a climax by Pugin's contemporary Viollet-le-Duc. Pugin's contribution to this tradition was less influential than his sociological and ethical interpretation of architecture as the true index of the state of society. This was the vision that fired the Victorian Gothicists Butterfield, Street, Pearson, and Bodley: Christian architects creating a Christian society with Christian buildings, schools, colleges, parsonages, convents, and churches. One of Pugin's principal contributions to the language of form was his insistence that the elevation of a building should be subservient to its plan. Though this principle was derived from his belief in truthfulness, it led, ironically, to a type of self-consciously asymmetrical architecture that closely resembled the products of the Picturesque that Pugin was committed to despise.

In Chapter 2 we emphasized the importance of Salvin's Scotney Castle, Kent (1835–43), in the Picturesque tradition, particularly because of its relation through a landscaped garden to the ruins of the medieval Scotney Castle. Salvin's new building (see illustration 33) was itself equally revolutionary. The asymmetrical separation of part from part on the entrance front, the apparently functional placement of windows and chimneys

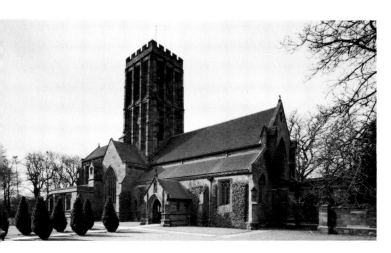

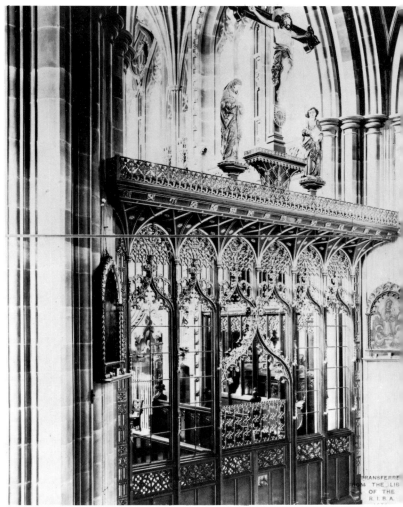

contrasting eloquently with areas of blank wall, the vigorous diagonality of
line—all this could be described as Puginesque, though, paradoxically, the
twenty-three-year-old Pugin was not yet capable of work of this quality.

The kind of buildings Pugin was designing in 1835 we can see at his own
house, St. Marie's Grange, Wiltshire. Here, though on a much smaller scale,
is the same determined asymmetry that characterizes Scotney, and that is
supposed to enable us to read the internal disposition of the building. The
house was altered and enlarged, probably by Pugin himself, but its original
appearance is recorded in a sketch by him of 1835 in which he is careful
to show its relation to the distant view of Salisbury cathedral (and here, of
course, is another parallel with Scotney). The cramped, narrow proportions
of St. Marie's Grange, the aspiring verticality of its all roofs and turrets, its
steeply sloping site and drawbridge are all unexpected reminders of another
pioneering house built by an architect for his own occupancy more than a
century earlier, Vanbrugh Castle, Greenwich.

Though Salvin's later career was prolific and in many ways distinguished,
he did not quite fulfill the particular promise of Scotney. It was Pugin who
developed the language of domestic Gothic in a paradoxical combination
of functional and Picturesque that was used to such brilliant effect by Richard
Norman Shaw. Between St. Marie's Grange and Shaw's superb Adcote,
Shropshire (designed 1875), lie Pugin's Scarisbrick Hall, Lancashire
(1837–45), and especially Alton Castle, Staffordshire (1847–51), with its
staccato separation of part from part, each functional element with its own
appropriate and distinct shape and roof. A humbler line of dwellings also
sprang from Pugin's early experiment at St. Marie's Grange. Between 1840
and 1843 he developed the theme of "Picturesque utility" (S. Muthesius,
The High Victorian Movement in Architecture, 1850–1870, 1971, pp. 4–10)

586. Edward Buckton Lamb, Nunn Appleton Hall, Yorkshire, 1864

588. William Butterfield, All Saints, Margaret Street, London, pulpit

587. William Butterfield, All Saints, Margaret Street, London, interior, 1849–59

589. William Butterfield, All Saints, Margaret Street, London, plan

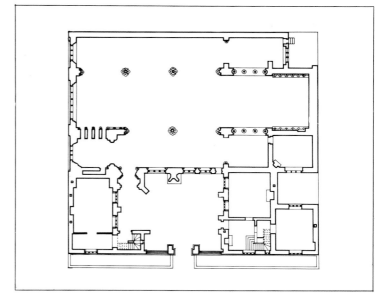

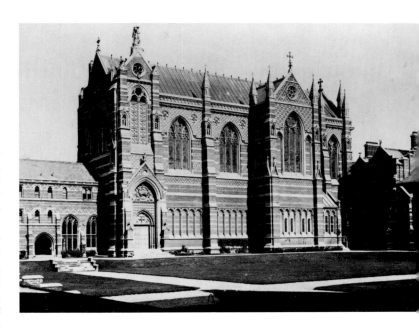

in a series of important and influential houses—Bishop's House, Birmingham (demolished), the Catholic school and teacher's house at Spetchley, Worcestershire, and his own house, The Grange, at Ramsgate, Kent. This earnest and supposedly "truthful" way of building caught on immediately with the Ecclesiological Society, which was busy popularizing in the Anglican church ideas Pugin had claimed were essentially Catholic. Butterfield's Coalpit Heath vicarage, Gloucestershire (1844), and the village of Baldersby, Yorkshire (1855–57); George Edmund Street's Colnbrook vicarage, Buckinghamshire (1853), and group of church, vicarage, and school at Boyne Hill, Maidenhead, Berkshire (1854); and William White's vicarages at Lurgashall, Sussex (1852), and Little Baddow, Essex (1857–58), are all unthinkable without the precedent of Pugin. Not least in importance is the building that stands at the end of this rather glum and cerebral development, Red House at Upton, near Bexleyheath, Kent, designed for William Morris (1834–1896) in 1859 by Philip Webb (1831–1915), which for so long, and so ironically, was hailed as a stepping-stone to the modern movement.

Pugin's church design had probably less influence on his contemporaries than his domestic design. Nonetheless, he has left us some singularly beautiful interiors, ranging from the early St. Chad's cathedral, Birmingham (1839), with its curiously attenuated proportions, to the solidly Early Victorian St. Giles, Cheadle, Staffordshire (1839–44)—elaborately stenciled in imitation of the treatment then being given to the Ste.-Chapelle in Paris—and finally to his late St. Augustine, Ramsgate, Kent (1845–50), possibly his finest church. At Ramsgate, which he paid for largely himself, Pugin was able to indulge his profound feeling for the powerful structure and profuse ornament of English early fourteenth-century Gothic. The result is a moving piece of living archaeology, which deeply influenced such followers of Pugin as Sir George Gilbert Scott, John Loughborough Pearson (1817–1897), and George Frederick Bodley (1827–1907). Pearson's opulent and sophisticated church of St. Mary at Dalton Holme, Yorkshire (1858–61), is a realization of the Puginesque dream as is the sumptuous, much later Holy Angels, Hoar Cross, Staffordshire (1872–1900), by Bodley, in whose career we can trace a Pugin revival. Bodley's All Saints, Cambridge (1861–70), came at the turning point when he rejected the exuberance of the 1850s for the calmer medievalism of Pugin.

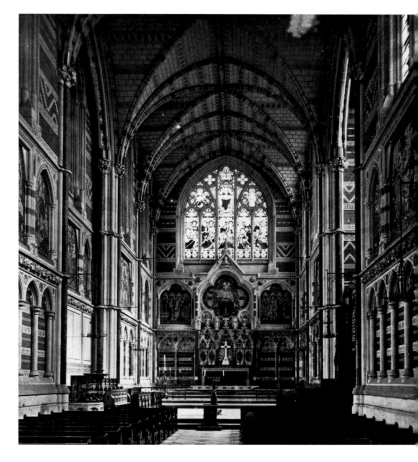

ENGLAND: *High Victorian Architecture*
We have just spoken of exuberance as characteristic of the 1850s. It is generally accepted that between 1850 and 1870 the Gothic Revival passed rather unexpectedly through a violent period recognizably different from what preceded and succeeded it. It is by turns muscular and geometrical, naturalistic and polychromatic, often unaccommodating and even brutal. It is particuarly associated with Butterfield, Lamb, Teulon, Burges, White,

Brooks, and Street and Bodley in their early work. The elaborate secular buildings of Scott and Waterhouse must also be considered as High Victorian.

The oldest architect working in this new manner was Edward Bruckton Lamb (1805–1869). His bizarre and assertive Gothic style had its origins in the Picturesque, pre-Puginesque world of John Claudius London (1783–1843) and his circle. He found it early and did not develop it according to the doctrines of Pugin and Butterfield. He was consequently spurned by the Ecclesiological Society, yet the violence of his work in the 1850s and 1860s—for example, at Nunn Appleton Hall, Yorkshire (1864)—justifies his placement in the High Victorian movement. The harsh but roguish complexities of the tower of his Christ Church, West Hartlepool, County Durham (1854), reappeared with undiminished vigor at St. Martin, Vicars Road, Gospel Oak, London (1862–65). Of St. Martin's tower, Sir John Summerson brilliantly observed, "Most towers answer a question. This one asks" (*Victorian Architecture: Four Studies in Evaluation,* 1970, p. 73).

An architect with an equally individual and strident language was William Butterfield (1814–1900). With Pugin he was the most original and influential of the mid-century ecclesiastical architects. The Ecclesiologists were much more concerned than Pugin with the problems of urban church-building; they were more attracted by force and power in architectural form, and, though deeply influenced by his appeal for constructional honesty, tended to interpret this in terms of structural polychromy: Thus, the English country church of the fourteenth century, which had been Pugin's ideal, was temporarily forsaken in favor of an original amalgam that drew on the more massive forms of the thirteenth century and in which the polychromatic effects of the medieval architecture in Italy and Spain were daringly elaborated in brick. Butterfield's "model church" for the Ecclesiological Society—All Saints, Margaret Street, London (1849–59)—is a doctrinal statement of this new reformed Gothic. It is a forceful and compelling work in which it is hard not to discern a desire to shock. In his distinguished monograph *William Butterfield* (1971) Paul Thompson has tried to absolve Butterfield from the attachment to a kind of creative ugliness that has sometimes been seen in his work. Yet we should not overlook the fact that the Ecclesiological Society's own organ referred to a "deliberate preference of ugliness" in an article on the consecration of the church in 1859 (*The Ecclesiologist,* vol. 20, p. 185). In the early 1850s Butterfield dropped his structural polychromy but returned to it with passion in such churches as St. Alban, Holborn (1859–62), and in one of his most powerful and best-known masterpieces, Keble College, Oxford (1866–83).

As brilliant as Butterfield, and possibly more versatile, was George Edmund Street (1824–1881). His early vicarage and theological college at Cuddesdon, Oxfordshire (1852), and church at Boyne Hill, Maidenhead, contained the seeds of that massive and deceptively simple style that led Charles Eastlake to believe that Cuddesdon College and East Grinstead

convent "have literally no architectural character beyond what may be secured by stout masonry, a steep roof, and a few dormer windows, though he claimed at the same time that "there is a genuine *cachet* on each design which it is impossible to mistake. They are the production of an artist hand" (*History of the Gothic Revival,* p. 323).

In 1855 Street published *Brick and marble of the Middle Ages: Notes of a Tour in the North of Italy,* in which he defended the combination of motifs from different styles and countries. In the late 1850s and 1860s he went on to produce a group of vividly original churches in which he developed his firsthand knowledge of the color and constructional detail of Italian Gothic. From the year 1859 date three remarkable churches in very different parts of the country: St. John the Evangelist, Howsham, Yorkshire; St. Philip and St. James, Oxford; and St. James-the-Less, Westminster, London. The massive chunkiness of St. John the Evangelist, Howsham, with its somewhat Italianate western porch, reappears in the bigger and more sculptural church at Oxford, but it is St. James-the-Less that reveals Street at his most forceful and most brilliant. Of striped and diapered red and black brick it is an electrifying blend of Butterfield's style with early French and north Italian details, dominated by a massive Ruskinian campanile, forty-one meters (one hundred thirty-four feet) of unbuttressed brickwork. Its forceful exterior geometry is echoed internally in the insistent patterning of tile, marble, and mastic. For Charles Eastlake, the whole church was "evidence of a thirst for change which Mr. Street could satisfy without danger, but which betrayed many of his contemporaries into intemperance. Even here there is something to regret in the restless notching of edges, the dazzling distribution of stripes, the multiplicity of pattern forms, and exuberance of sculptural detail" (*History of Gothic Revival,* p. 321).

The "intemperance" Eastlake noted can surely be found in the work of William White (1825–1900) and Samuel Sanders Teulon (1812–1873). Notched, polychromatic, and willful is White's bizarre church of St. Michael at Lyndhurst, Hampshire (1858–59), which has many features in common with Street's St. James-the-Less but markedly lacks its overall balance. But even White's work pales into normality by the side of Teulon's Shadwell Park, Norfolk (1856–60), freakishly muscular, or Burges's additions to Gayhurst, Buckinghamshire (1859). Teulon's early work—for example, Tortworth Court, Gloucestershire (1849–53)—is rather in the busy manner of E. B. Lamb, but by the late 1850s he was producing work in a sculptural idiom similar to Street's but more assertive, exemplified by such buildings as St. Mark, Silvertown, Essex. But it was in country-house design that Teulon's idiosyncratic genius found its fullest expression. His Elvetham Hall, Hampshire (1859–62), for the fourth Lord Calthorpe, is a secular counterpart of Street's contemporary St. James-the-Less, as is also John Prichard's and John Pollard Seddon's Ettington Park, Warwickshire (1858–63). Perhaps the climax of this instantly recognizable and permanently unforgettable Teulon manner is Bestwood Lodge, Nottinghamshire

596. John Loughborough Pearson,
St. Peter, Vauxhall, London,
1860–65

597. James Brooks, St. Columba,
Haggerston, London, 1867

598. William Burges, Cardiff Castle,
Glamorganshire, Smoking Room
ceiling, 1868–74

599. William Burges, Cardiff Castle,
Glamorganshire, Banquet Hall,
c. 1872–81

600. Deane and Woodward,
University Museum, Oxford
1854–60

(1862–64), a sensational building, which has inspired Mark Girouard to observe: "Anything striped, spiky, knobbly, notched, fungoid, or wiry fascinated him" (*The Victorian Country House,* 1971, p. 69). Bestwood was built for one of Teulon's characteristically aristocratic clients, the tenth duke of St. Albans, which forces us to question the popular modern notion that the High Victorian style was so vigorously self-assertive it must have been created for the new crude and self-educated captains of industry spawned by Victorian capitalism.

In 1857 John Loughborough Pearson, who had worked in Salvin's office, produced for a clergyman a High Victorian country house, Quar Wood, Gloucestershire (mutilated 1954), in a manner similar to but more ordered than Teulon's. Pearson's quietly geometrical St. Peter, Vauxhall, London (1860), with its echoes of Street and Teulon, leads us stylistically to the work of James Brooks (1825–1901). Brooks became known for his powerful and moving churches in the slum areas of London: St. Michael, Shoreditch (1863); St. Saviour, Hoxton (1864); St. Columba (1867) and St. Chad (1868), both in Haggerston; and Christ Church, Clapton (1870).

One of the most attractive of this close-knit group of High Victorian designers was George Frederick Bodley. Poet, musician, and Christian gentleman, strongly disliking the business aspects of his work, he lived richly and well, surrounded by beautiful objects. Disapproving of architectural competitions as much as Butterfield did, he eventually turned to designing luxurious but fastidious churches for artistic dukes. But before this costly Puginesque sensitivity overtook him, he was essentially a part of the "vigour and go" of the High Victorian decades. Like Street and White, he was a pupil of Scott, and his early Normal School at Cheltenham, Gloucestershire (1854), derives, via Pugin, from Street's Cuddesdon of 1852. Bodley's St. Michael and All Angels, Brighton, Sussex (1858–62), is a brick urban church with early French plate-tracery and bands of Italianate structural polychromy. Far more engaging is his All Saints, Selsley, Gloucestershire (1858–62). In some sense Selsley might be regarded as the jewel of the whole High Victorian movement, combining with sobriety and originality on a small scale so many of the characteristics we have described in this chapter. The bold massing, the contrasts of voids and solids, the beautiful grouping on a sloping site—extraordinarily and eloquently emphasized by the external stone staircase leaping up to the two-storied sacristy—the French plate-tracery and the Germanic saddleback tower, effortlessly contained within a design that is still in many ways English, the beautiful Morris glass (possibly the firm's first ecclesiastical commission), with the Nativity in the apse and the Creation in the western rose window: All this adds up to an unforgettable reflection of the mid-Victorian Christian dream of Reformed Gothic and a reformed Anglican church.

In total contrast to Bodley was the architect William Burges (1827–1881), who produced some of the most exuberant and colorful buildings of the 1860s and 1870s. His extraordinarily imaginative remodelings of Cardiff

601. Deane and Woodward,
*University Museum, Oxford, interior,
1854–60*

Castle, Glamorganshire (1868 onward), and Castel Coch, Glamorganshire (c. 1875 onward), for his principal patron, Lord Bute, contain interiors which have to be seen to be believed.

It would be wrong to imply that the High Victorian aesthetic was expressed only in church and country-house design. The manner is also recognizable in certain public buildings, though the Second Empire style radiating from Paris to England and North America was generally found more convenient for such buildings, particularly those on a monumental scale. A seminal building was the Oxford University Museum, designed in 1854 by Benjamin Woodward, of the firm of Deane and Woodward. Displaying all the polychromy and abrupt angularity of detail and mass required by the "realist" High Victorians, the museum is nevertheless steadied by an impressive, symmetrical entrance facade dominated by a central tower. This memorable formula caught on immediately. It was employed, for example, by Sir George Gilbert Scott in his unexecuted schemes for the City Hall, Hamburg, Germany (1854), and for the Foreign Office, London (1856); by Edward William Godwin (1833–1886) in his impressive town halls at Northampton (1860–64) and Congleton, Cheshire (1864); and by Jeffery and Skiller at Winchester Guildhall (1870–73). More spectacular is Scott's St. Pancras Station Hotel, London (1867–74) with its pinnacled Gothic skyline and its dramatic staircase supported on exposed iron beams.

The competitions held for government offices in Whitehall in 1856 and for the Law Courts in the Strand ten years later produced a rich crop of paper architecture adhering with varying degrees of fantasy to High Victorian modes of thought. Apart from the design by Scott already mentioned, those by Street, by Deane and Woodward, and by Prichard and Seddon for the Foreign Office were even more exuberant: Burges conducts us to a dream world of twelfth-century France as it never was; the proposals of John Pollard Seddon (1827–1906) seem equally other-wordly until we remember that he contrived to build something similar at Castle Hotel (subsequently University College), Aberystwyth, North Wales (1864); while the gusto of Alfred Waterhouse (1830–1905) shows him at a stage halfway between his early Scott- and Woodward-inspired Manchester Assize Courts (1859–64) and his Manchester Town Hall (1868–77), more freely Picturesque.

After 1870 the urgency of the demand for "truth" and "reform" could no longer be sustained. Something softer and more compromising seemed desirable. Richard Norman Shaw (1831–1912), in some ways the most brilliant architect of the century, is certainly the dominant figure in the story of Late Victorian architecture, yet much of the strength which prevented his architecture from going soft was derived from his High Victorian training in the office of G. E. Street. Such early works by Shaw as his unexecuted Exchange at Bradford, Yorkshire, and his now-demolished Holy Trinity, Bingley, Yorkshire, both designed in 1864, show his complete mastery of the style of Street, Butterfield, and Burges. His dazzling

Leyswood, Groombridge, Sussex, designed in 1866 for a successful businessman, was a turning point. This theatrical and captivating building caught the "Old English" spirit in an impressionistic rather than a "truthful" way, and thus the step from High Victorian to Late Victorian was made.

FRANCE

During the seventeenth and eighteenth centuries, interest in Gothic in France was firmly subordinated to the tenets of the rational, classical tradition. The architecture of the Middle Ages was studied with the closest attention, even with enthusiasm, but the result of this careful inspection—and it was more painstaking than that conducted anywhere else, England included—was not that the outlines and details of Gothic architecture were imitated, rather that something of the structural finesse they thought to be discernible in Gothic was infused into classical buildings. Soufflot, as we have seen, in designing the greatest church of the eighteenth century, Ste.-Geneviève, sought to put up a building Gothic in its structural principles, classical in appearance. And this curious equation was attempted by a host of other architects in France. Toward the end of the eighteenth century, when they had learned to appreciate the solid, sculptural qualities of mass, French architects found the elegant refinements of Gothic of far less interest. Indeed, their study of Gothic virtually ceased at that time. This waning interest in what one might call the rational characteristics of the style coincided, however, with a new responsiveness to its visual effects. This was part of an English import: the cult of the Picturesque and the natural landscape-garden. In many respects no more than a frivolous fashion, this cult was yet a vital element in the development of the French architectural imagination. Architects felt free, for the first time since their rejection of the rococo style, to cultivate purely visual pleasures. The most earnest and serious practitioners delighted to build an array of exotic pavilions and kiosks—Chinese, Tartar, and Turkish, no less than Gothic—that were in no part addressed to their academic training and reason. They were awakening thus their visual responses. All too soon—as we have noted in the case of Boullée—this new-found pleasure in variety and richness of effect was subsumed into a theory of lighting and giant, geometrical formality, somewhat curiously described in the jargon of English Picturesque theory. But the fashion for Picturesque gardens, once initiated, persisted unchecked until the end of the second decade of the nineteenth century. Gothic garden pavilions continued to be built in considerable numbers. But their design demanded no great knowledge of Gothic architecture, and learning was scarcely enhanced by this activity.

Nor did the fashion impinge much on the mainstream of architecture. Throughout the period we have been considering, only one large building was erected in the Gothic style, the cathedral of Ste.-Croix at Orléans. This was begun in 1599, as a monument to Catholic continuity after its

destruction by the Huguenots, and finished only in 1829, a monument to religious conservatism. Many of the greatest architects of the eighteenth century worked on the design of the west front—Gabriel, Trouard, E.-F. Legrand, and Pâris—and in this connection studied and measured a number of Gothic buildings; but they made no attempt to build anything else of the kind. Outside the field of garden follies nothing was built in France to constitute a Gothic Revival until well into the nineteenth century.

Though a frivolous, lighthearted Gothic Revival did not take hold in architecture, it penetrated the other arts. In the field of literature, for instance, the troubadour novel enjoyed an astonishing vogue in the closing years of the *ancien régime,* and the bland and rather lackluster tone of the genre was tainted with the sinister thrill of Gothic horror itself when, in 1764, F.-T.-M. de Baculard d'Arnaud's *Le Comte de Comynges* was first produced. New sentiments, new emotions, were at once brought into play. The school of history painting was affected. Within ten years Horace Walpole's *Castle of Otranto* had been translated into French, and in the years immediately after the Revolution Mrs. Radcliffe's novels were to be read with particular pleasure. The *roman noir* became immensely popular. F.-G. Ducray Duminil's *Coelina; ou, l'enfant du mystère,* of 1799, is said to have sold more than a million copies.

Whatever these new and exaggerated sentiments may have owed to English inspiration—and its impact was to be reinforced in the years that followed, when the novels of Sir Walter Scott were translated—the French sought always to identify them with their own medieval past. National pride was strong. A.-L. Millin's *Antiquités nationales; ou, recueil de monumens pour servir à l'histoire générale et particulière de l'empire français,* published in six volumes between 1790 and 1796, is typical of this enhanced interest in medieval history. Such romantic tastes were to be even more effectively elaborated and satisfied in the Musée des Monuments Français that Alexandre Lenoir started to set up in 1795 in the Couvent des Petits Augustins, and that is now a part of the École des Beaux-Arts. Here Lenoir gathered together treasures and bric-a-brac, stained-glass windows, and bits of sculpture and architectural details from buildings ravaged during the Revolution, and reassembled them with artifice and considerable inaccuracy to conjure up romantic sensations of the past. In the garden was a celebrated tomb, said to be that of Héloise and Abelard, made from fragments from the abbey church of St.-Denis and plaster figures modeled by Louis-Pierre Deseine. Within the museum the aura of myth and mystery was even more strongly evoked. Tombs and sculptural figures in the thirteenth-century rooms were dimly lit, and the low vaults of the old refectory of the Petits Augustins were painted in ultramarine and scattered with stars of gold. The fourteenth-century rooms were decorated in a more lively and buoyant manner. Lenoir moved thus through the centuries, producing a pageant of French history that profoundly inspired such men as Jules Michelet—"Que d'âmes," he wrote in the sixth volume of his *Histoire de la Révolution,* "ont pris dans ce musée l'étincelle historique, l'intérêt des grands souvenirs, le vague désir de remonter les âges! . . . C'est là, et nulle autre part que j'ai reçu d'abord la vive impression de l'histoire" (p. 117). Lenoir's museum was dismantled in 1816, but by then he had colored the imagination of more than one generation of Frenchmen.

François-Auguste-René de Chateaubriand himself was fascinated, inspired, and also enraged by what he called Lenoir's "Élysée." The opening lines of the short chapter on Gothic, in that chaotic work of genius *Le génie du christianisme,* were an indictment of Lenoir's methods. "Chaque chose," Chateaubriand wrote, "doit être mise en son lieu, vérité triviale à force d'être répétée, mais sans laquelle, après tout, il ne peut y avoir rien de parfait" (vol. 3, bk. 1, chap. 3).

The setting of a work of art, he said, was vital to it; to displace it was to destroy the *genius loci* and to dispel the veil of sanctity woven about it through the centuries. Age was a criterion of greater value than beauty. Chateaubriand sought thus to identify the spirit of ancient France with all vestiges and remains of Gothic architecture, however rude. He went even further: He offered Gothic architecture as a symbol of a renewed religious faith. Chateaubriand was not a devout Catholic when, in exile in England, he wrote *Le génie du christianisme* (he described his spiritual state then as "une nostalgie de dieu"), yet the publication of the work in 1802 was carefully timed to coincide with the signing of the Concordat and was at once looked upon as a Catholic creed.

Chateaubriand's Gothic metaphor was inevitably popularized; more people than ever before looked bemused at Gothic architecture. A welter of guidebooks was published. Writers, playwrights, and painters evoked Gothic images, but architects, as we have seen, remained largely aloof. On the occasion of Napoleon's coronation in 1804, Percier and Fontaine did put up a pretty, patterned portico in front of Notre-Dame, but the internal decorations were classical in spirit. What was needed to effect a serious Gothic Revival was archaeological knowledge. Such knowledge was but slowly accumulated.

The impetus came, once again, from England: from English scholars, active in Normandy, investigating the origins of the pointed arch. Andrew Coltee Ducarel's *Anglo-Norman Antiquities* was published in London in 1767, but more important were the studies of George Downing Whittington, who worked in Normandy during the very early years of the nineteenth century. He died before he could complete his investigations, but the results of his research were published by his friend the fourth earl of Aberdeen, in 1809, as *An Historical Survey of the Ecclesiastical Antiquities of France.* Whittington confirmed what the French had long believed, that Gothic was of French origin, and—in accord with the Benedictine historians of the eighteenth century—he upheld the excellence of the thirteenth-century style above all others. Small wonder that the French responded to his ideas. Auguste Leprévost (1787–1859), a local scholar who had been inspired also by the

Scots antiquary James Anderson, translated Whittington's book into French. In 1823 Leprévost, together with C.-A.-A.-D. de Gerville (1769–1853), another Norman scholar inspired by English antiquaries (he lived as a refugee in England from 1793 to 1801), founded the Société des Antiquaires de la Normandie. The third founding member was Arcisse de Caumont (1801–1873), the youngest, but even then the most learned. In the following year he read to the society his paper "Essai sur l'architecture religieuse du moyen-âge, particulièrement en Normandie" and was at once recognized as the soundest authority on Gothic architecture. His analysis and his method of dating buildings provided the basis for all future studies. He forged the science of Gothic archaeology. His greatest work, the *Cours*

d'antiquités monumentales, was published between 1830 and 1841; his *Abécédaire* did not appear until 1851. In 1834 he founded the Société Française d'Archéologie, organizing congresses each year in different parts of France and publishing in the *Bulletin monumental* the papers that were read. The *Bulletin* was from the start, and has remained, a stern, authoritative journal. It demonstrated that the romantic ghost could be exorcised from medieval studies.

Not that an archaeological standard of taste was at once accepted by exponents of Gothic; such men were as much inspired by the rhetoric of Michelet's circle, and in particular by that of Victor Hugo, whose rallying cry was contained in the novel *Notre-Dame de Paris,* first published in 1831. He spurred two of the most active propagandists of the first phase of the Gothic Revival, Adolphe-Napoléon Didron (1806–1867) and Charles Forbes, Comte de Montalembert (1810–1870). Didron, then a young civil servant, wrote to Hugo enraptured when he had read *Notre-Dame de Paris.* Hugo advised him to travel to Normandy. During the following months he walked, rucksack on his back, from one medieval building to another, thus initiating those archaeological studies that he was to diffuse first as editor of the *Bulletin monumental,* then after 1844 in the pages of the *Annales archéologiques.* In 1845 he published the *Manuel d'iconographie chrétienne grecque et latine.* Montalembert's fascination with Hugo had been stirred earlier, in 1830, with the production of *Hernani.* He, too, was dispatched to Normandy, which he explored by carriage, moving thence to England and then to Ireland, before returning to take up the romantic Catholic revival preached by Félicité-Robert de Lamennais and J.-B.-Henri Lacordaire. Neither of these men had much liking for Gothic architecture. Lacordaire listened long to Montalembert's expositions on Gothic only to find that even Ste.-Croix at Orléans escaped his understanding; "Je crois avoir un peu compris," he wrote to Montalembert on September 1, 1831. Yet Montalembert managed to initiate in their paper, *L'avenir,* the policy of which he was to become the most consistent and effective exponent in France: of regarding Gothic architecture as the Catholic style par excellence. The papal suppression of *L'avenir* in 1832 diminished none of his fervor; rather, it served to increase it. In Rome, where he traveled with Lamennais and Lacordaire, Montalembert met the German Nazarene painter Johann Friedrich Overbeck; in Florence he found a childhood acquaintance, Alexis François Rio (1797–1874), whom he inspired with his new-found passion. The result was *De la poésie chrétienne dans son principe, dans sa matière et dans ses formes,* the first volume of which Rio published in 1836. This won no immediate success: After five months no more than twelve copies had been sold. But in 1840 the English *Quarterly Review* devoted a long article to the book, and it later earned John Ruskin's respect, influencing much of the second part of his *Modern Painters.* The second part of Rio's book, *De l'art chrétien,* was published in 1855.

The only architect Montalembert inspired, Louis-Alexandre Piel (1808–

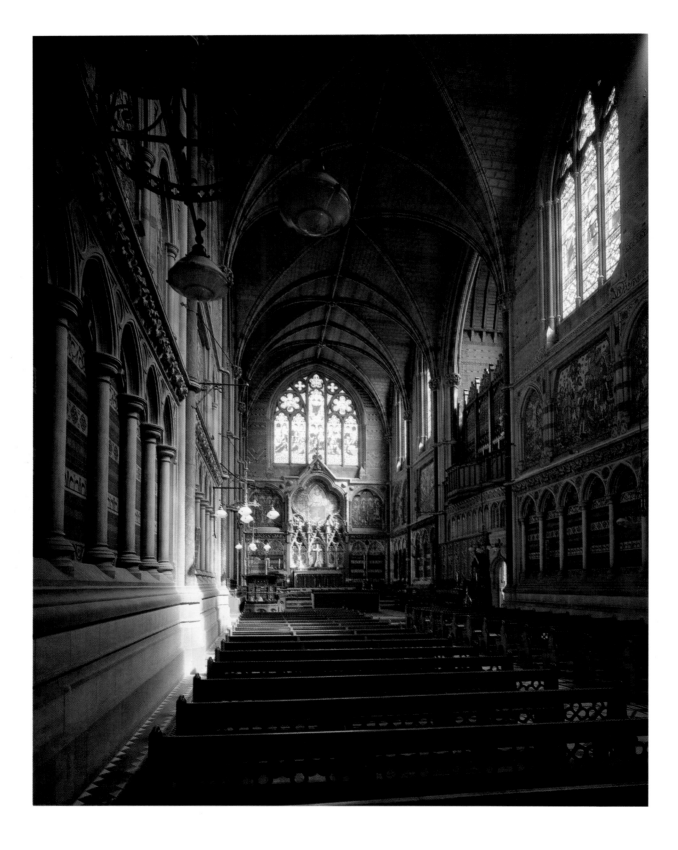

XLV. William Butterfield, interior
of chapel, Keble College, Oxford,
1873–76

609. Sir George Gilbert Scott,
St. Pancras Station Hotel, London,
stair hall, 1867–74

1841), is likewise little known. His active career was extremely short. He was a pupil of Francois Debret but, spurred by Montalembert, he traveled to Germany (writing a series of articles in 1836, "Voyage en Allemagne," for *L'européen*) and returned to design a village church in the Franche-Comté and then, in 1837, St.-Nicolas at Nantes (which was to be taken over by J.-B.-A. Lassus). In 1840 he left for Rome, where he was received into Lacordaire's Dominican order. In 1841, at the age of thirty-three, he died. But his influence was not ineffectual. He had written two more articles for *L'européen*, "Le temple de la Madeleine" and "Déclamation contre l'art païen," which served to set fashionable opinion against the adaptation of classical forms for church architecture.

Montalembert's own collection of articles *Du vandalisme et du catholicisme dans l'art,* issued in 1839, was shallow and unsustained by vigorous thought. He relied largely on the ideas of Hugo, Overbeck, and Pugin; but although he described St. Marie's College at Oscott and employed the methods of the *Contrasts,* he made no mention of Pugin by name. Yet Montalembert's influence was felt strongly in France, and even in England. In 1844 the Camden Society made him an honorary member, an honor he hastened to reject, publishing a pamphlet in English in which he accused the members of the society of being guilty of mortal sin. Gothic in France was to be practiced as a Catholic religious discipline, and the first phase of the revival was thus confined—almost exclusively—to the design of churches.

For all practical purposes the Gothic Revival in France began about 1840. There were several earlier experiments: a Protestant chapel with Gothic trimmings, in the Rue d'Aguesseau, Paris, dating from 1835, and another in a thirteenth-century style, begun in the same year, for the Dames de la Congrégation Notre-Dame, 84 Rue de Sèvres, Paris (now demolished), by François-Marie Lemarié (1795–1854), a pupil of Debret. But the only noteworthy project of the Gothic Revival to date from before 1840 is that for St.-Paul at Nîmes, designed in competition with thirty other architects, in 1835, by Charles-Auguste Questel. This church is one of the great representative buildings of the Romanesque Revival in France and also, by a curious freak, the first. It is the work, moreover, of an architect who does not figure as an important influence in either the Romanesque or the Gothic revivals. However, it is fair to note that Questel's restoration of St.-Martin d'Ainay at Lyons and, in particular, the magnificent copper-gilt altar front and the furnishings he designed for that church were acclaimed and thoughtfully scrutinized by a great many visitors, French and foreign, when they were exhibited at the international exhibition in 1855, alongside Viollet-le-Duc's similar altar front and furnishings for the cathedral of Clermont-Ferrand. But Questel is remembered today for a dull, classical *palais de justice* at Nîmes or the livelier, if still academic, *préfecture* and library on the Place de Verdun at Grenoble.

St.-Paul was begun only in 1838, after the drawings had been considerably revised in accordance with the dictates of the Conseil Général des Bâtiments

610. Charles-Auguste Questel,
St.-Paul, Nîmes, designed 1835, built
1838–50

611. Charles-Auguste Questel,
St.-Paul, Nîmes, interior, designed
1835, built 1838–50

Civils, and was not completed until November 1850. It emerged then as an adequate if slightly gutless interpretation of southern Romanesque architecture, with ribbed vaults over the nave and aisles, an apse colorfully decorated with murals by Jean-Hippolyte Flandrin, and stained-glass windows by Maréchal Guyon of Metz, but all handled with greater confidence and maturity than one might be led to expect from a pupil of Duban, even a precocious one. Much was no doubt due to the help of the archaeologist Charles Lenormant, Questel's brother by adoption.

There were far more uncertainty and awkward lapses of knowledge in other early attempts to revive the medieval styles: in St.-Clément at Nantes, for instance, built between 1841 and 1847 by François-Léon Liberge (1800–1860); or in the large church that Alexandre-Charles Grigny (1815–1867) erected between 1842 and 1846 for the sisters of the Adoration Perpétuelle du Saint Sacrement at Arras. And even more laxity and indecisiveness are in that handful of maverick commissions awarded by Louis-Philippe: the chapel dedicated to Saint Louis at Carthage, designed by Charles-Joseph Jourdain and consecrated on April 25, 1841 (now gone); the fanciful Gothic *cloche* that was placed in 1842 by Pierre-Bernard Lefranc (1795–1856) over the family chapel at Dreux, built initially by Cramail in the form of a Doric temple between 1816 and 1822; and, most astonishing of all, the mausoleum for Ferdinand d'Orléans, the Chapelle St.-Ferdinand (now the Place de la Porte des Ternes), Paris, built between July 1842 and July 1843, in something of a Romanesque manner, by none other than P.-F.-L. Fontaine, with windows to the design of Ingres and surrounds drawn by Viollet-le-Duc. Other oddities and disasters could be listed, for, the liturgical enthusiasms of the clergy having once been aroused, there was much experimentation throughout France. But only a few of the early provincial exponents of Gothic need be considered before turning our attention to the focus of the revival, which was in Paris.

In Normandy, as was appropriate, two architects of more than usual distinction emerged, H.-C.-M. Grégoire (1791–1854) and Jacques-Eugène Barthélemy (1799–1882). Grégoire, who had studied under Percier, began his career in 1837 with a small chapel in brick with trimmings of stone for the *hospice* at Yvenot (the similar chapel built there two years later for the seminary was by C.-L.-N. Robert). His major work was the fragile facade that he added to the late Gothic church of St.-Ouen at Rouen between 1845 and 1851. This was an architectural tour de force that displays neither originality nor real scholarship, yet evinces genuine powers of compositional skill. Not that Didron agreed: "Ce travail est inutile, nuisible, impossible," he wrote in the *Annales archéologiques* (p. 320) in 1845, when work was just begun; a year later he described the church as "l'édifice hybride et disgracieux [sic]" (p. 188). Barthélemy, who later became diocesan architect to Rouen, was better informed. In 1840 he began Notre-Dame-de-Bon-Secours at Blosseville, just outside the town. By 1847 building was complete. The fittings and colorful decorations inside were added during

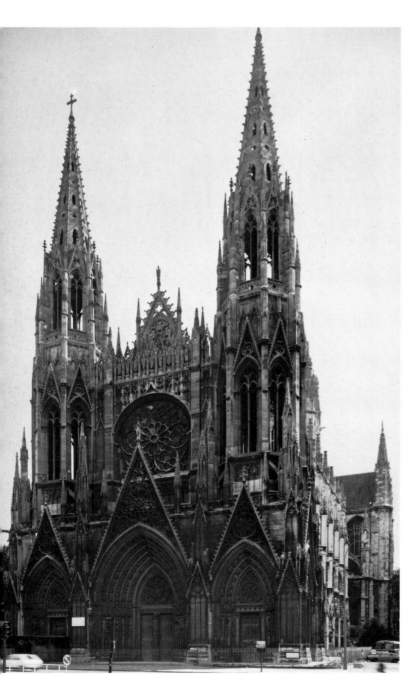

613. H.-C.-M. Grégoire, St.-Ouen,
Rouen, west facade, 1845–51

the reign of Louis-Napoleon. The church, entirely of stone, was in the thirteenth-century style. The composition is careful rather than interesting, though Barthélemy showed himself singularly resourceful in adapting recondite elements and details. Altogether, it gives evidence of archaeological sensibility and stands thus as a landmark for the beginning of the Gothic Revival in France. It bears comparison, moreover, with many of Pugin's early works. In 1844 Barthélemy started on a chapel in the thirteenth-century style at the Château du Plessis, near Port Audemer; two years later he built a small church in the same manner at St.-Aubin, near Elbeuf. However, when in 1847 he was commissioned to design the church of Ventes-St.-Rémi, near Saint-Saëns, he chose a Romanesque style. All his works have pretensions to archaeological accuracy—pretensions that are not altogether unfounded.

Less well known though no less earnest than Barthélemy were the architects Hippolyte-Louis Durand (1890-1881), Victor Gay, and the brothers Charles-Victor and Gustave Guérin. Hippolyte Durand studied under Lebas and Vaudoyer at the École des Beaux-Arts. When he left the school he took to sending studies of Gothic buildings to the Salons and was soon rewarded with the commission to restore St.-Rémy at Rheims—a work that won Montalembert's praise. In 1845 Durand exhibited designs for a number of small churches in the thirteenth-century style and conceived the idea, together with Didron, of publishing a catalogue of them, "Parallèle de projets d'églises en style ogival du XIIIᵉ siècle." The project was abandoned. But in the same year Durand began his first Gothic building, a thirteenth-century chapel for M. d'Orjault at Beaumont (Allier). In the following year he designed a church in the same style for Peyrehorade (Landes)—a church, as we shall see, that was to be the subject of some controversy at the Conseil Général des Bâtiments Civils. In 1849 Durand was made diocesan architect in the Basses-Pyrénées and in the years that followed built a number of churches in that area, all of them orthodox but dull. He was an architect of no great distinction.

Victor Gay, of whom much less is known, is perhaps more important. In 1846 he designed a large church—it was thirty-eight meters (one hundred twenty-five feet) long—for St.-Sulpice-les-Feuilles, near Arnac (Haute-Vienne). The church was conceived as a frame construction—the buttresses, the piers, and the ribs of the vaults of granite, the rest of the masonry of a light, less durable stone. The significance of the arrangement was at once apparent to all French theorists of Gothic construction, foremost among them Viollet-le-Duc, who was at that time publishing a series of articles on the subject in the *Annales archéologiques*. In the same year Gay designed a similarly organized chapel at Nanterre—it was exhibited at the Salon in 1846—but this seems to have aroused little interest in the architectural world. Indeed, almost nothing is known of Gay's activities after his early outburst. He designed some notable church furnishings, made by L. Bachelet, but, like Piel, may well have ended up in Rome, for the church

614. Gustave Guérin and Charles-
Victor Guérin, St. Étienne, Tours,
interior, 1869–74

615. Gustave Guérin and Charles-
Victor Guérin, St.-Étienne, Tours,
1869–74

614. Gustave Guérin and Charles-
Victor Guérin, St. Étienne, Tours,
interior, 1869–74

616. Jean-Baptiste-Antoine Lassus
and Eugène-Emmanuel Viollet-le-Duc,
chapter house, Notre-Dame, Paris,
1846–50

617. Jean-Baptiste-Antoine Lassus
and Eugène-Emmanuel Viollet-le-Duc,
chapter house, Notre-Dame, Paris,
interior, 1846–50

of the Corpus Domini, on the Via Nomentana, is said to have been built by him.

It is Gustave Guérin who emerges as the first representative of the type that becomes so familiar with the advance of the Gothic Revival in France: the architect obsessed with Gothic as an exemplar of structural finesse. He was the son of Charles-Mathias Guérin, an architect of Tours. His first important commission was the restoration of the cathedral there. In 1844 he was asked to design the church of St.-Étienne at Tours, but he found, as many men must have found, that he was ill equipped to design and supervise the construction of a church in the Gothic style. Together with his brother Charles-Victor he began to inspect and to measure Gothic churches of the area. They planned a book on Gothic construction but published only one article, in 1847, in the *Revue générale de l'architecture*. The building of St.-Étienne was delayed until 1869, finished five years later, and it was not before April 1855, when Guérin started to restore his most famous church, Ste.-Anne, at Lariche Extra, Tours, that his ideas were to be given adequate expression. The rebuilt church is a complex structure, suggesting a deep understanding of Gothic construction, but little of the art of architecture.

Lassus and Viollet-le-Duc are the great representative figures of the Gothic Revival. The focus of their activity was in Paris, in particular on their works of restoration, where they trained the builders and craftsmen needed to sustain the revival. Jean-Baptiste-Antoine Lassus was a classically trained architect, a pupil of Henri Labrouste, but like other Labrouste disciples—Suréda, E. Boeswillwald, E.-L. Millet, J.-J.-G. Lisch, and J.-E.-A. de Baudot—he turned early to the study of thirteenth-century Gothic. In 1835 he was awarded a prize at the Salon for a restoration of the Ste.-Chapelle; two years later he submitted an analysis of the construction of the refectory of St.-Martin-des-Champs in Paris. Also in 1835, together with another of Labrouste's pupils, Adolphe-Gabriel Gréterin (1806–1852), he began the restoration of the late Gothic church of St.-Severin in Paris. Then, in 1838, he was made *Inspecteur* under Godde at St.-Germain-l'Auxerrois, and under Duban at the Ste.-Chapelle. Within another year he was in charge of the renovation of both these churches. He restored them to an almost unbelievable and highly colored medieval splendor. The painting on the porch at St.-Germain-l'Auxerrois, together with most of the internal furnishings, has now disappeared, though the window of the Passion, in the chapel behind the main altar, on which Didron, Louis-Adrien Lusson, and Louis-Charles-Auguste Steinheil collaborated, and which was made by Rebouleau, stands witness still to the beginnings of the stained-glass revival in France, heralded in 1837 by the publication of Ferdinand Charles Lasteyrie's *Histoire de la peinture sur verre*. At the Ste.-Chapelle, where Lassus was joined in 1840 by Viollet-le-Duc and, soon after, by Suréda, the sumptuousness of the work is still evident and is daily admired by throngs of visitors. Pugin was one of the first. Didron took him to look at it in 1844.

618. Eugène-Emmanuel Viollet-le-Duc, Maison du Personnel (Custodian's house), Notre-Dame, Paris, 1866

"I have seen the most glorious things," he wrote on May 28 to his patron, the earl of Shrewsbury, "far beyond my expectations; the restoration of the Ste.-Chapelle in Paris is worthy of the days of St. Louis. I never saw images so exquisitely painted." He returned, inspired, to design the colored wall paintings for St. Giles at Cheadle. Didron traveled, in turn, to England to witness the consecration of this church.

In April 1844 Lassus and Viollet-le-Duc were appointed architects for the restoration of Notre-Dame and the building of the new chapter house. Within a few years most of the craftsmen trained at St.-Germain-l'Auxerrois and the Ste.-Chapelle were working on the new site. The restoration proceeded steadily until 1864, when the spire of the crossing was finally finished, to the design of Viollet-le-Duc. The other altogether original feature of the building, the chapter house, was largely designed by Lassus. The fabric was complete by 1850, and the rich decorations were added in the years immediately following. The Maison du Personnel to the right of the west front, dating from 1866, is Viollet-le-Duc's alone.

Lassus's independent work is inevitably of interest, though of little appeal. In August 1843 he took over the design of St.-Nicolas at Nantes, begun by Piel. The church that he put up in the following years, however, was all his own. It was modeled in its parts on the cathedral at Chartres (restored by Lassus from 1848 onward) and was probably one of the most severe and rigorous interpretations of thirteenth-century work to be found in France at that period. It is a disappointment, though it is more coherent within than without. A few years later Lassus started on a chapel for the Château de Gezaincourt (Somme), consecrated in August 1848, but his most important building was the church of Sacré-Coeur, Place d'Allier, Moulins, where, in 1852, he was to begin a nave in the thirteenth-century style for the cathedral of Notre-Dame (taken over later by E.-L. Millet). A local architect, L.-D.-G. Esmonnot (1807–1880), who had originally been asked to prepare designs for the Sacré-Coeur, in 1844 proposed a building in the Romanesque style, but this was judged to be too expensive and in 1849 Lassus was called in to design the new church. As before he took the cathedral of Chartres as his model, on this occasion providing twin towers for the facade. Esmonnot supervised building activities.

Four years later Lassus started on the smaller and simpler church of St.-Pierre at Dijon (July 1853-October 1858), an undertaking that was once again accompanied by related works of restoration, this time on the thirteenth-century church of Notre-Dame at Dijon. One year later be began St.-Jean-Baptiste-de-Belleville, Paris (June 1854–August 1859): "un monument ogival," his biographer Alfred Darcel wrote in 1858, "vigoureux et solide, dont la nef est de proportions excellentes, et la façade un vrai chef-d'oeuvre par l'ajustement des flèches sur les tours qui l'accompagnent." Contemporary opinion is more equivocal. The junction between the spires and the supporting towers is gauche, and Lassus was at such great pains to subordinate his artistic personality to the dictates of archaeological knowl-

619. Jean-Baptiste-Antoine Lassus,
Sacré-Coeur, Moulins, 1849 onward

620. Jean-Baptiste-Antoine Lassus,
Sacré-Coeur, Moulins, interior, 1849
onward

354

621. Jean-Baptiste-Antoine Lassus, St.-Jean-Baptiste-de-Belleville, Paris, 1854-59

622. Eugène-Emmanuel Viollet-le-Duc, De Courmont House, Paris, 1846–49

623. Eugène-Emmanuel Viollet-le-Duc, Viollet-le-Duc House, Paris, 1861–62

edge that he must be judged to have blunted his sensibilities. His design is dull, attenuated, and lacking in all vitality. But in this at least it gives an impression of truthfulness to its period, and in particular to the stage that the Gothic Revival had then reached in France. In the competition for the cathedral of Notre-Dame-de-la-Treille at Lille, of 1855, for which Lassus submitted a similar design, he was awarded only third prize, being easily overtaken by the Englishmen William Burges—the winner, then quite unknown—and G. E. Street, who came in second. *The Ecclesiologist* marked Lassus's work down as "meager."

Lassus's other architectural works are of little interest. He added a porch to and designed the fittings for Lemarié's chapel in the Rue de Sèvres and carried out alterations and additions for other religious foundations. His domestic work is not exciting. He built a country house at Maisons Lafitte in a Louis XIII manner; a town house on the corner of the Rue Taitbout and the Rue de Provence, Paris, with thirteenth-century details; and in 1848 began a complex structure in the Avenue Montaigne, Paris, for Prince Soltykoff—at once a house and a museum for a mass of medieval and Renaissance *objets d'art*. The building, of brick and stone, was in the fifteenth-century style. The attracting feature, however, was a large rib-vaulted room copied from Mont Saint-Michel.

Lassus's literary contributions to the Gothic Revival were legion: articles on scale ("le module humain") in the *Annales archéologiques;* a great *Monographie de la cathédrale de Chartres* (1842–67), carried out with the help of Didron and the painter Eugène-Emmanuel Amaury-Duval; and the *Album de Villard de Honnecourt* (1858), completed after his death by Alfred Darcel. This work, dedicated to Henri Labrouste, contains an introduction in which the problems of the Gothic Revival are clearly outlined.

Viollet-le-Duc's contributions to the movement were even more solidly literary and intellectual. He was, in addition, the most active restorer in all France. But he was responsible also for a number of original works of architecture in which he tried, with failing conviction, to demonstrate how Gothic might be used as the basis for a nineteenth-century style. He began in 1846 with a house in the Rue de Berlin (now 28 Rue de Liège), Paris, for Henri de Courmont, a high-ranking official and a close friend of Prosper Mérimée. By 1849 the house was complete, the first of its kind (the gimcrack Maison des Goths, 116 Rue St.-Martin of 1826, apart) in which Gothic details were applied to a traditional Parisian street frontage. The stepped stringcourses, brackets, and moldings were not, of course, intended as mere decorative devices but rather as functioning elements. They are nonetheless deployed with remarkable firmness to produce an attractive pattern of horizontals and verticals. The facades on the court, of brick with stone trimmings, have a more grim, functional expression, with little overt Gothicism, the single pointed relieving arch in the brickwork carrying with it an air of appropriateness. In his later Parisian apartment buildings (15 Rue de Douai, of 1857–60, for instance, or his own house at 68 Rue

Condorcet, of 1861–62) there are occasional hints of this fondness for Gothic, but Viollet-le-Duc seems to have rejected the style thereafter as unsuitable for city architecture. He used it, of course, for tombs (for Montalembert's family's in the Cimetière de Picpus, of 1850, and for Lassus's in the Cimetière Père-Lachaise, of 1857) and for a sequence of projects for funerary chapels, none of great interest; but only for church-building did he adopt it with conviction, and later, on occasion, for country houses—but only for those built up on older, existing structures. These last were of little enough consequence and may be briefly listed: the Château de Montdardier, Le Vigan (Gard), for the Comte de Ginestou (1861–68; extended 1884–88); a project of 1861 for the Château de Chamousset, St.-Laurent-de-Chamousset (Rhône), for Comte Paul de Saint-Victor; the Château de Pupetières, Chabons (Isère), for the Marquis de Virieu (1861), executed by Denis Darcy (1823–1904); the Château de La Flachère (Rhône) for the Comte de Chaponay (1863); and the Château d'Arragori, just outside Hendaye, for Antoinine d'Abbadia (1864–66), largely the work of a pupil, Edmond Duthoit. All these commissions arose from Viollet-le-Duc's close connection, through Prosper Mérimée, with the court of Louis-Napoleon. They were indiscriminate works for undiscriminating courtiers, parodies of that giant burlesque for Louis-Napoleon in which Viollet-le-Duc was indulging, the Château de Pierrefonds (Oise).

He had first proposed as a summer retreat for the court a restoration of a small château at Bonaguil (Lot-et-Garonne), but in April 1855 the emperor and empress traveled to England. They did not see Balmoral Castle, then barely complete, but they returned determined to emulate it. A month later Viollet-le-Duc prepared drawings for the conversion of the Château de Coucy (Aisne). Work was started at once and pursued for three years, but in 1858, on Viollet-le-Duc's persuasion, Coucy was rejected in favor of Pierrefonds. In February of the same year his designs were accepted. His presentation drawings of the following year show that the whole enterprise was considered as something of a medieval fantasia. Cavaliers and armored knights parade the court, kirtled ladies lean from the turrets, and buxom peasants are shown roasting oxen in the kitchen. Not that Viollet-le-Duc was constrained by such romantic images: He unflinchingly displayed girders of his drawbridge and introduced trusses of iron and steel under his high-pitched roofs. His later sketches for the interiors, never to be completed, are intriguing also for indications of a new sense of style, sinuous and softly curving, especially in the design of the sofas and chair. The emperor himself was enchanted: "J'ai là," he told Mérimée in 1866, "une chose *unique.*" William Burges, long an admirer of Viollet-le-Duc and to a limited degree his emulator, was bitterly disappointed by his visit to Pierrefonds; he returned from France in 1873, horror-struck, to denounce the work: "I wish to point out to the younger members of the Institute," he said, "that antiquarianism and archaeology do *not* make an architect" (*The Architect,* 1873, p. 331).

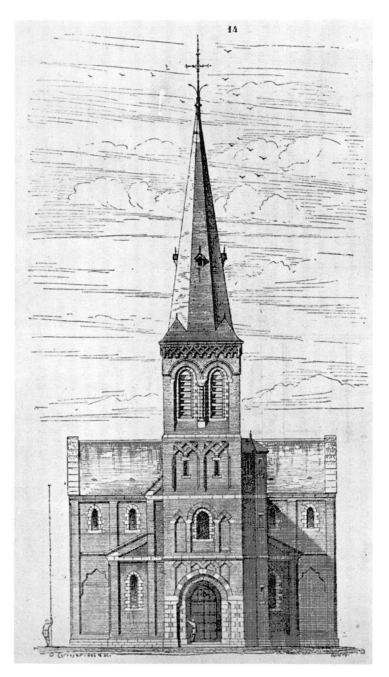

626. Émile Boeswillwald, church,
Masny, elevation of the west façade,
designed 1860

14

Viollet-le-Duc's designs for churches, though far more seriously studied, serve only to confirm this opinion. He began in 1852 with a project for St.-Gimer outside Carcassonne, built with much difficulty and dispute as to costs, between 1853 and 1858. This brutal building—asymmetrical on account of foundation difficulties rather than compositional preferences— must be regarded essentially as a restoration study, related to the architect's rebuilding of the walled town close by. In 1855 he prepared drawings for a church at La Nouvelle (Aude) of an etiolated Gothic, happily not to be built; between 1859 and 1861 he put up a simple if colorfully decorated chapel for the Petit Séminaire, Rue de Vaugirard, Paris, which was moved in 1898 to Fontenay-aux-Roses, and enlarged; but not until 1860, when he designed St.-Denys-de-l'Estrée at Saint-Denis, outside Paris, and 1861, when he drew up the project for the church at Aillant-sur-Tholon (Yonne), did Viollet-le-Duc indicate the form that he might give to a considered revivalist work. The church at Aillant-sur-Tholon, built between 1863 and 1865 under the direction of the local architect, Adolphe-Auguste Lefort, is strong and assertive and carefully composed with regard to the Picturesque balance of the townscape, but scarcely suitable as a model for other architects; St.-Denys-de-l'Estrée, erected between 1864 and 1866, was marginally more attractive, equally carefully related to the town, secular in its overtones, certainly more influential. This building showed Viollet-le-Duc at his most determined. The materials were chosen with the greatest care; all the capitals and carvings were drawn out to full scale. Internally one is struck by the unusually wide and generous proportions of the bays, designed *ad quadratum,* the fullness of the moldings and profiles; but the suppression of the cross-ribs in the vaults—lightly decorated instead with painted arabesque motifs and scattered stars—seriously weakens the effect of the whole. The building is lacking in nobility and power; it is an ungainly and depressingly uninspired interpretation of a thirteenth-century structure. Modest as to his architectural abilities, Viollet-le-Duc might well have agreed. Yet Duban, reporting on the church in 1867, evidently regarded it with respect. In 1866 Viollet-le-Duc tried his hand at a far more ambitious variant, a design for St.-Pierre-de-Chaillot, intended for the site of the present Place des États-Unis, Paris; but though this was approved in 1868, it was to be rejected four years later. Viollet-le-Duc's only other excursion into ecclesiastical Gothic was the Protestant chapel on the Avenue de Rumine, Lausanne, built between 1876 and 1877, under the direction of the local architect Jules-Louis Verrey. This neat, domesticated building is perhaps the most successful, if unadventurous, of his Gothic essays. Clearly, he was inhibited in such endeavors. He was unable to give the lead expected, indeed demanded, of him.

Whatever Viollet-le-Duc's failings as an architect, he determined the course of the Gothic Revival virtually unaided, in particular through his power of patronage as architect to the Commission des Monuments Historiques and, perhaps even more effectively after 1853, as one of the

three *Inspecteurs Générals* of the Service des Édifices Diocésains (of the other two inspectors, one was Henri Labrouste, said to be too old and infirm to mount the scaffolds, the other Paul Abadie, a pupil and unabashed admirer of Viollet-le-Duc). Indeed, all the serious acceptable architects who emerged in the 1850s and 1860s to support the Gothic Revival either had been trained by Lassus and Viollet-le-Duc or had worked for one of the two organizations dominated by the latter. It is fair to note, however, that they had, almost to a man, begun their careers under the aegis of Henri Labrouste. It was with no little perception that the critic Redon, writing in both *Le Figaro* and *La construction moderne* in 1900, should have remarked the final result of this influence, beginning with the works of the master himself: "L'architecture de Viollet-le-Duc est sèche, sectaire et sans âme; c'est une sorte de gothique *néo-grec*" (*La construction moderne,* p. 613).

At the Ste.-Chapelle Lassus and Viollet-le-Duc trained Suréda, who traveled to Spain in 1855 to set up a commission on historic monuments, and later became architect to the king; at Notre-Dame they indoctrinated Abadie, Boeswillwald, M.-A.-G. Ouradou, and Millet. Paul Abadie (1812–1884), the son of an architect of the same name from Angoulême, was a pupil of Achille Leclère, who was later to restore the cathedrals of both Angoulême and Périgueux. He started his independent career as diocesan architect with the churches of St.-Martial (1850–53) and St.-Ausone (1851–68), both at Angoulême. In 1854 he designed the church of Notre-Dame at Bergerac (first commissioned from Viollet-le-Duc), soon after, another at Valeyrac (Gironde), and then the Hôtel de Ville at Angoulême (1858–65) and the church of Ste.-Marie (1864–86) in the Bastide quarter at Bordeaux. His greatest work was the Sacré-Coeur at Montmartre, Paris, which he won in a competition with seventy-seven other architects in 1874. This was completed only in 1919. It confirmed him, even then, as the greatest exponent of the Romano-Byzantine style—a style sustained from the first by Félix de Verneilh's *Architecture byzantine en France, Saint Front de Périgueux ezt les églises à coupoles de l'Aquitaine,* published in 1851. Émile Boeswillwald (1815–1896), the son of a Strasbourg stonemason, had studied with Henri Labrouste before becoming *Inspecteur* at Notre-Dame in Paris in 1845. Within two years he had been appointed to restore the cathedral at Luçon and soon after began on Notre-Dame at Laon. In 1849 he became diocesan architect at Soissons, Orléans, and Bayonne. At Soissons he erected the dull, stripped Gothic church of St.-Waast; at Masny, near Douai (Nord), he built an equally ungainly but far more original church, designed in 1860 (the year in which the fourth volume of Viollet-le-Duc's *Dictionnaire raisonné de l'architecture française* appeared, with its challenging article on construction). This church incorporates columns of cast iron— once painted and stenciled in green, red, yellow, and black—with a brick superstructure, all exposed, and is equally harshly decorated inside and out with corbels and patterns and lintels of open brickwork set at forty-five-degree angles. This was clearly intended as more than a revivalist exercise;

it was a determined attempt to give expression to Viollet-le-Duc's latest doctrines, and was acknowledged as such when it was finished, in 1864. The curé's house and the village hall, also by Boeswillwald, are in the same style, with an attempt at Picturesque grouping. But the architecture cannot be judged a success; nor was it of any great influence, though its decorative motifs were taken up later by Félix Narjoux for his schools in Paris. In the south of France, in the hills to the southeast of St.-Jean-Pied-de-Port, Boeswillwald built the small chapel of St.-Sauveur; at Biarritz, starting in 1863, and later at Beaumetz, he built other chapels, covered inside and out with geometrical designs in colored stone, brick, and tile. These were crude, self-conscious adaptations of Byzantine and other Eastern models to which the medieval architecture of the region was thought to relate. They owed something, no doubt, to A. L. Couchaud's *Choix d'églises byzantines de la Grèce,* of 1842, and even more, perhaps, to C. F. Texier's and R. P. Pullan's *Architecture byzantine,* of 1864. Boeswillwald's one ambitious domestic undertaking was the grotesque rebuilding of the Château de Montigny, near Masny (Nord), complete with octagonal towers of varying diameters and crow-stepped gables—all derived, it would seem, from an unexecuted project by Viollet-le-Duc, of May 1863, for the Château de Merinville. Boeswillwald was, through life, a close friend of Viollet-le-Duc and also of his mentor, Mérimée. In the autumn of 1854 he traveled with them to Germany; he owed the commission of the Biarritz chapel to Mérimée and in 1860 succeeded him as *Inspecteur Général des Monuments Historiques,* the first architect to be appointed to the post.

Maurice-Augustin-Gabriel Ouradou (1822–1884), a pupil of Lebas, the third of the early disciples of Viollet-le-Duc to be trained at Notre-Dame, became his son-in-law in 1857 and worked thereafter in close conjunction with him; indeed, such houses as that for Auguste Griois, at Ambrières-les-Vallées (Mayenne), designed in 1857 but begun only in 1865, and the Hôtel Duranti, 184 Boulevard Haussmann, Paris, both to be credited on completion to Ouradou, were commissioned from and first sketched by Viollet-le-Duc. One can well understand his reluctance to accept credit for these miserable works. Ouradou did little else to match even their small distinction—some minor restorations, church furnishings, and tombs. Eugène-Louis Millet (1819–1879), a pupil of Labrouste, entered the École des Beaux-Arts in 1837; three years later he was working for Viollet-le-Duc. He started in 1848 to restore the cathedrals of Châlons-sur-Marne and of Troyes, where he was to build the Chapel des Soeurs de la Providence, and in 1855 was commissioned to restore the Château de St.-Germain-en-Laye, near Maisons Lafitte, where in 1867 he began the new church in the Rue de la Muette. Three years after Lassus's death in 1857 Millet took over the work of the cathedral at Moulins and, similarly, succeeded to the restoration of the cathedral at Rheims in 1874, after Viollet-le-Duc's resignation as *Inspecteur Général des Édifices Diocésains.* Millet's special influence on the Gothic movement was exerted, however, not as an architect but as a teacher

*XLVI. George Edmund Street,
SS. Philip and James, Oxford,
1860-62*

of craftsmen, in particular, the members of the Cercle des Ouvriers maçons et Tailleurs de Pierres, for whom he built a small center in Paris, at 9 Rue des Chantiers.

To the list of architects already considered one might add the names of Jean-Charles Laisné (1819–1891), Victor-Marie-Charles Ruprich-Robert (1820–1887), Jean-Juste-Gustave Lisch (1828–1910), Joseph-Eugène-Anatole de Baudot (1834–1915), Édouard-Jules Corroyer (1835–1904), Félix Narjoux (1836–1891), and Edmond-Armand-Marie Duthoit (1837–1889). All of these men worked long and with distinction both for the Commission des Monuments Historiques and for the Service des Édifices Diocésains and upheld, if in some cases only to a limited extent, the ideals of Viollet-le-Duc. But they were certainly not consistent Gothic Revivalists. Ruprich-Robert, a pupil of Constant-Dufeux, in 1840 became Viollet-le-Duc's assistant and later his successor at the École de Dessin. He began three churches in 1855, with the plates of the *Dictionnaire raisonné de l'architecture française* in mind: the church of Athis (Orne), St.-Jean-Baptiste at Flers (Orne; 1855–68), and the Chapelle du Petit Séminaire at Sées (Orne). He built little else in this manner, but instead demonstrated his attachment to Viollet-le-Duc in theories of ornamental design, proposed first in 1866 in the *Flore ornamentale: essai sur la composition de l'ornement, éléments tirés de la nature et principes de leur application,* a work of considerable importance, completed in 1876. His great literary contribution, however, was *L'architecture normande aux XIᵉ et XIIᵉ siècles en Normandie et en Angleterre,* published posthumously.

Juste Lisch, a pupil of both Vaudoyer and Labrouste, likewise showed early Gothic sympathies, with his design for the bishop's palace at Luçon, though he turned soon after to classical sources for inspiration. His late works, the Gare de Le Havre and a host of buildings set up for the Paris exhibition of 1878—in particular, the Gare du Champ de Mars—and others for the Paris exhibition of 1889 (one of which survives as the Gare de Javel) were all designed with exposed frameworks of iron filled in with luridly colored panels of glazed bricks and tiles. They show undivided loyalties to the doctrines set down by Viollet-le-Duc in the second volume of the *Entretiens sur l'architecture.* Édouard-Jules Corroyer and Félix Narjoux, pupils of Constant-Dufeux, allied themselves always with Viollet-le-Duc and were active and sympathetic restorers of Gothic monuments. Corroyer began with the restoration of Mont Saint-Michel, a project later taken over by another of Viollet-le-Duc's disciples, his biographer, Paul-Émile-Antoine Gout (1852–1923). Narjoux started his career in 1857 with the restoration of the cathedral of Limoges. Both were early supporters of the Gothic Revival, Narjoux most notably in a house he built in his native Chalon-sur-Saône, closely modeled on the thirteenth-century houses of Cluny. Despite this interest in Viollet-le-Duc and Gothic architecture, both Corroyer and Narjoux spent most of their active careers developing a style that was far closer to the heart of Charles Garnier than that of Viollet-le-Duc. Only the three schools that Narjoux built in Paris (after 1872, when the Paris council

630. Louis-Jean-Antoine Héret,
Notre-Dame-de-la-Croix, Paris,
1863–80

voted to erect thirty-five such buildings) were to be organized and detailed in a manner responsive to the teachings of Viollet-le-Duc.

Anatole de Baudot and Edmond Duthoit alone of this group should be considered as determined and evolving exponents of the Gothic cause. Even so, their roles must be carefully defined. Duthoit was the son and the nephew of stone carvers at Amiens, trained and employed first by Viollet-le-Duc. But he spent much of his life outside France—in north Africa, where from 1872 onward he was actively engaged in restoration work, and in the Middle East, in Palestine and Syria in particular, where he traveled first in 1861, on the expeditions of the Comte de Vogüé and W. H. Waddington. There he measured and sketched a number of Early Christian and Byzantine churches, regularly sending drawings to the Salons and articles to the *Gazette des architectes et du bâtiment.* He was even tempted to try his hand at designing in the Eastern manner: He built two churches in Beirut. Yet his most adventurous work was done in France. For Viollet-le-Duc he supervised the reconstruction of the fifteenth-century Château d'Arragori, near Hendaye, on the Spanish border, designed for the explorer and astronomer Antoinine d'Abbadia. He greatly elaborated Viollet-le-Duc's designs, introducing an array of highly colored decorative motifs, partly Gothic in character but equally inspired by Eastern sources. "Mon arabe," he said, "sent le gothique, et mon gothique a un arrière goût d'arabe ou de byzantin." His Château du Roquetaillade, southeast of Bordeaux, near Langon, once again begun on the basis of Viollet-le-Duc's designs in 1864, on this occasion for M. de Mauvesin, was even more spectacular. No detail, no piece of furniture, even, fails to show something of the exotic image Duthoit had evolved. The Rose Bedroom, the Green Bedroom, and the chapel are Duthoit's alone. It is the only building in France that may be compared—if unfavorably—to William Burges's contemporary work at Cardiff Castle (see illustrations 598, 599). Duthoit, unfortunately, produced little else: churches of a modest sort at Champeaux (Deux-Sèvres; c. 1878), Bryas (Pas-de-Calais; 1880-84), and Souverain-Moulin (Pas-de-Calais; c. 1883), and of a spectacular sort at Albert (Somme; 1883-97), where he erected the highly colored, almost exotic pilgrimage church of Notre-Dame-de-Brebières.

Anatole de Baudot was perhaps a more fitting heir to Viollet-le-Duc, his defender and constant support. He came to him first when Labrouste closed his *atelier* in 1856. By 1857 he had been set to work on the restoration of the cathedral at Puy-en-Velay (Haute-Loire) and was soon after appointed diocesan architect at Clermont-Ferrand. During the years that followed he restored no fewer than twenty-five churches. His original buildings are almost as numerous, usually adventurous. However, it is difficult to assess his particular genius at this period, for his early works were designed under the watchful eye of Viollet-le-Duc, and only after his death did de Baudot learn to extend his abilities. Then he emerged as an innovator of great distinction. Not, of course, that he did not himself early inflect the works of his mentor. The house that Viollet-le-Duc built about 1863, for M.

Sauvage, a building contractor, on a site bounded by Rue Le Peletier, Rue La Fayette, and Rue Chauchat in Paris, is largely the work of de Baudot, and undoubtedly owes much of its decoration in the form of outsized grotesques and gargoyles to his supervision. "Réussie ou non," de Baudot wrote in 1865 in the *Gazette des architectes et du bâtiment,* "cette façade a le mérite de l'originalité" (p. 83). At the same time he erected a more conventional building, with scarcely a hint of Gothic in its detailing, 21 Rue de Leningrad (originally Rue de Saint Petersbourg); then another at 34 Rue Saint-Lazare, finished in 1866, more boldy—one might say clumsily—detailed. This has something of the quality of Viollet-le-Duc's apartments for M. Milon, put up between 1857 and 1860, at 15 Rue de Douai. The Gothic features in the design, as one might expect at this period, are not obtrusive. De Baudot's slightly later church at La Roche Millay (Nièvre), of 1870, was likewise derived from a design by Viollet-le-Duc; the second for the tower and west front of St.-Martin at Ussel (Corrèze), dating from 1852 (the first was done in 1843), which was supervised by Millet and later credited to him. It is just possible that Viollet-le-Duc was indeed the designer of the La Roche Millay church also, for early sketches relating to it are still among his papers.

De Baudot's first important church, St.-Lubin at Rambouillet, designed in 1865 in competition with fifty-four other architects, relates rather to Viollet-le-Duc's more venturesome theories, taken up already, as we have seen, by Boeswillwald for the church at Masny. Along the nave are columns of iron, set two feet in front of piers of stone, serving together to support the walls and stone vaults above. The arrangement, taken perhaps from the lower chapel of the Ste.-Chapelle, or, more probably, from the fourteenth-century church of Tour (Calvados), restored later by de Baudot, avoids the use of flying buttresses while retaining an air of lightness internally. Though technically sound, the design was strongly attacked. Bourgeois de Lagny ridiculed it as a naive paraphrase of Gothic in the *Moniteur des architectes,* in 1866. César Daly followed up the attack in the *Revue générale de l'architecture* thirteen years later, when the church was finally completed. De Baudot determined not to use exposed ironwork in his later designs for churches, three of which—Levallois-Perret (1869), Sèvres (1870), and St.-Bruno at Grenoble (1870)—were won in competition and were at once castigated in the established architectural press, and then not built—though St.-Justin at Levallois-Perret was eventually erected, in a modified form, between 1892 and 1911. The project for the church at Privas (Ardèche), which de Baudot exhibited at the Salon in 1876, was, however, carried out. All were thoughtful if straightforward adaptations of simple thirteenth-century structures. They were related to Viollet-le-Duc's designs for the church at Aillant-sur-Tholon and, in particular, to St.-Denys-de-l'Estrée. What distinguishes all these churches, whether by Viollet-le-Duc or by his followers, is that they were modeled on the parish churches of France, not the cathedrals that Lassus and his contemporaries had sought to emulate,

632. Joseph-Auguste-Émile
Vaudremer, St.-Pierre-de-Montrouge,
Paris, 1864–72

if only in miniature. The limited extent of the aspirations of both Viollet-le-Duc and de Baudot at this period is to be measured by the two lackluster volumes of their manual of instruction, *Églises de bourgs et villages,* published in 1867. Only long after Viollet-le-Duc's death did de Baudot demonstrate the truly startling quality of his imagination, beginning in 1882 with the building of the Lycée Lakanal at Sceaux, in which some of Boeswillwald's innovations at Masny were to be exploited and developed, but especially after 1890, when he initiated his astonishing experiments in reinforced brickwork and concrete, including the Lycée Victor Hugo, 27 Rue de Sévigné (1894–96), and the church of St.-Jean-de-Montmartre (1894, 1897–1904), both in Paris. This development culminated in 1914 in his famous design for a giant exhibition hall, in all things a presage to the works of Pier Luigi Nervi. In de Baudot the intellectual promise of the Gothic Revival might be held to have been fulfilled.

There is a great deal more in the history of the Gothic Revival in France outside the orbit of Viollet-le-Duc urgently requiring investigation: the two early churches that Ferdinand Leroy is reported to have built at Châteauroux (Indre), by 1844, for example; or the ten that Paul Pechinet, an architect active at Langres, is said to have built in the Haute-Marne by 1846; or that extraordinary series on the outskirts of Paris, all by Claude Naissant (1801–1879), of a spare and taut geometry derived from Romanesque models. The critic of *The Ecclesiologist* had begun to remark upon some of the latter as early as 1855: St.-Lambert, Rue Bausset, Vaugirard (1848–56); Notre-Dame-de-la-Gare, Place Jeanne d'Arc, Ivry (now Gobelins; 1855–64); St.-Charles-Borromée at Joinville-le-Pont (1856–66); St.-Pierre, Place de l'Église, Charenton-le-Pont (1857–59): Ste.-Geneviève, Rosny-sous-Bois (1857–66); and Notre-Dame-de-la-Médaille-Miraculeuse, 80 Avenue Pierre Larousse, Malakoff (1861). Also of interest is the imposing church of Notre-Dame-de-la-Croix, Rue Julien Lacroix, at Ménilmontant in Paris, by Louis-Jean-Antoine Héret (1821–1899), another of Lebas's pupils, built between 1863 and 1880, all in stone apart from the ribs of the vaults of the nave, which are of iron lattice construction. Even more demanding of comment is St.-Pierre-de-Montrouge, on the Place Victor Basch, Paris, built between 1864 and 1872 by Joseph-Auguste-Émile Vaudremer (1829–1914), the most outstanding of Blouer's and Gilbert's pupils. This church, though once again based on Romanesque models, was even more consciously indebted to a restoration study of Qal'at Saman, in Syria, that Duthoit had showed at the Salon and had then published in the *Gazette des architectes et du bâtiment* in 1864, the year before the Comte de Vogüé's two great volumes *La Syrie centrale* started to appear. Vaudremer was attempting to produce a building of solid dignity—a quality noticeably lacking in the works of Viollet-le-Duc and his followers—that was clearly ecclesiastical in character, but in no way attested to the Gothic Revival. And he succeeded. St.-Pierre is perhaps the only church of the period of any architectural quality. He was less adept in his subsequent experiments—Notre-Dame-

d'Auteuil, Place d'Auteuil, Paris, of 1876–80, which hints at a knowledge of Abadie's work; the gable-fronted Protestant Temple de Belleville, 97 Rue Julien Lacroix, Paris, put up between 1877 and 1880; the Greek Orthodox church in the Rue Georges Bizet, Paris, of 1890–95—though his last, St.-Antoine-des-Quinze-Vingts, 66 Avenue Ledru-Rollin, Paris, of 1901-3, reveals unusual and surprising powers of asymmetrical composition. Other classically trained architects sought similar evasive expedients along the lines suggested by the engineers François-Léonce Reynaud, in his *Traité d'architecture,* of 1850–58, and F. de Dartein in his *Étude sur l'architecture lombarde,* issued between 1865 and 1882. Lombard Gothic, it seemed, had the merit of being Italian, not French. Louis-Joseph Duc adopted it for the chapel of the Lycée Michelet, Paris, as did P.-R.-L. Ginain, to much less pleasing result at Notre-Dame-des-Champs, in the Boulevard du Montparnasse, Paris, of 1867–76. Such compromises, however, had little convincing effect. They made no impact on subsequent architecture.

Whether or not one notes and pursues the instances listed above, the pattern of the development of the Gothic Revival in France must already be clear. Support came in the first instance from the Commission des Monuments Historiques and later and more forcefully, after 1850, from the Service des Édifices Diocésains. Nearly all the architects we have considered had restored at least one Gothic building before they undertook to build anything new. They were thus amateur archaeologists and at once acknowledged an archaeological standard of taste. The focus for all their discussion, their source of information and ideas, was thus the *Annales archéologiques,* started by Didron in 1844. The tone of this review was from the first stridently militant. Didron delighted to provoke friends and enemies alike. The Gothic Revival was deliberately encouraged by scores of articles on medieval music, stained glass, and, above all, architecture. Félix de Verneilh established the national status of Gothic in a series of articles in 1845; Lassus preached the merits of the thirteenth-century style in the same year; while Viollet-le-Duc, as we have seen, beginning in 1844 and continuing until 1847, outlined in full those theories on Gothic that he was to elaborate later in life. These were the years of the highest hopes and excitement. Building in the Gothic style started just before 1840, though the first admired achievement, Barthélemy's Notre-Dame-de-Bon-Secours, was not completed until 1847. The Gothic movement during the 1840s was being firmly consolidated. In 1852 Didron estimated that two hundred churches of a mock-medieval kind had been built or were under construction in France. The chapter house of Notre-Dame in Paris was then complete, resplendent with murals and rich new furnishings, but the mature works of Lassus and Viollet-le-Duc were yet to come. At just this period, however, the sap and savor that had sustained the whole movement failed. Lassus remained a convinced revivalist, but Viollet-le-Duc, though he continued to design in a Gothic style, was no longer wholehearted in his support. He had given notice of this crisis of faith as early as 1844, concluding one of

365

his articles in the *Annales archéologiques* with the words, "Ces secondes poussées n'ont jamais le vigueur, la sève des premières; elles sont souvent pâles et étiolées. Mais enfin ce sont encore les rejetons d'une bonne souche, et il faut bien se garder de les dédaigner" (p. 179). Already he was looking for an alternative form of architecture, Gothic in its principles but not in its appearance. He was determined to forge a new style. Although he remained friendly with Didron after 1848, he ceased to provide propaganda in the *Annales archéologiques*. Instead, he wrote after 1852 for the *Revue générale de l'architecture* and then for the *Encyclopédie d'architecture*, the review founded in 1851 by Adolphe Lance (1813–1874) and Victor Calliat (1801–1881). Viollet-le-Duc was not alone in his misgivings; many of the most active and serious-minded adherents of the Gothic movement sought a solution to the dilemmas of nineteenth-century architecture outside the restrictions of a revivalist doctrine. They built churches in the Gothic style—or in an interpretation of it—but little else. They were not sure of their cause. Apart from the limited creative ability of the architects involved, this lack of strong conviction must be held largely accountable for the rapid decline into eclecticism of the Gothic Revival in France. Very little of value in the way of building was to emerge.

The cause, the catalyst of this crisis of faith, was, paradoxically, the erection of Ste.-Clotilde, in Paris, the most conspicuous of the early monuments to the Gothic Revival, and one for which Didron and all his host fought tenaciously. The history of this battle is little known. It begins, surprisingly, in 1834, when Prosper Mérimée, as *Inspecteur Général des Monuments Historiques*, suggested, wisely enough, that all plans for restoration work to be undertaken by the Commission des Monuments Historiques be submitted to the Conseil Général des Bâtiments Civils. This procedure was followed happily for five years and more, for Jean Vatout, president of the Commission, was at the same time president of the Conseil. But at the end of 1839 control of the Conseil was transferred from the Ministère de l'Intérieur to the Ministère des Travaux Publics. Vatout was obliged to resign his position on the Commission, which was thus deprived of its president and of the intimate cooperation of the staff of the Conseil. The Commission, now presided over by Ludovic Vitet, decided to assert its independence; in this it was successful, but at the expense of the Conseil's trust. Thereafter the two bodies were in all things opposed. And their antipathy became more marked with the quickening interest in Gothic, for, though the members of the Commission were by no means Gothic enthusiasts to a man, almost all the members of the Conseil opposed the Revival. They were, for the most part, members of the Académie.

The changes in administration had an irritating consequence for the Commission: the virtual loss of control over several important historic monuments, among them the church of St.-Denis, which François Debret had been restoring for a number of years. In 1839 he began work on the west front. More than an inch of stone was cut from the face of the building;

niches and altogether unwarranted detail were also added to the north tower, which had been struck two years before by lightning. The Commission complined repeatedly. It demanded Debret's removal. Then, in 1844, the north tower was found to be collapsing under its own weight. All Gothic men were aghast. Didron attacked Debret and the Conseil viciously in the *Annales archéologiques.* The members of the Conseil lost no time in retaliating. Early in 1845 they arbitrarily refused to allow construction of three churches in the Gothic style strongly championed by Didron: St.-André, a diminutive version of St.-Nicaise, at Rheims; St.-Aubin at Toulouse, designed in competition the year before by Gaston Virebent; and St.-Étienne at Tours, by Gustave Guérin. The plans of St.-Étienne had already been passed and work was stopped only at the last moment by telegram. Didron was furious. He launched a new offensive. St.-André and St.-Aubin were not built, and St.-Étienne was begun only in 1869; but Didron's campaign resulted in the acceptance of the plans of the more conspicuous, and thus even more controversial, church of Ste.-Clotilde. Th earliest plans for this, in the classical style, were by Jean-Nicolas Huyot (1780–1840). Two years before he died he was succeeded as architect by his friend Franz Christian Gau (1790–1854), a native of Cologne who had crossed the Rhine in 1809 to study under Lebas and Debret. The *Préfet de la Seine,* Claude-Philibert-Barthelot Rambuteau, a friend of Mérimée, demanded a church in the Gothic style. After some delay Gau produced a project in a fourteenth-century style. This was rejected by the Conseil in 1840 on the grounds that too many iron cramps and tie-rods were proposed in the construction. In the years that followed Gau modified his design no fewer than three times. On each occasion it was rejected. By 1845 Rambuteau had lost patience. He demanded acceptance of the desaign. The Conseil made no move. Then, early in 1846, the north tower of St.-Denis, collapsing slowly for two years, had to be hastily demolished. Debret was dismissed, but he was made a member of the Conseil. Rambuteau responded at once. Under the threat of a full-scale enquiry into the conduct of the work at St.-Denis, he forced the Conseil to approve the plans of Ste.-Clotilde. They were passed by one vote. Didron was triumphant. He disliked Gau and he disliked Gau's design, but he was overjoyed that a victory had been won for the Gothic cause in the teeth of the Conseil's—and thus the Académie's—opposition. The Académie was no yet prepared to concede the victory. A.-N. Caristie, a member of both the Conseil and the Commission, submitted a specially prepared questionnaire to the Académie. "Est-il convenable à nôtre époque," he asked, "de construire une église dans le style dit gothique?" This memoir and the discussion that followed were summarized by Désiré-Raoul Rochette and published at once as an academic encyclical. A copy was sent to the Ministère de l'Intérieur. Didron, Lassus, and Viollet-le-Duc all responded with vigor, and no fewer than six other pamphlets were written to support them. Viollet-le-Duc was appointed architect for the restoration of St.-Denis. In the same year, the Conseil

attempted to prevent the election of Hippolyte Durand's church at Peyrehorade, but was thwarted. By 1847 eighteen of the twenty plans for churches passed by the Conseil were in some medieval style or other.

Work was at once begun on Ste.-Clotilde. Responsibility, however, was placed in the hands of Théodore Ballu rather than of Gau, who had become deaf and unduly querulous. Ballu kept to Gau's designs as far as possible, being forced to reduce the height of the towers for reasons of economy. He retained the two spires, modifying their design. By December 1857 the church was complete. Didron disliked it with a rare intensity, as indeed did all committed revivalists. They thought it too florid in detail and were not proud of their victory.

The dispute forced many admirers of Gothic architecture to consider seriously the merits of a Gothic Revival; they had been unnerved by the feebleness of their own arguments, Viollet-le-Duc no less than anyone else, and there is ample evidence to suggest that they soon found the style insupportable. Churches like Gau's were not worth fighting for. The movement declined. It would not be unfair to say that it failed. The French had for only a very few years felt impelled to imitate Gothic.

637. Joseph-Auguste-Émile Vaudremer, Lycée Buffon, Paris, courtyard, 1885–90, 1895–99

Historians of modern architecture have looked to the nineteenth century, if at all, for prophets of the modern movement. Such theorists who have held rational, apparently utilitarian ideals—Horatio Greenough, A. W. N. Pugin, Edward Lacy Garbett, and Viollet-le-Duc—have been singled out and upheld as extraordinary visionaries who owed nothing or almost nothing either to their predecessors or to the societies in which they lived. Yet they evolved their ideas in relation to both, and if we hope ever to understand their intentions and meanings we must assess them in relation to the complex contexts from which they emerged. To abstract and isolate their ideas is to falsify them and to give them new meanings. This might, indeed, be stimulating. But to view history as triumphant progress toward the present is to view it through a distorting glass.

The nineteenth-century radicals were not what they have seemed. Those moments in their careers when they have appeared to err or to falter have for the most part been ignored or set aside as embarrassments. Take Sir Joseph Paxton (1801–1865), the duke of Devonshire's head gardener at Chatsworth, who had already designed for the estate the Great Conservatory in 1836 and the *Victoria regia* greenhouse in 1850, before he put up the Crystal Palace, in London, in 1850–51. This marvel of prefabrication, of iron and glass—and also, it must be stressed, a great deal of timber construction—has a forceful clarity of expression that has rarely failed to satisfy. But it was not always thought of as "Architecture," which is how we have been taught to consider it. Paxton himself regarded the structure only as a specific solution to a particular dilemma. Iron and glass were not generally applicable to Victorian architectural needs, nor were the methods of building he had developed. When he launched into, among many other careers, that of architect after the Great Exhibition, he started to build Mentmore House in Buckinghamshire, a solid Elizabethan pastiche, for the Baron de Rothschild. He built much more of this sort. For the Rothschilds in France, with whom he had business dealings, he started a whole sequence of houses, beginning in 1853 with Ferrières, outside Paris, and ending, as we have seen, with the Château de Pregny, outside Geneva, where he was to be joined by Viollet-le-Duc. These great ungainly châteaux are all in a rich and florid style. They were clearly conceived as appropriate solutions to the problems Paxton considered as set; they were as fitted to their purposes as the Crystal Palace. And the lessons we have derived from this particular building—if lessons are wanted from history—we might as readily have read into the stones of Pregny.

Owen Jones (1809–1874), an architect of as clear and commonsensical a cast of mind as Paxton, was appointed Superintendent of the Works at the Crystal Palace with the injunction to give it something of the effect of Architecture. He applied, as we might think proper, no ornamentation; instead, he invented a system of colored decoration designed to give body and depth to the framework of iron and timber. He painted the interior with stripes of red, yellow and blue, all separated by white, an arrangement

based on Michel Eugène Chevreul's *De la loi du contraste simultané des couleurs,*
of 1839—a law that Hittorff had tried to interpret so very differently at
St.-Vincent-de-Paul—and also based on the color experiments of George
Field. The theory was all science and calculation, but the effect was as of
a fairy palace. "Looking up the nave with its endless rows of pillars," wrote
the correspondent of the *Illustrated London News* on May 1, 1851, "the scene
vanished from extreme brightness to the hazy indistinctness which Turner
alone can paint." The outside was all blue and white. In 1856 Jones
published his *Grammar of Ornament,* in which he made clear his belief that
the generative forces of the nineteenth century—like religious or moral
belief in the past—were science, industry, and commerce, and that it was
the business of designers to express these. The artistry that was to give style
to this utilitarian form—outlined in his thirty-seven propositions—consisted
in proportion systems, geometrical arrangements of pattern and color,
scientifically applied. At the end of his book were suggested decorative
appliqués evolved from plant forms, a fashion that may have begun in
England with Pugin's *Floriated Ornament,* of 1849. It was certainly taken up
and marvelously expanded there by such men as James Kennaway Colling,
John Lindley, Ralph Nicholson Wornum, Christopher Dresser, Frederick
Edward Hulme, and Lewis Foreman Day. In France, as we have seen,
Viollet-le-Duc and Ruprich-Robert pursued this path to somewhat different
ends. The magical aura that Owen Jones had conjured up with his science
at the Crystal Palace he successfully captured once again in his halls of arts
and commerce—St. James's Hall, off Regent Street, London, of 1855 to
1858, the Crystal Palace Bazaar, between Great Portland and Oxford streets,
London, of 1858, and Osler's shop, Oxford Street, of 1858 to 1860—all
long since gone. Each had a roof of iron and glass and plaster painted in
primary colors. They caused a sensation. But when it came to providing
homes for the solid citizens who paid to hear music or shopped in these
emporiums Owen Jones chose to design in a heavy Italianate style, as he
did, for example, No. 8 Kensington Palace Gardens, London. He
considered it appropriate to the station and needs of his clients.

When one turns to the career of that febrile French seer Hector Horeau
(1801–1872), who in 1849, even before Paxton, submitted an iron and glass
structure in the Crystal Palace competition, one finds the same candid
acceptance of common propriety in the field of domestic and other
architecture. A pupil of Eugène-Charles-Frédéric Nepveu (1777–1862) and
then of François Debret, he failed to win the Grand Prix in 1826 but, like
Owen Jones, traveled for three years throughout Europe and later, in 1837,
to North Africa, before settling down to his chosen, constantly frustrating
career. He published a spectacular and highly colored *Panorama de l'Égypte
et de la Nubie* in 1841. But first he made a name for himself as a builder
of iron and glass structures: In 1846 he designed a *jardin d'hiver* at Lyons
(built in the following year) and the Château des Fleurs (a bandstand, in
effect) for the corner of the Rue Vernet and the Rue Galilée, off the

Champs-Elysées, in Paris, much praised in 1847 in the *Revue générale de l'architecture* (pp. 254, 410). He published a number of ambitious schemes for improving the drainage of the city, for *abattoirs,* markets, and exhibition buildings. His design for the Halles Centrales, the central market of Paris, a great iron and glass structure similar in appearance to Philibert de l'Orme's design for the Salles des Fêtes Royales, the forerunner of C.-L.-F. Dutert's Galerie des Machines, was first presented in 1844 and developed in the following years. When Victor Baltard and F.-E. Callet were appointed to build that market and began with a ponderous pavilion of stone, Horeau initiated a campaign that brought Baron Haussmann, in 1853, to order its demolition—thus leading to the erection of the iron and glass structures that Baltard and Callet eventually designed. Horeau was furious. He moved in 1855 to England, where he suggested a whole new range of street improvements and exhibited them all, four years later, in the Hanover Square Rooms, London. By then he had built a house in Surrey (untraced) and another at Primrose Hill, London (probably The Poplars, at 18 or 20 Avenue Road; demolished in 1934), illustrated in the review established by Viollet-le-Duc's son, the *Gazette des architectes et du bâtiment,* in 1868. The plan is imaginative, if symmetrical, with splayed wings, but the elevation is decorated with conventional Italian-inspired motifs. In the first volume of the elder Viollet-le-Duc's *Habitations modernes,* of 1875, another of Horeau's houses is illustrated, a farmstead at Ostend, in Belgium, with clumsy brick decoration around the door and window openings, and boldly projecting timber bargeboards and balconies with frets and rude arabesques. A Swiss chalet, it seems, has strayed. Later in life Horeau moved to Madrid, where in 1868 he designed an iron and glass market for the Plaza Cebada. A few years after—while serving a prison sentence in Paris for overenthusiastic support of the Commune—he sketched proposals for a new *hôtel de ville,* once again an ordinary enough, unpretentious sort of builiding, but with a great glass-roofed court in which all business was to be conducted. Horeau was a hard thinker and a man of immense enterprise and no little adventure, but he, too, accepted, without qualm it seems, that for certain types of building, the conventional hybrid modes were the best.

In America James Bogardus (1800–1874), a manufacturer of machinery, was making four- and five-story fronts for buildings, all of iron and glass, from the late 1840s onward, but he chose to cast them in classically modeled molds, and with his increasing success made them ever more rich and intricate in decoration. The Renaissance style that he applied was to him an essential and fitting part of the whole conception. And, though he had an arrogant disregard of all conventional opinion and ranked the products of engineering extremely high, even James Fergusson (1808–1886), that bombastic philistine, one-time indigo merchant, and archaeologist, the architectural historian who was probably more widely read than any other during the nineteenth century, thought that such buildings as the Crystal Palace were lacking in a sense of solidity and mass, and could not, as he

642. Owen Jones, No. 8 Kensington
Palace Gardens, London, c. 1850
643. Plate from John Ruskin's
Seven Lamps of Architecture,
1849

expressed it, "be elevated to the class of the Fine Arts." Fergusson, it is to be remarked, was general manager, from 1856 to 1858, of the Crystal Palace Company, at Sydenham, where Paxton and Jones had set up an even grander variant of the Hyde Park structure. His most entertaining and certainly most provocative book was *History of the Modern Styles of Architecture,* of 1862 (published together with his *Illustrated Handbook of Architecture,* of 1855, as part of the even more compendious *History of Architecture in All Countries, from the Earliest Times to the Present Day,* issued between 1865 and 1867). At the end of his *History of the Modern Styles of Architecture,* having rejected Greek and Gothic as moribund, and having ranted and raved at the shams of modern architecture, Fergusson yet felt compelled to recommend to his contemporaries that they take up a Renaissance style. "There is yet one other style within whose limits progress still seems possible," he wrote despairingly. "The Renaissance Italian is by no means worked out." Fergusson sought an architecture that was altogether sensibly designed and built, strong and durable, reflecting both in its forms and in its decoration—which he considered of the highest importance—the aspirations and the communal sense of the society that produced it: a banal aim, one might judge, but one that, together with so many other contemporaries, he thought best fulfilled in the Renaissance manner.

No less bathos attaches to those agonized theories offered in that now little-known but, in the nineteenth century, much-read *Rudimentary Treatise on the Principles of Design in Architecture,* first printed in 1850. The author was Edward Lacy Garbett, who was to appeal so much to Horatio Greenough and later American theorists. He staunchly upheld the importance of structural principles, recognizing two systems of structural purity, the Greek and the Gothic, but rejected them at length in favor of a third, as yet unresolved—that of the Italian Renaissance.

Other nineteenth-century prophets—those who most strongly affected nineteenth- and even twentieth-century sensibilities—came to somewhat different conclusions, though they inclined to agree with Fergusson as to the merits of the Crystal Palace. A. W. N. Pugin, that brilliant proselytizer of Gothic, described the building in casual asides in his letters as "the crystal humbug" and "a glass monster." This was not because he disapproved of iron construction or other modern devices and inventions, for he wrote in 1843 in *An Apology for the Revival of Christian Architecture in England,* "Any modern invention which conduces to comfort, cleanliness or durability should be adopted by the consistent architect." Moreover, he made clear in other of his works his approval of modern plumbing systems, gaslights, all manner of mechanical devices, and even the railways, provided that they were designed directly and simply with reference to their use. He liked best what he called "the substantial manner." He loathed the evident lack of mass of the Crystal Palace, and even more the evident indifference to Gothic that it reflected. The Medieval Court he set up in Paxton's building was, in its rich intensity, in sharp contrast to that pared-down structure. The

XLVIII. Augustus Welby Northmore Pugin, Houses of Parliament, Houses of Lords, the library, London, 1844-52

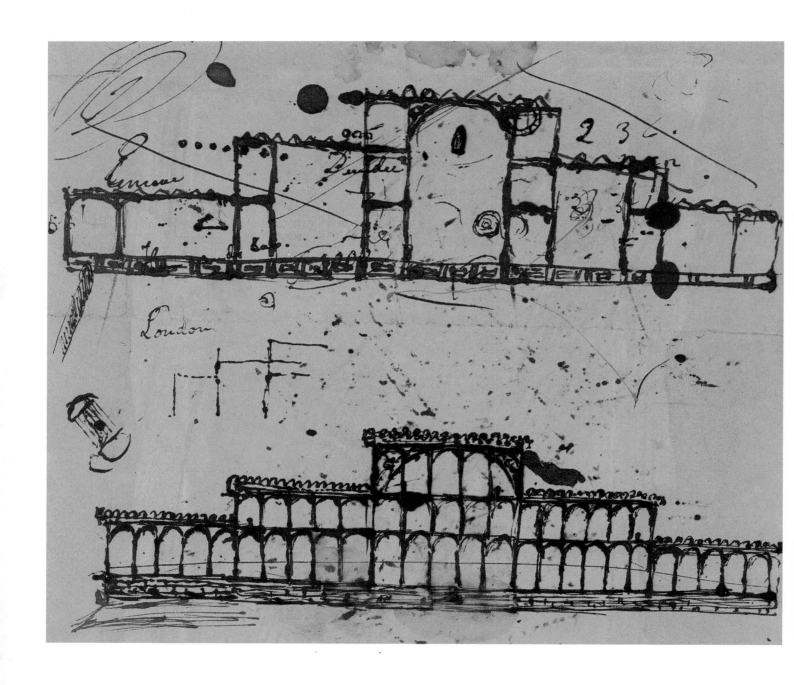

*644, 645. Louis-Auguste Boileau,
project for a chapel at Saint-Denis,
exterior and interior, 1854*

principles that Pugin laid down in 1841 on the first page of *The True
Principles of Pointed or Christian Architecture* have nothing overtly to do with
Gothic. "The two great rules for design are these: 1st, that there should
be no features about a building which are not necessary for convenience,
construction, or propriety; 2nd, that all ornament should consist of
enrichment of the essential construction of the building." However, it is
evident throughout this book, and made quite plain in the second edition,
that the only acceptable style is Gothic. Pugin countenanced no other. He
fought throughout his short and active life for its revival, for it represented
to him the last historical stage at which architecture had been a complete
expression of communities imbued with a true spiritual faith. Pugin had been
converted to Roman Catholicism in 1835. The Reformation, and all that
was associated with it, was thus to him a second fall from grace. In his early
years he adopted the late Gothic style, but as his belief grew that the
Reformation was not the root cause of the fall, merely part of a more general
decay in faith, he retreated to the styles of the early fourteenth and late
thirteenth centuries; these became for him the only true architecture for the
Revival.

Pugin's principles and much of his attitude toward Gothic—even his
identification of it as the true Catholic style—may be traced back,
surprisingly, to so academic a source as Jacques-François Blondel's *Cours
d'architecture,* to which Pugin was no doubt introduced by his father, an
architectural illustrator from France. But Pugin's perfervid moralism is new
to architectural theory. It was most forcefully expounded right from the start,
in the most devastating of all his books, *Contrasts; or, A Parallel Between the
Noble Edifices of the Fourteenth and Fifteenth Centuries, and Similar Buildings of
the Present Day,* issued in 1836. The text is short, but the sixteen contrasted
plates make his meaning clear: All the towns and buildings of the nineteenth
century are degraded and mean; those of the Middle Ages are rewarding
and full, burgeoning with ancient feelings and sentiments. " 'Tis they alone
that can restore pointed architecture to its former glorious state: without
it all that is done will be a tame and heartless copy, true as far as the
mechanism of the style goes, but utterly wanting in that sentiment and
feeling that distinguishes ancient design" (2d ed., 1841, p. 43).

The moral note struck by Pugin was to be the real contribution of England
to nineteenth-century architectural thought. John Ruskin (1819–1900) was
the most eloquent spokesman of the ethical—though not the Catholic—
attitude. His social convictions, however, were to be forcefully and
dogmatically expressed only later in life. Yet already in his very first
writings, "The Poetry of Architecture," published in 1837 and 1838, under
the pseudonym Kata Phusin ("According to Nature"), in *Loudon's Architectural Magazine,* was his whole future understanding made evident. His editor
Johan Claudius Loudon, it is worth remarking, was a man of a different
stamp. All his activity was in sharp contrast to Ruskin's—his obsessive
writing apart. Loudon was a caricature of the dour, industrious Scot; he got

up at seven each morning, breakfasted, and then worked without a break until eight in the evening, writing in the course of his life over four million words, mostly on estate management and horticulture but on much else besides. He was forever producing practical proposals for such things as drainage systems and heating devices. He sought out the woman he was to marry because she had written what must rank as one of the first works of science-fiction, *The Mummy: A Tale of the Twenty-Second Century* (1827). He was building greenhouses years before Paxton and established the techniques of construction that Paxton was later to use at Chatsworth and the Crystal Palace. He was a very early protagonist of iron and glass architecture. But in his myriad publications he also offered all manner of architectural styles (he employed Charles Barry and those rogues E. B. Lamb and S. S. Teulon indiscriminately to make his designs), for, though he had explicit and very commonsensical ideas about architecture, he cared not a jot what it should look like provided that it be usefully organized and soundly built. He cared for everything that Ruskin did not; yet he did care for Ruskin and was generous in his praise of his writings. Ruskin's "The Poetry of Architecture" dealt with qualities of landscape and the manner in which a chalet, a cottage, or a farmhouse might relate to it, in the tradition of Picturesque theory already widely applied in England. However, Ruskin's particular view of the way in which such inevitable, unassuming, and "natural" architecture is a reflection not only of the skills but of the whole way of life of the people who made it was new—though it may well have derived from Jean-Jacques Rousseau's enraptured description of the life and form of a mountain village near Neuchâtel contained in his polemic of 1758 addressed to d'Alembert "*. . . Sur le projet d'établir un théâtre de comédie en [Genève].*" Goodness in architecture, for both men, arises from goodness in man. Later, in those two works most memorably concerned with architecture, *The Seven Lamps of Architecture,* of 1849, and *The Stones of Venice,* issued in three volumes in 1851 and 1853, Ruskin was to enlarge on this theme. In *The Queen of the Air,* of 1869, he was to turn it into an aphorism: "A foolish person builds foolishly, and a wise one sensibly; a virtuous one, beautifully; and a vicious one, basely."

The seven lamps—Sacrifice, Truth, Power, Beauty, Life, Memory, Obedience—have not much to do with architecture, certainly not in any conventional fashion. Ruskin was not greatly interested in the way a building might work, in its organization, or in its structure (though he was vehement in his denunciation of what he recognized as structural deceit). There are no more than one or two plans illustrated in his published works, and no sections; nor, if we are to judge by his drawings and descriptions, was he much taken with mass or volume in architecture. His skill as a draftsman and his passion in writing are directed to details: to doorheads and windows, to capitals and moldings. He focused always on discrete fragments. Architecture itself, he thought, resided in surface adornment, in moldings and sculpture. "Thus," he wrote in "The Lamp of Sacrifice," "I suppose

648. William Slater, project for a
church in the Gothic style with cast-
iron columns, 1856

no one would call the laws architectural which determine the height of a breastwork or the position of a bastion. But if to the stone facing of that bastion be added an unnecessary feature, as a cable moulding, *that* is Architecture." But what excited him above all else was surface pattern, the texture of things, whether in architecture or nature. His delight in drawing or describing such patterns was sensual, almost erotic. He saw in the surface, whether worked by man or weathered by time, the imprint of all nature, to be caressed by the hand and the eye. No matter if the surface was rough and ungainly, scarred and broken, provided it be a truthful expression. He abominated all restoration in architecture, battling furiously against it through life, and in 1874 refusing the Gold Medal of the Royal Institute of British Architects became the company included men who were defacing the ancient buildings he loved. The surface of structures had for him a sanctity that must not be disturbed (shades here of Chateaubriand). There was more to it than visual delight. The surface revealed the nature of the man who had worked it, giving expression to all his joys, passions, and beliefs; it thus also expressed the nature of the society of which that man was a part. For good architecture to arise, those responsible must have good lives and be happy.

Ruskin's ideal society was set somewhere in the Middle Ages, a notion he had derived first from Thomas Carlyle and later from Pugin. However, good Evangelical that he was and fearing lest he be tainted by Pugin's Catholicism, he sharply denied any such influence. He thus rejected all Renaissance architecture as a sham and upheld Gothic as an image of the good and the true. But just as there is not as much as one might expect of architecture in the *The Seven Lamps,* so there is not much in it on Gothic—nor is there even in *The Stones of Venice.* Ruskin's crusade was not a national one. He disliked the damp and the gloom of the north and did not look long at the Gothic monuments of England, or even at those of France (though in time he learned to admire some of the latter). He preferred the south. Italian Gothic became for him the symbol of all he loved in architecture— Giotto's tower at Florence and, even more, the Doges' Palace, at Venice. Hastily written and added almost haphazardly to the second volume of *The Stones of Venice,* his chapter "The Nature of Gothic" served nonetheless as a catechism for the serious-minded architects of England. William Morris, of whom nothing need here be said, solemnly printed a separate edition at the Kelmscott Press in 1892. He described it then as "one of the very few necessary and inevitable utterances of the century." It was the spur to his career, and to that of Philip Webb, William Lethaby, and a great many others. "The Nature of Gothic" is, as might be expected, unspecific. Ruskin approaches his subject through broad categories: savageness, imperfection, changefulness, redundance, and rigidity. Yet one emerges from it inspired with a new reverence and feeling for the idea of Gothic. Absolutely, it was the most potent of all Ruskin's writings on architecture.

In time he turned his attention away from architecture: He thought rather

649, 650. Louis-Auguste Boileau, St.-Paul, Montluçon (Allier), interior, 1864–69

on the nature of society and on what it might be. He became one of the most radical thinkers of his age. He aimed to make England a good, egalitarian society—with equal wages for all (he himself had been left 197,000 pounds on his father's death). Architects, he saw, were impotent; only when the nature of society changed would good architecture arise. In 1864 he was invited to lecture at the Mechanics Institute at Bradford, where a competition was being held for the design of a new exchange. He was expected to advise on the style, which no one doubted he would designate as Gothic. Instead, he told the assembled burghers and businessmen that *he* didn't care a damn what style they got, because *they* didn't. All that concerned them was the making of money. And he thundered on and on about the immorality of their lives and the consequent ugliness of their city. "The only absolutely and unapproachably heroic elements in the soldier's work," he told his audience, "seems to be—that he is paid little for it—and regularly: while you traffickers, and exchangers, and others occupied in presumably benevolent business, like to be paid much for it—and by chance. I never can make out how it is that a *knight*-errant does not expect to be paid for his trouble, but a *pedlar*-errant always does;—that people are willing to take hard knocks for nothing, but never to sell ribands cheap; that they are ready to go on fervent crusades, to recover the tomb of a buried God, but never on any travels to fulfil the orders of a living one;—that they will go anywhere barefoot to preach their faith, but must be well bribed to practise it, and are perfectly ready to give the Gospel gratis, but never the loaves and fishes.

"If you chose to take the matter up on any such soldierly principle; to do your commerce, and your feeding of nations, for fixed salaries; and to be as particular about giving people the best food, and the best cloth, as soldiers are about giving them the best gunpowder, I could carve something for you on your exchange worth looking at. But I can only at present suggest decorating its frieze with pendent purses" (*The Works of Ruskin*, ed. E. T. Cook and A. Wedderburne, vol. 18, p. 450).

The one building with which Ruskin was said to have been closely involved, the University Museum at Oxford, by Sir Thomas Deane and Benjamin Woodward, was not a successful expression of his ideals. He was less involved, though, than is usually thought. He was out of England for much of the building period and was writing hard for most of the rest of the time. The final design was made in 1854, and construction began in the following year, with workmen brought over from Ireland led by the rumbustious James O'Shea. He was to demonstrate in his work all Ruskin's cherished obsessions, thought his insolent disregard for the dignitaries of Oxford led to his deportation in 1860, before the work of carving was complete. Woodward died in the following year, and funds were lacking, so little more was done. The bulk of the work was, however, by then largely executed, with a fantastical covered court all in iron and glass, Gothic in style. Ruskin cannot have much approved of the use of iron, but he was

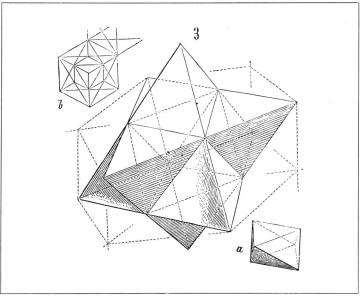

651. *Eugène-Emmanuel Viollet-le-Duc, project for a concert hall with a ceiling vaulted in iron and brick, from his twelfth.* Entretien sur l'architecture, *c. 1866*

652. *Eugène-Emmanuel Viollet-le-Duc, diagram showing that the equilateral triangle must be the basic principle of all architecture, from his* Dictionnaire raisonné de l'architecture française, *1866*

never strongly critical about it. His concern for the joy of a man in his work and for the way he might make his mark on the finished surface had led him, inevitably, to reject the large-scale use of iron in architecture as well as all methods of prefabrication. The workman, he said, was thus degraded. Critics might see the effects of a painting by Turner (a painter he revered) in the nave of the Crystal Palace, but 1851, Ruskin retorted, was the very year in which Turner had died. In fact, Turner was keenly interested in the Crystal Palace. But for Ruskin there was nothing in it either of Turner or of Architecture. "The quantity of thought it expresses is, I suppose," he wrote in 1855 in a note to the second edition of *The Seven Lamps*—a note, incidentally, directed against Garbett—"a single and very admirable thought of Sir Joseph Paxton's, probably not a bit brighter than thousands of thoughts which pass through his active and intelligent brain every hour—that it might be possible to build a greenhouse larger than ever greenhouse was built before. This thought, and some very ordinary algebra, are as much as all that glass can represent of human intellect" (*Works,* vol. 9, p. 456). When he viewed the influence of his own works and writings in 1874 in the preface to the third edition of *The Stones of Venice,* "which has mottled our manufactory chimneys with black and red brick, dignified our banks and drapers' shops with Venetian tracery, and pinched our parish churches into dark and slippery arrangements for the advertisement of cheap coloured glass and pantiles," he felt bound to reject them, too, as pernicious.

On the Continent ethics and social morality were not permitted to dominate architectural theory: No one of any great influence took up architecture as a religious crusade, no one veered from architecture to political theory. Nonetheless, many—indeed, all the key figures—held strong, sometimes violent, political views. Gottfried Semper, the German spokesman, was forced to flee to Belgium and then to France when the antimonarchical revolution in which he was involved had failed. In France, Horeau, as we have seen, was imprisoned for his part in the Commune. Earlier, Gilbert, Blouet, Labrouste, and Duc had been passionately stirred by the ideas of Saint-Simon and Comte, while César Daly, editor of that most influential and sumptuous of journals, the *Revue générale de l'architecture,* was a Fourierist, and even designed a *phalanstère,* which he illustrated in outline in his *Revue.* But there was little else of this sort in it.

Viollet-le-Duc himself had fought on the barricades when young and, after the Franco-Prussian war, when the mood of the country was at a very low ebb, he thought to take up an active political stance. He started to write regularly for *Le centre gauche, Le peuple,* and *Le bien public.* In 1873 he stood in the first municipal elections and was chosen as Republican candidate for Montmartre, a position he was to hold for no more than a year, for he decided then that the Republican government was without morality. He denounced it in *Le centre gauche* and resigned his seat and all government appointments, including that of *Inspecteur Général des Édifices Diocésains.* He was reelected to the city council, although under a different political banner,

653. Eugène-Emmanuel Viollet-le-
Duc, section of a Gothic church, from
his Dictionnaire raisonné de
l'architecture française 1859

and sat on it until his death in 1879. These were honest and courageous steps to take, but there is no need to exaggerate their importance. Viollet-le-Duc had for too long been a compliant courtier under the Second Empire; he had done nothing then to use his influence to improve the world.

The focus of all Viollet-le-Duc's interest in architecture was on construction. He was determined to show that the proper expression of structural principles would produce proper architecture. No one who has read Henry Adam's *Mont-Saint-Michel and Chartres,* packed with quotations from Viollet-le-Duc, can be in any doubt that he was also a man of sensitivity and feeling, acutely responsive to the poetry of Gothic architecture, and that he may be interpreted also in this light; but in his battle against the established architectural conventions, and in particular those established by the École des Beaux-Arts, he was forced to steel his arguments with the most ruthless logic and to interpret Gothic architecture—indeed, all good architecture, in which he included Greek and also Byzantine—as the readily explicable results of determined ends. The principles he adduced in his analysis were to be applied in the fashioning of an architecture for the nineteenth century and even after. He emerges thus as a harsh materialist, crude and overbearing. Yet even those structural principles he had so early explained in the pages of the *Annales archéologiques* were to be but tentatively applied to the exigencies of nineteenth-century architecture. From the first he accepted that new materials, especially iron, must serve as an essential part of nineteenth-century renewal. He was even prepared to use iron for restoration work: He ordered iron window frames for Ste.-Madeleine at Vézelay in 1845, just as Lassus had done for St.-Germain-l'Auxerrois. However, in a report to the Commission des Monuments Historiques of 1850 on the ridiculous cast-iron spire that J.-A. Alavoine had set on top of Rouen cathedral in 1824, Viollet-le-Duc firmly rejected—in much the same manner as had Pugin—the notion that iron might be used to reproduce forms or ornaments that had evolved under different circumstances. There was to be no cast-iron Gothic. He was vehement in his denunciation of all such experiments. On January 11, 1854, Louis-Auguste Boileau (1812-1896), the son of a joiner and himself the maker and carver of the organ loft at St.-Germain-l'Auxerrois, the architect also of a simple mock-Gothic church at Mattaincourt (Vosges) that included cast-iron pews, published a proposal in *La presse* for a church with columns of cast iron to be erected in the Chaussée-d'Antin. On February 18 this was again published, in *L'illustration,* with an enthusiastic commentary by Albert Lenoir. Within a short time a pupil of Percier and Fontaine, Louis-Adrien Lusson (1790–1864), had taken up the idea and proposed it to the archbishop of Paris for a site on the corner of the Rue Monthyon (now Rue Ste.-Cécile) and the Rue du Conservatoire. Work began in the month of March. Boileau, as might be expected, protested most strongly. He replaced Lusson as architect and by December 21, 1855, his new church of St.-Eugène had been consecrated. Externally it is an ordinary enough red-brick box, stuccoed here

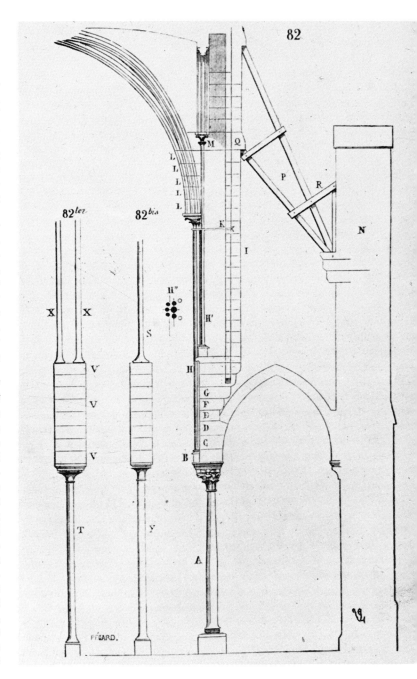

and there and broken by pointed windows, with three gables on the entrance facade. Internally it is a curious Gothic paraphrase similar to that designed (possibly in the same year) in England for the Ecclesiological Society, by William Slater, Richard Cromwell Carpenter's pupil and successor, but published in *Instrumenta ecclesiastica* only in 1856. All the columns and ribs and even the traceries of Boileau's church are of iron. The vaults are covered with sheets of metal. The building caused much excitement and comment. César Daly condemned it early, in February 1855, long before its completion, in the *Revue générale de l'architecture,* as a conception of the utmost naivety. Two years later he was to reject it as too much the railway shed: "Dans lesquelles toutefois la colonne en fonte réussit très bien, parce que là l'effet d'art résulte uniquement de l'aménagement, non pas le plus monumental, dans le sens propre du mot, mais le plus commode, d'un grand espace qu'on doit disposer, autant que possible, de façon à en utiliser toutes les parties et à y laisser largement pénétrer le jour; dans une église, au contraire, la colonne, il nous semble, est tout à la fois faite pour soutenir et pour meubler" (p. 100). But Michel Chevalier published a highly appreciative account of Boileau's paraphrase in the *Journal des débats* on June 1, 1855, and at once proposed that the system be adopted for the cathedrals of Moulins and Marseilles and also for the new churches at Montpellier and Lille. Chevalier's tribute drew forth a rude reply from Viollet-le-Duc. In the *Encyclopédie d'architecture,* in the same month, he wrote, "Un système dont toute la solidité réside dans l'extrême précision des assemblages se rapproche plus de l'art du mécanicien que de l'art de l'architecture. . . . M. Boileau, le directeur de la construction de Saint-Eugène, quelque ingénieux qu'il soit, n'était pas architecte, c'était un fort habile menuisier, et quoi qu'on fasse, la première éducation pratique ne se remplace pas." It was, he added, a puerile pastiche in bad taste. Boileau replied in the following month with more restraint than might be expected. He was doing no more, he said, than Viollet-le-Duc himself had suggested in his writings. Approving of the principles of Gothic construction, he had tried to interpret them in the way in which thirteenth-century masons themselves might have done had they had present-day resources. Viollet-le-Duc's distaste, he suggested, was aroused because the forms and arrangements of Gothic had not been slavishly copied. Viollet-le-Duc was enraged. He responded in the same issue of the *Encyclopédie d'architecture,* raising a host of technical issues and also that question pertinent to the whole problem: "Pourquoi des arcs, quand on peut avoir des poutres de fonte ou de tôle d'une énorme portée? Pourquoi ne pas se servir de ces matières comme les ingénieurs anglais et français sont arrivés à le faire, c'est-à-dire en simplifiant de jour en jour les formes, en rompant franchement avec les vieilles traditions imposées par la routine?" But there is small cause to think that Viollet-le-Duc would have liked St.-Eugène any better had it resembled more closely a railway shed. Along with César Daly and most of his fellow critics in France, he had not admired the Crystal Palace. Henri Sirodot had dismissed it in the *Revue*

655. Jules Saulnier, Menier chocolate factory, Noisiel-sur-Marne, 1869, 1871–72

656. Eugène Train, Collège Chaptal, Paris, 1863–75, a celebrated example of mixed brick, terra-cotta, colored ceramic, and exposed iron construction that started a fashion even before its completion

générale de l'architecture in 1851 as no more than a giant greenhouse, without pretensions to architecture (p. 154).

Boileau was unabashed. Already in a small brochure issued in September 1854 he had published his first, and even more startling, project for a church of iron as *La nouvelle forme architecturale.* He showed tenuous columns of iron supporting a system of segmental arches and ribs of iron, carrying in turn an array of ribbed vaults, built up one against another to form a pyramidal composition. The curved vaults are exhibited both inside and out. The columns of iron, boldly expressed inside, are sheathed on the outside perimeter with stone. But the window areas between remain unusually large. The traceries with which they are filled are yet more unusual. They are made up of intersecting arcs to form a pattern of lines that relates to the segmental arches of the vaults. Two towers of a similar idiosyncratic composition stand at the west end of the church. Altogether, the design is freakish, inspired not only by Gothic examples but also, there is little doubt, by Moorish architecture (extracts from Owen Jones's lavish book on the Alhambra were published in the *Revue générale de l'architecture* in 1844, and one plate in particular seems to have provided the prototype for Boileau). He was later to produce many and far more ambitious variations on this design, to illustrate them, and to issue them together with the most persuasive of literary propaganda: In 1881 he published *Les principes et exemples d'architecture ferronière,* five years later the *Histoire critique de l'invention en architecture,* and in 1889 *Les préludes de l'architecture du XXᵉ siècle et l'exposition du centenaire,* a work of prophetic intention. But, apart from the great Magasins du Bon Marché, a department store begun, together with his son Louis-Charles, in 1869, his executed works showed little advance on St.-Eugène, if indeed they attained its standard of consistency. He added an iron-ribbed dome to his early reinforced-concrete church of Le Vésinet (Yvelines) in 1863, in the same year began St.-Paul, Place J. Dormoy, at Montluçon (Allier), and then in 1869 started work on St.-Étienne at Juilly (Seine-et-Marne)—where Lamennais and his disciples had installed themselves in 1830—a church not unlike St.-Eugène. In 1868 he built Notre-Dame-de-France in Leicester Place, London, a curious, iron-framed structure (demolished in 1957) set within the circular shell of Robert Barker's old panorama.

Viollet-le-Duc ignored this activity. His disciple J.-E.-A. de Baudot, however, attacked Boileau's designs for the church at Le Vésinet in 1863 in the *Gazette des architectes et du bâtiment* and three years later castigated the project Boileau had submitted in the Rambouillet competition (won, it may be remembered, by de Baudot himself, with a design incorporating columns of iron). "Le parti général adopté par l'architecte," he wrote, "n'est pas un système, mais simplement l'application de métal à des formes qui ne résultent pas des propriétés des matériaux employés" (p. 97). De Baudot sought thus firmly to disassociate his design from Boileau's. Later he was to find that Boileau was, after all, a liberating stimulus; when he came to design a church at Montmartre he took up a great deal from him. But the dispute with

Boileau forced Viollet-le-Duc at once to consider more seriously the role of iron in architecture. In the article on construction in the fourth volume of the *Dictionnaire raisonné de l'architecture française,* issued in 1860, he showed very simply how iron, and timber, too, might be substituted for the structural members of a Gothic church, suggesting in this way how iron might be used in the nineteenth century. He himself used it thus unenterprisingly (as Butterfield and other such Gothic enthusiasts had done earlier in England) for the trusses of the sacristy of the cathedral at Rheims, designed in July 1862, but not built until 1870, and also for the more adeptly designed trusses for the roofs of the Château de Pierrefonds (1862). The Maison du Personnel at Notre-Dame in Paris, also with simple trusses of iron, was built in 1866. The use of iron was a particularly sensitive issue for Viollet-le-Duc at this period (hence de Baudot's shamefaced attack on Boileau's Rambouillet design) because Alfred Darcel, reviewing architecture at the Salon of 1864 in the *Gazette des beaux-arts* and, more important, César Daly in the editorial and in an assessment of a confessional designed twenty years earlier by Lassus for St.-Germain-l'Auxerrois included in the *Revue générale* in 1866, and also Bourgeois de Lagny in his review of the Salon of the same year in the newly founded *Moniteur des architectes,* had all vigorously attacked those tendencies that they associated then with Viollet-le-Duc. The Rambouillet church designs were a particular pretext for scorn. "L'école rationaliste," wrote Daly (thus categorizing Viollet-le-Duc and his disciples), "qui tend en ce moment à transformer l'*art architectural* en *architecture industrielle,* proclam[e] ainsi devant tous son scepticisme en matière d'art, son respect exclusif pour la science et l'utile" (p. 5). Bourgeois de Lagny, like Darcel earlier, even associated Viollet-le-Duc and his disciples with Boileau—an association they dreaded. Everyone regarded Boileau as a crank. But Bourgeois de Lagny was perhaps even more damaging when he linked them with the Realists, then being so widely discussed. "Le réalisme architectural (ou la construction avec l'absence d'art)," he concluded, "n'a qu'un rôle très-secondaire à remplir dans le développement de l'art monumental" (p. 81). Viollet-le-Duc had long been a friend of Champfleury and, in the *Journal des débats,* on August 7, 1863, had reviewed his collected essays, *Réalisme,* with what best tact he could. However, when he commented on other products of the Realist school, the novels of Flaubert, in letters to Mérimée, he was unequivocal in his contempt. Mérimée shared his opinions: "J'ai lu le roman de Flaubert," he wrote on December 29, 1869, of *L'éducation sentimentale.* "Hélas! C'est un mathématicien qui se trompe," a remark that both Daly and Bourgeois de Lagny would willingly have applied at that time to Viollet-le-Duc.

Viollet-le-Duc's answer to this onslaught was the astounding designs contained in the twelfth *Entretien,* dating from 1866 or just after. There, in illustrations for a *hôtel de ville* supported by V-poles and for other large halls combining struts and frameworks of iron supporting masonry vaults— but especially in his hall for three thousand people—he showed how an

architecture for the future might be forged. Modest in his estimation of his creative abilities, he no doubt saw that his designs were ungainly and lacking in style, but they were yet an attempt of a determined and desperate sort to achieve style. The polyhedral hall is indeed a naive illustration of style as defined in that very same year, 1866, not in the *Entretiens,* as one might expect, but in the eighth volume of the *Dictionnaire raisonné de l'architecture française.* "Le style," Viollet-le-Duc wrote (no longer part, if it ever had been for him, of period styles), *"est la manifestation d'un idéal établi sur un principe"* (p. 475). To him, this great guiding principle was, ultimately, that of the world, of the universe itself. The secret of all its structure, of all its stability, was the equilateral triangle, upon which all the structure of all matter, all fine form, was based. The earth's crust had style. There is a lot more to his argument, and more subtlety than is here indicated, but even this short exposition is enough to demonstrate how he had moved from Gothic Revivalism to the most inclusive of guiding principles and how he hoped that they might be interpreted. No one would say that he succeeded, but the breadth of his outlook was without equal.

Not many of his contemporaries were better equipped than Viollet-le-Duc to take up his challenge or to provide an example of his intentions. Those that did make the attempt were not trained by him. A pupil of Horeau, Jules-Désiré Bourdais (1835–1915), about 1868 built a small chapel at Négreplisse (Tarn-et-Garonne) with a roof supported by four conspicuous timber struts, composed in a manner reminiscent of the illustrations offered in the *Entretiens.* Jules Saulnier completed a series of great brick structures for the Menier chemical factory at Saint-Denis in 1865; then, four years after, began the design of that celebrated iron-framed building across the Marne at Noisiel, for the Menier chocolate works. Building did not start for another two years but was sufficiently advanced for Viollet-le-Duc to draw it to the attention of his readers in the eighteenth *Entretien,* written in 1871 or early in 1872. It was illustrated in full in the *Encyclopédie d'architecture* in 1874 and in the years that followed, together with Saulnier's subsidiary buildings and remarkable workers' housing. The splendid building over the river gleaming with richly colored and patterned glazed bricks is thought to be the first complete iron-framed structure ever erected. This may indeed be the case. But the diagonal metal framework that is so boldy exposed on the facade commemorates a timber-framed structure erected on the same site between 1840 and 1855 by Saulnier's master, Bonneau, which in turn was based on a surviving medieval construction. Viollet-le-Duc may, nonetheless, have acted as a stimulus to Saulnier. Less doubtful is his influence on the architect of the library of the École de Droit, Rue Cujas, Paris, built between May 1876 and June 1878 by Louis-Ernest Lheureux (1827–1898), a pupil of Henri Labrouste. Lheureux had worked with Labrouste on the Collège Ste.-Barbe, just across the street, where he also built the Salle de Dessin. All these buildings—the facade of the College apart—are now gone, as is the second hall that Lheureux added to the first, beginning in 1880.

659. Louis-Ernest Lheureux,
Bibliothèque de l'École de Droit,
Paris, second reading room, 1880,
1893–98

In both, arrangements of cast-iron brackets and ceiling beams, with infilling panels of brickwork, were striking interpretations of Viollet-le-Duc's ideas but they were even more notable as examples of the reserve and monumental splendor that one associates with the name of Labrouste. The stone facade of the first hall, admirably articulated with three tall arches and a panel of lettering, was among the finest examples of French nineteenth-century architecture. Lheureux did little else of this quality, though his designs for the Entrepôt, the wine warehouses, at Bercy, Paris, approved in 1877 by Viollet-le-Duc himself—in his role as committee member for the city council—were not unworthy successors; iron-framed buildings, with infilling panels of glazed brickwork. The first phase of building was complete by 1886, but this has now disappeared. There is not much else dating from this period to bear witness to the theories of Viollet-le-Duc.

"Nous faisons de l'architecture de sentiment," Viollet-le-Duc wrote angrily in 1871 in the seventeenth *Entretien,* "comme nous avons fait de la politique de sentiment, la guerre de sentiment. . . . Il faudrait songer à faire intervenir en tout ceci la froide raison, le bon sens pratique, l'étude des nécessités du temps, des perfectionnements fournis par l'industrie, des moyens économiques, des questions d'hygiène et de salubrité" (p. 296). This was the note he struck again in the conclusion to the *Entretiens,* an emphasis upon practical wisdom and analytical investigation, which he believed was best expressed in the work of engineers: in particular, that engineer of the École des Ponts et Chaussées Auguste Choisy (1841–1919).

Choisy, in his studies of the art of construction in history, even more perhaps in his devasting *Histoire de l'architecture,* of 1903, fittingly resolved all these issues, over which Viollet-le-Duc had pondered and puzzled, in a most ruthless conclusion. Choisy's brilliant illustrations reduced the complexities of all architecture to a few simple lines. Choisy provides the natural ending to the period we have studied, for he condensed not only Viollet-le-Duc's but all architectural theory into the simplest of aphorisms and diagrams. His very last work was an edition of Vitruvius, published in 1909, the final occasion on which that old Roman was edited for architects—and how very different it was from Perrault's, though one can see the connection. But there is yet one more architect who demands consideration before our conclusion is reached. That man is Gottfried Semper, a pupil of Gärtner, an architect of a distinctly lackluster kind.

Semper, like Viollet-le-Duc, was ultimately concerned with the problem of style. His preoccupation with this question antedated even Viollet-le-Duc's. His first attempt to explain it was in *Die vier Elemente der Baukunst,* published in Brunswick late in 1851, but based on lectures he had prepared in London, where he was established from 1851 to 1855. While in London, he was in close contact with Owen Jones and Henry Cole, for whom he acted as an investigator of Meyer's enameling process at Sèvres and Minton's tileworks at Trent. Semper was also responsible for the arrangement of some of the exhibits at the Crystal Palace. He could not, however, approve of

660. *Auguste Choisy, isometric view of J.-G. Soufflot's Ste.-Geneviève, Paris from Choisy's* Histoire de l'architecture, *1903*

661. *Gottfried Semper,* Wreath, *plate from his* Der Stil, *vol. 1, 1860*

this building since he believed that iron, when thus logically used, was unable to produce monumental form. One of his pupils, whom we know only by his initials, L. H., writing in 1900 in *La construction moderne,* summed up his beliefs: "Il y a deux catégories de constructions: 1ᵉ celles dont chaque élément est en lui-même stable (comme le temple de Paestum). C'est ce qui caractérise la construction monumentale; 2ᵉ celles dont les éléments ne doivent leur stabilité qu'à leur assemblage; c'est ce qui caractérise la construction des meubles, des chaises, par example. Entre ces deux extrêmes il y a toute une série de degrés qui donnent des structures plus ou moins monumentales suivant qu'elles se rapprochent de l'un des systèmes ou de l'autre. La cathédrale gothique serait donc moins monumental que le temple de Paestum, et le Palais de cristal ne serait pas du tout monumental" (p. 525). But it was there, at the Crystal Palace, overwhelmed by the sheer number and variety of artifacts, that he determined to evolve some system whereby the meaning of all such creative endeavor might be grasped and explained. He had earlier marveled in Paris at the ordering devices adopted at the Jardin des Plantes by that great biologist Georges Cuvier, who had first put forward a classificatory system based not on the resemblance of creatures and their parts but rather on the functioning of their organs and other vital processes. The key to the theory that Semper was to propose for the works of man was a small exhibit at the Crystal Palace, a model of a Carib hut, from the village of Arima, near Port of Spain, Trinidad. This was the work of Manuel Sorzano and was filled with utensils and other objects, mostly of Spanish or modern West Indian origin. It was not a primitive hut, but it made manifest the four processes that Semper was to uphold as the prime generators of everything made by man. He made no differentiation between the arts and the crafts. His developed theory is contained in *Der Stil,* published in Munich in two volumes, in 1860 and 1863. The third volume, which was to treat of architecture, was never completed. But this scarcely matters. The tenor of the theory is clear. Semper conceived four essential processes of making: weaving, molding, building in timber, and building in stone, sometimes reduced to heaping (to which he reluctantly appended metalworking). Each of these involved particular materials: textiles, ceramics, wood, and stone. Each in turn resulted in a particular element of architecture: the enclosing wall and all decorative pattern; the base and the hearth; the system of support; and the masonry wall, which might eventually serve to replace any of the former. Everything in art and architecture and all the crafts he held to be reducible to these processes and the materials associated with them. The highest form of expression was architecture, as it contains them all. But it was not, as must already be evident, the first of the arts to emerge; indeed, it derived from the four crafts, and thus suggests that Semper upheld a theory of the practical and useful origin of all art and architecture. His "materialist" stance has often been derided. But this is to misinterpret him willfully, for he believed that the crafts were originally developed for symbolical purposes. Long before man

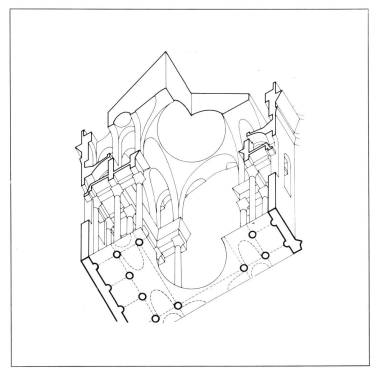

ter in 1872. There was a lot more besides, but his architecture is all undistinguished. In the prolegomena to *Der Stil* he was able to hold up no more challenging a style for future development than that of the cinquecento, it "not being complete in itself." "Die Gefahr für die Erhaltung jener Baukunst der Wiedergeburt die, zugleich mit der Malerei und der Bildnerei des Cinquecento, und in gleichem Grade, unübertroffen dasteht, ohne, wie das Gothische, in sich fertig zu sein, keine Seite zu weiterer Entwicklung zu bieten, liegt in der Thatsache, dass sie nur durch wahrhaft künstlerische Hand ausführbar ist, aber durch Pfuscherei, die heutzutage verlangt wird, sofort in trivialste Formengemeinheit ausartet" (vol. 1, p. xvii). Semper despised Gothic, in particular after 1844 when he was overtaken by Sir George Gilbert Scott in the Nikolaikirche competition at Hamburg. The ideas of the three great European theorists—Ruskin, Viollet-le-Duc, and Semper—were not readily absorbed. They were not to be taken up outside their own countries until late in the century. Semper's stay in England from 1851 to 1855 no doubt ensured an early interest in his work, in particular in the orbit of the South Kensington Schools of Design, but none of his works was translated. His ideas on the design of urns or vases were adopted in 1862 by Christopher Dresser (1834–1904) for *The Art of Decorative Design,* and later, without acknowledgment, for *Principles of Decorative Design* (1873). Yet as late as 1884, when Lawrence Harvey read "Semper's Theory of Evolution in Architectural Ornament" to the Royal Institute of British Architects, he began with the words, "Perhaps many of my British colleagues have never heard of Semper" (*Transactions,* 1885, vol. 1, p. 29).

One might think that Semper's earlier sojourns in France, in 1826 and 1827, in 1829 and 1830, and from 1849 to 1851, also ensured a heightened interest in his works when they appeared, but there is no hint of any. Viollet-le-Duc owned a copy of *Der Stil,* but was not equipped to read it. His analysis of urns or water vessels in the sixth *Entretien,* which might be taken as a rebuke to or even as a parody of Semper's, was written in 1859, before the publication of Semper's book. Semper, however, had read the four *Entretiens* issued in 1858, for he was quick to reject Viollet-le-Duc's notions on the design of Doric columns; he mocked him in *Der Stil* as a materialist.

Ruskin, so widely read in England, was but slowly acknowledged in France. Mérimée intended to write an article on him as early as 1856, a few years after Mérimée's return from England with Viollet-le-Duc, but nothing came of it. Viollet-le-Duc made no mention of Ruskin. The first article to appear in France on Ruskin, signed "J. C.," in the *Revue britannique* of 1856, was hostile. The first important studies were J.-A. Milsand's two articles in the *Revue des deux mondes* of July 1860 and August 1861, issued together as a book in 1864. But it was not for his architectural criticism that Ruskin was admired. Robert de La Sizeranne's celebrated *Ruskin et la religion de la beauté* produced the same reaction in France in 1897 that had been provoked exactly twenty years before in England, when Walter Pater's blasphemous

made a house, before he molded a hearth or a pot, he had started to weave and to plait, to make a wreath. The wreath is offered at the beginning of *Der Stil* as the first of the fully fashioned, expressive products of man.

According to Semper's theory, most patterns spring from the art (or the craft, if we prefer to call it that) of weaving. Patterns thus precede the development of structural form, so that ornament may be seen as more basic than structure. The developed theory also includes the way in which religious, social, and political institutions condition the processes of making to give fit and poetic expression to forms. But Semper himself was never to succeed in giving adequate shape to his ideas—not even to the extent that Viollet-le-Duc did. He built hugely—in Dresden, where he put up two successive opera houses (begun in 1837 and 1871); in Zurich, where he became professor in 1855 at the Eidgenössische Technische Hochschule and began to build the new school in 1859; and in Vienna, where he started construction on the Kunst und Naturhistorisches Museums and Hofburgthe-

essay "The School of Giorgione" was published in the *Fortnightly Review.* "Art, then," Pater wrote (and he thought this of architecure too), "is ... always striving to be independent of the mere intelligence, to become a matter of pure perception, to get rid of its responsibilities to its subject or material" (p. 530). Ruskin's message was seen in France in this light; the moral and intellectual elements in art that he so staunchly upheld were largely overlooked—though it is fair to note that Charles Lucas, writing his obituary in *La construction moderne,* in January 1900, described Ruskin as a moralist. Marcel Proust became his greatest admirer; to him Ruskin and Pater represented all that Viollet-le-Duc was not. By 1904 Proust had published his translation of *The Bible of Amiens.* Four years earlier *The Seven Lamps of Architecture* had appeared in French. By then Ruskin had died, like Pugin, mad.

Ruskin himself, surprisingly, looked upon the works of Viollet-le-Duc with a measured respect. He saw to it that the great *Dictionnaire raisonné de l'architecture française* was purchased for his students at Oxford, though he mentioned it only with passing scorn in his lectures of 1873; but he returned to the subject eleven years later as Slade Professor: "And here I must advise you that in all points of history relating to the period between 800 and 1200, you will find M. Viollet-le-Duc, incidentally throughout his *Dictionary of Architecture,* the best-informed, most intelligent, and most thoughtful of guides. His knowledge of architecure, carried down into the most minutely practical details—(which are often the most significant,) and embracing, over the entire surface of France, the buildings even of the most secluded villages; his artistic enthusiasm, balanced by the acutest sagacity, and his patriotism, by the frankest candour, render his analysis of history during that active and constructive period the most valuable known to me, and certainly, in its field, exhaustive. Of the latter nationality his account is imperfect, owing to his professional interest in the mere *science* of architecture, and comparative insensibility to the power of sculpture" (*Works,* vol. 33, p. 465).

This passage, long, eloquent, and rambling, it typical of the late Ruskin, but its general tone is unexpected in its sympathy. For, though fully conscious of what he regarded as Viollet-le-Duc's failings in sensibility, and horrified by them, Ruskin was yet willing to recognize the achievement represented by the *Dictionnaire raisonné de l'architecture française:* "Were you not glad when that book came out?" Sir Sidney Cockerell asked him in 1888. "No, I was very jealous," he replied, "I ought to have written it myself." Certainly he read it again and again, and recommended it often. He was fascinated by it, and also by Viollet-le-Duc. On October 18, 1882, he recorded this poignant note in his diary: "Disturbed sleep, dreaming I had introduced myself to M. Viol[let]-le-Duc and that he wouldn't have anything to say to me."

But perhaps more revealing of Ruskin's relation to Viollet-le-Duc is his response to another of his books, *Le massif du Mont Blanc,* of 1876. Almost

exact contemporaries, strongly opposed in sentiment and outlook, Ruskin and Viollet-le-Duc yet shared interests to an uncanny degree. Both were passionate geologists, both traveled on all possible occasions to view the Swiss Alps. After the disappointments of 1863, when he was hounded out of the École des Beaux-Arts by the students he had thought to indoctrinate, Viollet-le-Duc first sought solitude, strength, and reassurance in the healing springs of alpine scenery. Thereafter he went back each year, for eight weeks in the summer. In 1872 he built himself a chalet at Chamonix, two years later a house at Lausanne, La Vedette (demolished in 1976), where he died and was buried. Viollet-le-Duc was not a climber, but his relentless urge to activity drove him up the mountains. He started to survey Mont Blanc, often climbing steadily for eight hours to reach a vantage point, only to find the mountains obscured by clouds. Undeterred, he would return the next day to take his readings. He was tireless in his task. By 1876 he was able to issue both a most detailed map of Mont Blanc and a study of that mountain. Cutting the leaves of that book in this same year, as he set out on his journey to Switzerland, Ruskin contemplated, he wrote, "the splendid dash of its first sentence into space—'La croûte terrestre, refroidie au moment du plissement qui a formé le massif du Mont Blanc,'—with

664. *Gottfried Semper, Town Hall, Winterthur, staircase, 1863–69*

something of the amazement, and some manner of the praise, which our French allies are reported to have rendered to our charge at Balaclava: 'c'est magnifique: mais ce n'est pas—la géologie.' '' From the Simplon inn, he wrote on September 2 to Dr. John Brown, "At last my enemy *has* written a book." There were more fallacies on physical laws, he noted, than one could count.

When Ruskin wrote of the Alps he remarked on the masses and forms, the patterns and textures and hues of the rocks, digressed on their formation, and read therein lessons of nature. He derived lessons also on human fortitude and dignity when he observed the manner in which people had adapted their ways of living and building to that world of violent contrasts. This was a note he had struck first, in his earliest writings, "The Poetry of Architecture." Viollet-le-Duc made no acknowledgment of the people; he liked best the high, desolate regions of rock and everlasting ice. And, though his work might have seemed and been intended to seem a straightforward technical account of the formation of Mont Blanc, there was another, not darker but certainly more wayward, purpose. His last chapters reveal his aim. He wished to present to the mind's eye the spectacle of the mountain as it once existed, hard and neat and new.

What Viollet-le-Duc offers is nothing less than a gigantic restoration study. There is no more than a sketch of his proposal in the book, but on the wall of his studio in Paris he hung a large, carefully colored vision of the mountain as it might be: "Fin de l'époque glacière: étude de restitution." He left this on his death to his mistress, Mme. Sureda. Restoration, of course, was anathema to Ruskin.

Le massif de Mont Blanc was among the first of Viollet-le-Duc's books to be translated and issued in England in its entirety. Charles Wethered translated an extract from the *Dictionnaire raisonné de l'architecture française—On Restoration*—in 1875. During the same period Benjamin Bucknall (1833–1895), who was to translate both *Le massif de Mont Blanc* in 1877 and the *Entretiens* (as *Lectures on Architecture*), in 1877 and 1881, issued three English versions of the popular studies that Viollet-le-Duc had contrived for the young, *How to Build a House, Annals of a Fortress,* and *The Habitations of Man in All Ages* (Viollet-le-Duc fondly envisaged these as equivalents of Jules Verne's stories). But Viollet-le-Duc had long since won fame in England: As early as 1855 Matthew Digby Wyatt had written to ask permission to translate the *Dictionnaire raisonné de l'architecture française* and had worked seriously at the task until he became convinced that no English publisher would support the scheme. Five years later another prospective translator appeared in Martin Macdermott, and once again nothing resulted. But Viollet-le-Duc's achievements were sufficiently esteemed by 1864 for the Royal Institute of British Architects to award him their Gold Medal (on the advice of Daly). He did not travel to England to receive this honor. Even before then a succession of admirers from Sir George Gilbert Scott to William Burges and Alfred Waterhouse had plundered the pages of both

Dictionnaires in search of gables, finials, crockets, and gargoyles, and all manner of medieval details. When Scott came to design the main stair of St. Pancras Station Hotel, it was clear that he had learned to respond—and swiftly—to the designs in the twelfth *Entretien.* Waterhouse used exposed iron girders and struts in the ways suggested by Viollet-le-Duc in many of his later works. Slowly Viollet-le-Duc won renown as a prophet of an independent architecture, based, indeed, on the principles abstracted from a study of the buildings of the Middle Ages, but owing nothing to them in appearance.

In America, as might be imagined, the reception of the three great theorists was not dissimilar from their reception in Europe. Ruskin's works were read and absorbed almost as soon as they were published in England, following, as early as 1839, Loudon's praise of "The Poetry of Architecture," reprinted in the *Journal of the Franklin Institute.* American editions of volumes one and two of *Modern Painters* were published in 1847 and 1848; the following year *The Seven Lamps of Architecture* appeared; and in 1851 the first volume of *The Stones of Venice* was issued—without plates. Critics found Ruskin both admirable and absurd, inspiring and confusing. He was accused of cant and inconsistency, but to judge from the many editions of his works that were printed, he was steadfastly read. Henry van Brunt (1832–1903), a young architect trained at Harvard University, no doubt reflected informed opinion when, in his paper "Cast Iron in Decorative Architecture," read to the Institute of Architects in December 1858, he judged Ruskin to be altogether sound in his observations on the art of the Middle Ages, but of little relevance to architects in the nineteenth century. These, van Brunt claimed, operated in an age of machines, not of handicrafts. "Labor," he concluded, "now is the means and not the end of life." Van Brunt had also read Owen Jones and, probably, Viollet-le-Duc, whose *Entretien* he was to translate two years before Bucknall as *Discourses on Architecture,* in 1875, the second volume appearing in 1885. This was not the first of Viollet-le-Duc's works to be printed in America. *Histoire d'une maison,* translated by G. M. Towle, had already appeared as *The Story of a House* in 1874. These were followed, in 1876, by Bucknall's translation of *Histoire de l'habitation humaine (The Habitations of Man in All Ages)* and, in 1881, by *Learning To Draw,* a translation of L'*histoire d'un dessinateur; comment on apprend à dessiner,* by Virginia Champlin (a pseudonym). The American equivalent of Scott's interpretation of the drawings in the *Entretiens* was the stupendous covered court of The Rookery, La Salle Street, Chicago, designed in 1885 by John Wellborn Root (1850–1891), of the firm of Burnham and Root. Root was also the man who first published translations from Semper's *Der Stil* in America—in the *Inland Architect and New Record,* in 1889–90—though Semper's works were certainly read in Chicago long before that. Indeed, it has even been suggested that the term "curtain walling," which is so strongly associated with the late nineteenth-century architecture of Chicago, commemorates Semper. In 1891, Bernard Maybeck (1862–1957), far away from Chicago, in California, started to translate *Der Stil,* but did not get very far.

After the turn of the century, Frank Lloyd Wright redecorated the covered court at The Rookery with surprisingly little tact—surprisingly, because of the many members of the Chicago School who responded to the writings of Viollet-le-Duc, Wright absorbed them to the most splendid and rewarding effect, regarding them always as the spur to his greatness. He even made his son read the *Dictionnaires.* Other architects, very different in their ways, gave to their interpretation of these teachings a wholeness of vision never achieved in Viollet-le-Duc's lifetime. One thinks of Antonio Gaudí in Spain, of Victor Horta in Belgium, of Hendrikus Petrus Berlage in Holland—all of whom based their thinking on his—and also, perhaps, of the whole school of Russian Constructivists.

SELECTED BIBLIOGRAPHY

GENERAL

Arts Council of Great Britain. *The Age of Neo-Classicism*. Council of Europe exhibition catalogue. London, 1972.

BRAUDEL, F. *Capitalism and Material Life*. Translated by Miriam Kochan. London, 1973.

CASSIRER, E. *The Philosophy of the Enlightenment*. Princeton, N.J., 1951.

COLLINS, P. *Changing Ideals in Modern Architecture, 1750–1950*. London, 1965.

ERDBERG, E. VON. *Chinese Influences on European Garden Structures*. Cambridge, Mass., 1936.

FORSSMAN, E. *Dorisch, Ionisch, Korinthisch: Studien über den Gebrauch der Säulenordnungen in der Architektur des 16.–18. Jahrhunderts*. Stockholm, 1961.

FRANKL, P. *The Gothic: Literary Sources and Interpretations Through Eight Centuries*. Princeton, N.J., 1959.

GERMANN, G. *Gothic Revival in Europe and Britain: Sources, Influences and Ideas*. London, 1972.

GIEDION, S. *Mechanization Takes Command*. New York, 1948.

GUSDORF, G. *Naissance de la conscience romantique au siècle des lumières*. Paris, 1976.

HAUTECOEUR, L. *Rome et la renaissance de l'antiquité à la fin du XVIIIe siècle*. Paris, 1912.

HITCHCOCK, H. R. *Architecture: Nineteenth and Twentieth Centuries*. Rev. ed. Baltimore and Harmondsworth, 1971.

HONOUR, H. *Chinoiserie: The Vision of Cathay*. 1961. Reprint. London, 1973.

———. *Neo-Classicism*. Harmondsworth, 1968.

IMPEY, O. *Chinoiserie: The Impact of Oriental Style*. Oxford, 1977.

KAUFMANN, E. *Von Ledoux bis Le Corbusier: Ursprung und Entwicklung der autonomen Architektur*. Vienna, 1933.

LAVEDAN, P. *L'histoire de l'urbanisme: renaissance et temps modernes*. Paris, 1941.

MAINSTONE, R. J. *Developments in Structural Form*. London, 1974.

MEEKS, C. L. V. *The Railroad Station: An Architectural History*. New Haven, Conn., 1956.

MICHEL, A. *Histoire de l'art*. Vol. 7. Paris, 1926.

OMONT, H., ed. *Athènes au XVIIe siècle: dessins des sculptures du Parthénon*. Paris, 1898.

PEVSNER, N., ed. *The Picturesque Garden and Its Influence Outside the British Isles*. Washington, D.C., 1974.

PEVSNER, N., and LANG, S. "Apollo or Baboon." *Architectural Review* 104 (1943): 271–79. Reprinted as "The Doric Revival" in *Studies in Art, Architecture and Design*, by N. Pevsner, vol. 1, pp. 196–211. London and New York, 1968.

———. "The Egyptian Revival." *Architectural Review* 119 (1956): 243–54. Reprinted in *Studies in Art, Architecture and Design*, by N. Pevsner, vol. 1, pp. 212–35. London and New York, 1968.

PRAZ, M. *An Illustrated History of Interior Decoration.*

London and New York (as *An Illustrated History of Furnishing*), 1964.

ROSENBLUM, R. *Transformations in Late Eighteenth-Century Art*. Princeton, N.J., 1967.

SELING, H. "The Genesis of the Museum." *Architectural Review* 141 (1967): 103–14.

SIRÉN, O. *China and Gardens of Europe of the Eighteenth Century*. New York, 1950.

VIERENDEEL, A. *L'architecture métallique au XIXe siècle*. Brussels, 1890.

———. *Esquisse d'une histoire de la technique*. 2 vols. Brussels, 1921.

ZEITLER, R. W. *Klassizismus und Utopia*. Stockholm, 1954.

———. *Die Kunst des 19. Jahrhunderts*. Berlin, 1966.

CONTEMPORARY SOURCES

ADAM, R. *The Works in Architecture of Robert and James Adam, Esquires*. 3 vols. 1773–1822. Reprint. London, 1931.

ALBERTOLLI, G. *Ornamenti diversi inventati*. Milan, 1782.

———. *Alcune decorazioni di nobili sale ed altri ornamenti*. Milan, 1787.

ALPHAND, A. *Les promenades de Paris*. Paris, 1867–73.

BARRY, A. *The Life and Works of Sir Charles Barry*. London, 1867.

BLONDEL, J.-F. *Cours d'architecture*. Paris, 1771–77.

BOILEAU, L.-A. *La nouvelle forme architecturale*. 1853.

———. *Histoire critique de l'invention en architecture*. Paris, 1886.

BUTTERFIELD, W. *Instrumenta ecclesiastica*. 1844–57.

CAMPBELL, C. *Vitruvius Britannicus; or, The British Architect*. 3 vols. London, 1715–25.

CARMONTELLE, L. C. de. *Jardin de Monceau*. 1779.

CHOISY, A. *Histoire de l'architecture*. 1903. Reprint. Paris, 1954.

CONSIDERANT, V. *Considérations sociales sur l'architecture*. 1834.

DRESSER, C. *Principles of Decorative Design*. London and New York, 1873.

DUMONT, G.-P.-M. *Recueil de plusieurs parties de l'architecture sacrée et profane de différents maîtres tant d'Italie que de France*. Paris, 1764–67.

DURAND, J. N. L. *Vues des plus beaux édifices publics et particuliers de la ville de Paris*. Paris, [1787?].

———. *Recueil et parallèle des édifices de tout genre anciens et modernes*. Paris, 1800.

———. *Précis des leçons d'architecture données à l'École royale polytechnique*. Paris, 1802–5.

EASTLAKE, C. L. *A History of the Gothic Revival*. 1872. Reprint. Leicester and New York, 1970.

FISCHER VON ERLACH, J. B. *Entwurff einer historischen Architektur*. Vienna, 1721.

GARNIER, C. *Le nouvel Opéra de Paris*. Paris, 1878–81.

GONDOIN, J. *Description des écoles de chirurgie*. Paris, 1780.

GOURLIER, C.-P. et al. *Choix d'édifices publics projetés et construits en France depuis le commencement du XIXe siècle*. Paris, 1825–50.

HITTORFF, J.-I. *Restitution du temple d'Empédocle à Selinonte; ou, l'architecture polychrome chez les grecs*. Paris, 1846–51.

HOPE, T. *Household Furniture and Interior Decoration*. 1807. Reprint. London, 1946.

[KENDALL, H. E.] *Modern Architecture*. [1856.]

KLENZE, L. von. *Sammlung architektonischer Entwürfe für die Ausführung bestimmt oder wirklich ausgeführt*. 10 pts. Munich, 1830–50.

KNIGHT, R. P. *An Analytical Inquiry into the Principles of Taste*. London, 1805.

KRAFFT, J. K. *Choix des maisons et d'édifices publics de Paris et de ses environs*. Paris, 1838.

KRAFFT, J. K., and RANSONNETTE, P. N. *Plans, coupes, élévations des plus belles maisons et des hôtels construits à Paris et dans les environs. 1771–1802*. Reprint. Paris, 1909.

LABORDE, A. de. *Description des nouveaux jardins de la France et de ses anciens châteaux*. Paris, 1808–15.

LANDON, C. P. *Annales du musée et de l'école moderne des beaux-arts. 1803–22*. Reprint. Paris, 1834.

[LAUGIER, M.-A.] *Essai sur l'architecture*. Paris, 1753.

LEDOUX, C.-N. *L'architecture considérée sous le rapport de l'art, des mœurs et de la législation*. Paris, 1804.

LEEDS, W. H. "An Essay on Modern English Architecture." In *The Travellers' Club House . . . and the Revival of the Italian Style*, by Charles Barry. London, 1839.

LE ROUGE, G.-L. *Description du Colisée élevé aux Champs Élysées*. Paris, 1771.

———. "Jardins anglo-chinois." *Cahiers* 13 (1785).

LE ROY, J.-D. *Les ruines des plus beaux monuments de la Grèce*. Paris, 1758.

MAROT, J. *Le temple de Balbec*. [c. 1680.]

NARJOUX, F. *Paris: monuments élevés par la ville, 1850–1880*. Paris, 1880–83.

NEUFFORGE, J.-F. de. *Recueil élémentaire d'architecture*. 9 vols. Paris, 1757–72.

DE L'ORME, P. *L'architecture de Philibert de l'Orme*. 1567. Reprint. Ridgewood, N. J., 1964.

PAINE, J. *Plans, Elevations and Sections of Noblemen's and Gentlemen's Houses Executed in the Counties of Derby, Durham, Middlesex, Northumberland, Nottingham and York*. 2 vols. London, 1767–83.

PATTE, P. *Monumens érigés en France à la gloire de Louis XV*. Paris, 1765.

PERCIER, C., and FONTAINE, P.-F.-L. *Journal des monuments de Paris*.

PERRAULT, C. *Les dix livres d'architecture de Vitruve*. Paris, 1673.

PETITOT, E.-A. *Mascarade à la grecque*. Parma, 1771.

PEYRE, M.-J. *Oeuvres d'architecture*. Paris, 1765. 2d ed. Paris, 1795.

PIRANESI, G. B. *Prima parte di architetture, e prospettive*. Rome, 1743.

———. *Le antichità romane*. 4 vols. Rome, 1756–.

————. *Parere su l'architettura*. Rome, 1765.

————. *Diverse maniere d'adornare i cammini*. Rome, 1769.

————. *Différentes vues de quelques restes de trois grands édifices qui subsistent encore dans le milieu de l'ancienne ville de Pesto*. Rome, 1778.

PUGIN, A. W. N. *Contrasts; or, A Parallel Between the Noble Edifices of the Fourteenth and Fifteenth Centuries, and Similar Buildings of the Present Day*. London, 1836.

————. *The True Principles of Pointed or Christian Architecture*. London, 1841.

————. *An Apology for the Revival of Christian Architecture in England*. London, 1843.

QUATREMÈRE DE QUINCY, A.-C. *Le Jupiter Olympien; ou, l'art de la sculpture antique considérée sous un nouveau point de vue*. Paris, 1815.

RONDELET, J. *Traité théorique et pratique de l'art de bâtir*. Paris, 1802–3.

RUSKIN, J. *The Seven Lamps of Architecture*. New York, 1849.

SCHINKEL, K. F. *Sammlung architektonischer Entwürfe*. 28 portfolios. Berlin, 1819–40.

————. *Werke der höheren Baukunst für die Ausführung erfunden*. 2 vols. 1842–48.

SCOTT, G. G. *Personal and Professional Recollections*. London, 1879.

SEMPER, G. *Der Stil in den technischen und tektonischen Kunsten*. Frankfurt-am-Main, 1860–63.

SOANE, J. *Plans, Elevations, and Sections of Buildings Erected in the Counties of Norfolk, Suffolk, Yorkshire, etcetera*. London, 1788.

————. *Sketches in Architecture*. London, 1798.

————. *Designs for Public and Private Buildings*. London, 1828.

————. *Description of the House and Museum on the North Side of Lincoln's Inn Fields, the Residence of John Soane*. London, 1835–36.

SPON, J. *Voyage d'Italie, de Dalmatie, de Grèce, et du Levant, fait aux années 1675 et 1676*. Lyons, 1676.

STUART, J., and REVETT, N. *The Antiquities of Athens*. 4 vols. London, 1762–1816.

TALLIS, J. *Tallis's History and Description of the Crystal Palace*. London and New York, 1852.

VIOLLET-LE-DUC, E.-E. *Dictionnaire raisonné de l'architecture française du XIe au XVIe siècle*. 10 vols. Paris, 1854–68.

————. *Entretiens sur l'architecture*. Paris, 1863–72.

FRANCE

BABEAU, A. A. *La ville sous l'Ancien Régime*. Paris, 1880.

BALLOT, M. J. *Le décor intérieur au XVIIIe siècle à Paris et dans la région parisienne*. Paris, 1930.

BELEVITCH-STANKEVITCH, H. *Le goût chinois en France au temps de Louis XIV*. 1910. Reprint. Geneva, 1970.

BENOIT, F. *L'art français sous la Révolution et l'Empire: les doctrines, les idées, les genres*. Paris, 1897.

BLOMFIELD, R. *A History of French Architecture from 1661 to 1774*. 2 vols. London, 1921.

BRAUNSCHWIG, M. *L'Abbé Dubos, renovateur de la critique au XVIIIe siècle*. Toulouse, 1904.

BRUNEL, G., ed. *Piranèse et les français, 1740–1790*. Rome, 1978.

CASSIRER, K. *Die ästhetischen Hauptbegriffe der französischen Architektur-Theoretiker von 1650–1780*. Berlin, [1909?].

CHANGNEAU, C. et al. *Jardins en France, 1760–1820*. Exhibition catalogue. Paris, 1977.

CHARVET, E.-L.-G. *Lyon artistique: architectes, notices biographiques et bibliographiques avec une petite note des édifices et la liste chronologique des noms*. Lyons, 1899.

CHOPPIN DE JANVRY, O. "Le Desert de Retz." *Bulletin de la Société de l'Histoire de l'Art Français*, Année 1970, pp. 125–48.

CLOZIER, R. *La Gare du Nord*. Paris, 1940.

CONTET, F. et al. *Les vieux hôtels de Paris*. 2 vols. Paris, 1908–37.

CORDIER, H. *Le Chine en France au XVIIIe siècle*. Paris, 1910.

COUSSILLAN, A. A. [HILLAIRET, J.]. *Dictionnaire historique des rues de Paris*. 2 vols. Paris, 1968.

DARTEIN, F. DE. *Études sur les ponts en pierre remarquables par leur décoration: Antérieurs au XIXe siècle*. 4 vols. Paris, 1907–12.

DELABORDE, H. *L'Académie des Beaux-Arts depuis la fondation de l'Institut de France*. Paris, 1891.

DESHAIRS, L. *Bordeaux, architecture et decoration au dix-huitième siècle*. Paris, 1907.

————. *Aix-en-Provence, architecture et décoration aux dix-septième et dix-huitième siècles*. Paris, 1909.

————. *Dijon, architecture et décoration au dix-septième et dix-huitième siècles*. Paris, 1909.

DREXLER, A., ed. *The Architecture of the École des Beaux-Arts*. New York, 1978.

ERIKSEN, S. *Early Neo-Classicism in France*. London, 1974.

D'ESPOUY, H., ed. *Les Grands Prix de Rome d'architecture: 1850–1900, 1900–1905*. 2 vols. Paris, n.d.

————. *Monuments antiques, relevés et restaurés par les architectes pensionnaires de l'Académie de France à Rome*. 2 vols. Paris, n.d.

GALLET, M. *Paris Domestic Architecture of the 18th Century*. London, 1972.

GANAY, E. DE. "Les jardins à l'anglaise en France." 1923. Ms. in 2 vols., Bibliothèque des Arts Décoratifs, Paris.

GIEDION, S. *Bauen in Frankreich, Eisen, Eisenbeton*. Leipzig, 1928.

GRUBER, A. C. *Les grandes fêtes et leurs décors à l'époque de Louis XVI*. Geneva, 1972.

HAUTECOEUR, L. *Histoire de l'architecture classique en France*. Vols. 3–4. Paris, 1950–57.

————. *Paris de 1715 à nos jours*. Paris, 1972.

————. "Les places en France au XVIIIe siècle." *Gazette des beaux-arts* 85 (1975): 89–116.

HÉLIOT, P. "La fin de l'architecture gothique dans le nord de la France aux XVIIe et XVIIIe siècles." *Bulletin de la Comm. Royale des Monuments et des Sites* 8 (1957).

HERMANN, W. *Laugier and 18th-Century French Theory*. London, 1962.

HUNT, H. J. *Le socialisme et le romantisme en France*. Oxford, 1935.

JARRY, P. *La guirlande de Paris; ou, maisons de plaisance des environs, au XVIIe et au XVIIIe siècle*. Paris, 1928–31.

KALNEIN, W. G., and Levey, M. *Art and Architecture of the Eighteenth Century in France*. Baltimore and Harmondsworth, 1972.

KIMBALL, S. F. *The Creation of the Rococo*. 1943. Reprint. New York, 1964.

LEITH, J. A. *The Idea of Art as Propaganda in France, 1750–1799*. Toronto, 1965.

LELIÈVRE, P. *L'urbanisme et l'architecture à Nantes au XVIIIe siècle*. Nantes, 1942.

LÉON, P. *La vie des monuments français: destruction, restauration*. Paris, 1951.

LEONARD, C. M. *Lyon Transformed: Public Works of the Second Empire, 1853–1864*. Berkeley and Los Angeles, 1961.

LOCQUIN, J. *La peinture d'histoire en France de 1747 à 1785*. Paris, 1912.

LUCAS, C. L. A. *Étude sur les habitations à bon marché en France et à l'étranger*. Paris, 1899.

MAGNE, L. *L'architecture française du siècle*. Paris, 1889.

MALLION, J. *Victor Hugo et l'art architectural*. Paris, 1962.

MARION, M. *Dictionnaire des institutions de la France aux XVIIe et XVIIIe siècles*. Rev. ed. Paris, 1968.

MAROT, P. *La Place Royale de Nancy*. Nancy, 1966.

MIDDLETON, R. D. "The Abbé de Cordemoy and the Graeco-Gothic Ideal: A Prelude to Romantic Classicism." *Journal of the Warburg and Courtauld Institutes* 25 (1962): 278–320; 26 (1963): 90–123.

MORNET, D. *Le sentiment de la nature en France de J.-J. Rousseau à Bernardin de Saint-Pierre*. Paris, 1907.

————. *Le romantisme en France au XVIIIe siècle*. Paris, 1912.

MORTIER, R. *La Poetique des ruines*. Geneva, 1974.

MOULIN, M. *L'architecture civile et militaire au XVIIIe siècle en Aunis et Saintonge*. La Rochelle, 1972.

MULLER, E., and CACHEUX, E. *Habitations ouvrières et agricoles*. Paris, 1855–56.

NIÈRES, C. *La reconstruction d'une ville au XVIIIe siècle: Rennes 1720–1760*. Paris, 1972.

NOLHAC, P. DE. *Hubert Robert*. Paris, 1910.

————. *Histoire du château de Versailles: Versailles au XVIIIe siècle*. Paris, 1918.

PARISET, F. G. *Histoire de Bordeaux, 1714–1814*. Vol. 5. Bordeaux, 1968.

PINKNEY, D. H. *Napoleon III and the Rebuilding of Paris*. Princeton, N.J., 1958.

SAISSELIN, R. G. *Taste in Eighteenth-Century France*. New York, 1965.

SCHNEIDER, R. *L'esthétique classique chez Quatremère de Quincy (1805–1825)*. Paris, 1910.

————. *Quatremère de Quincy et son intervention dans les arts (1788–1830).* Paris, 1910.

STAROBINSKI, J. *The Invention of Liberty, 1700–1789.* Geneva, 1964.

————. *1789: les emblèmes de la raison.* Paris, 1973.

STEINHAUSER, M. *Der Architektur der Pariser Oper.* Munich, 1969.

SUTCLIFFE, A. *The Autumn of Central Paris: The Defeat of Town Planning, 1850–1970.* London, 1970.

THIBERT, M. *Le rôle social de l'art d'après les Saint-Simoniens.* Paris, 1926.

TOURNIER, R. *Les églises comtoises: leur architecture des origines au XVIIIᵉ siècle.* Paris, 1954.

————. *Maisons et hôtels privés du XVIIIᵉ siècle à Besançon.* Paris, 1970.

VAUDOYER, A.-L.-T., and BALTARD, L. P., eds. *Grands Prix d'architecture, 1801–1831.* 3 vols. Paris, 1818–34.

VERLET, P. "Le mobilier de Louis XVI et de Marie-Antoinette à Compiegne." 1937. Ms., Louvre, Paris.

————. *French Furniture and Interior Decoration of the Eighteenth Century.* London, 1967.

GERMANY AND AUSTRIA

BEENKEN, H. *Schöpferische bauideen der deutschen romantik.* Mainz, 1952.

DU COLOMBIER, P. *L'architecture française en Allemagne au XVIIIᵉ siècle.* 2 vols. Paris, 1956.

GROTE, L., ed. *Die deutsche Stadt im 19. Jahrhundert.* Munich, 1974.

MANN, A. *Die Neuromanik: eine rheinische Komponente im Historismus des 19. Jahrhunderts.* Cologne, 1966.

MUTHESIUS, S. *Das englische Vorbild.* Munich, 1974.

PLAGEMANN, V. *Das deutsche Kunstmuseum, 1790–1870.* Munich, 1967.

ROBSON-SCOTT, W. D. *The Literary Background of the Gothic Revival in Germany.* Oxford, 1965.

VOGT, G. *Frankfurter Bürgerhäuser des Neunzehnten Jahrhundert.* Frankfurt, [1970?].

WAGNER-RIEGER, R. *Wiens Architektur im 19. Jahrhundert.* Vienna, 1970.

WAGNER-RIEGER, R., ed. *Die Wiener Ringstrasse: Bild einer Epoche.* Cologne, Graz, and Vienna, 1969–. (9 vols. to date.)

GREAT BRITAIN

ALLEN, B. S. *Tides in English Taste (1619–1800).* 2 vols. 1937. Reprint. New York, 1969.

AMES, W. *Prince Albert and Victorian Taste.* London and New York, 1968.

ANSON, P. F. *Fashions in Church Furnishings, 1840–1940.* Rev. ed. London, 1965.

ARMYTAGE, W. H. G. *Heavens Below: Utopian Experiments in England, 1560–1960.* London, 1961.

BOASE, T. S. R. *English Art, 1800–1870.* Oxford, 1959.

BURKE, J. *English Art, 1714–1800.* Oxford, 1976.

CHADWICK, G. F. *The Park and the Town: Public Landscape in the 19th and 20th Centuries.* London and New York, 1966.

CLARK, K. *The Gothic Revival.* London, 1928. Reprint. New York, 1974.

CLARKE, B. F. L. *Church Builders of the 19th Century.* 1938. Reprint. Newton Abbot, Devon, 1969.

————. *Parish Churches of London.* London, 1966.

CLIFTON-TAYLOR, A. *The Pattern of English Building.* Rev. ed. London, 1972.

COLVIN, H. M. *A Biographical Dictionary of British Architects, 1600–1840.* London, 1978.

CRAIG, M. J. *Dublin, 1660–1860.* Rev. ed. London, 1969.

CROOK, J. M. *The Greek Revival: Neo-Classical Attitudes in British Architecture, 1760–1870.* Feltham, 1968.

————. *The British Museum.* London and New York, 1972.

CROOK, J. M., and PORT, M. H. *The History of the King's Works.* Vol. 6 (1782–1851). London, 1973.

DYOS, H. J. *Victorian Suburb: A Study of the Growth of Camberwell.* Leicester, 1966.

DYOS, H. J., and WOLFF, M., eds. *The Victorian City: Images and Reality.* 2 vols. London, 1973.

FAWCETT, J., ed. *Seven Victorian Architects.* London, 1976.

FERRIDAY, P., ed. *Victorian Architecture.* London, 1963.

FOWLER, J., and CORNFORTH, J. *English Decoration in the 18th Century.* London, 1974.

GARRIGAN, K. O. *Ruskin on Architecture: His Thought and Influence.* Madison, Wis., 1973.

GIROUARD, M. *The Victorian Country House.* Oxford, 1971.

————. *Sweetness and Light: The Queen Anne Movement, 1860–1900.* Oxford, 1977.

GOMME, A., and WALKER, D. *Architecture of Glasgow.* London, 1968.

GOODHART-RENDEL, H. S. *English Architecture Since the Regency.* London, 1953.

HITCHCOCK, H.-R. *Early Victorian Architecture in Britain.* 2 vols. 1954. Reprint. New Haven, Conn., 1972.

HOBHOUSE, H. *Lost London.* Boston and London, 1971.

HOPKINS, H. J. *A Span of Bridges.* New York and Newton Abbot, 1970.

HUNT, J. D., and WILLIS, P., eds. *The Genius of the Place: The English Landscape Garden, 1620–1820.* London, 1975.

HUSSEY, C. *The Picturesque.* 1927. Reprint. New York, 1967.

————. *English Country Houses: Late Georgian, 1800–1840.* London, 1958.

————. *English Country Houses: Mid-Georgian, 1760–1800.* Rev. ed. London, 1963.

JERVIS, S. *High Victorian Design.* Ottawa, 1974.

KELLET, J. R. *The Impact of Railways on Victorian Cities.* London, 1969.

London, County Council. *Survey of London.* London, 1896–. (39 vols. to date.)

MACAULAY, J. *The Gothic Revival, 1745–1845.* Glasgow and London, 1975.

MACLEOD, R. *Style and Society: Architectural Ideology in Britain, 1835–1914.* London, 1971.

MORRIS, W. *Collected Works of William Morris.* Edited by M. Morris. 24 vols. London, 1910–15.

MUTHESIUS, H. *Die neuere kirchliche Baukunst in England.* Berlin, 1901.

MUTHESIUS, S. "The 'Iron Problem' in the 1850's." *Architectural History* 13 (1970): 58–63.

————. *The High Victorian Movement in Architecture, 1850–1870.* London, 1971.

OLSEN, D. J. *Town Planning in London: The Eighteenth and Nineteenth Centuries.* New Haven, Conn., 1964.

————. *The Growth of Victorian London.* London, 1976.

PEVSNER, N. *The Buildings of England.* 46 vols. Harmondsworth, 1951–74.

————. *Some Architectural Writers of the 19th Century.* Oxford, 1972.

Port, M. H. *Six Hundred New Churches: A Study of the Church Building Commission, 1818–1856.* London, 1961.

PORT, M. H., ed. *The Houses of Parliament.* New Haven, Conn., 1976.

RICHARDSON, A. E. *Monumental Classic Architecture in Great Britain and Ireland During the Eighteenth and Nineteenth Centuries.* London, 1914.

Royal Institute of British Architects (RIBA). *Catalogue of the Drawings of the Royal Institute of British Architects.* London, 1969–. (17 vols. to date.)

RUSKIN, J. *The Works of John Ruskin.* Edited by E. T. Cook and A. Wedderburn. 39 vols. London, 1903–12.

SAXL, F., and WITTKOWER, R. *British Art and the Mediterranean.* London, 1948.

SHERBURNE, J. C. *John Ruskin; or, The Ambiguities of Abundance.* Cambridge, Mass., 1972.

STEEGMANN, J. *Consort of Taste, 1830–1870.* London, 1950.

SUMMERSON, J. *Heavenly Mansions, and Other Essays on Architecture.* 1949. Reprint. New York, 1963.

————. *Architecture in Britain, 1530–1830.* 5th ed. London, 1969.

————. *Georgian London.* Rev. ed. London, 1970.

————. *Victorian Architecture: Four Studies in Evaluation.* New York, 1970.

————. *The London Building World of the 1860s.* London, 1973.

————. *The Architecture of Victorian London.* Charlottesville, 1976.

WATKIN, D. J. *Morality and Architecture: The Development of a Theme in Architectural History and Theory from the Gothic Revival to the Modern Movement.* Oxford, 1977.

WHIFFEN, M. *Stuart and Georgian Churches: The Architecture of the Church of England Outside London, 1603–1837.* London and New York, 1948.

WHITE, J. F. *The Cambridge Movement: The Ecclesiologists and the Gothic Revival.* Cambridge, 1962.

WOODBRIDGE, K. *Landscape and Antiquity: Aspects of English Culture at Stourhead, 1718 to 1838.* London, 1970.

YOUNGSON, A. J. *The Making of Classical Edinburgh, 1750–1840.* Edinburgh, 1966.

GREECE

RUSSACK, H. H. *Deutsches Bauen in Athen.* Berlin, 1942.

SINOS, S. "Die Gründung der neuen Stadt Athen." *Architectura* 1 (1974): 41–52.

TRAVLOS, J. *Architecture néoclassique en Grèce.* Athens, 1967.

ITALY

ANGELINI, L. *L'avvento dell'arte neoclassica in Bergamo.* Bergamo, 1966.

BASSI, E. *Architettura del sei e settecento a Venezia.* Naples, 1962.

BORSI, F. *La capitale a Firenze e l'opera de G. Poggi.* Rome, 1970.

BRUSATIN, M. *Illuminismo e architettura del '700 Veneto.* Castelfranco Veneto, 1969.

HASKELL, F. *Patrons and Painters: A Study in the Relations Between Italian Art and Society in the Age of the Baroque.* 1963. Reprint. New York, 1971.

LAVAGNINO, E. *L'arte moderna dai neoclassici ai contemporanei.* 2 vols. Turin, 1956.

MEZZANOTTE, G. *Architettura neoclassica in Lombardia.* Naples, 1966.

POMMER, R. *Eighteenth-Century Architecture in Piedmont:* *The Open Structures of Juvarra, Alfieri and Vittone.* London and New York, 1967.

PROZZILLO, I. *Francesco Milizia, teorico e storico dell' architettura.* Naples, 1971.

VENDITTI, A. *Architettura neoclassica a Napoli.* Naples, 1961.

WITTKOWER, R. *Art and Architecture in Italy, 1600 to 1750.* 3d ed. Baltimore and Harmondsworth, 1973.

ZUCCA, L. T. *Architettura neoclassica a Trieste.* Trieste, 1974.

PORTUGAL

FRANCA, J. A. *Lisboa Pombalina, e o iluminismo.* Lisbon, 1965. (First published as *Une ville des lumières: la Lisbonne de Pombal.* Paris, 1965.)

RUSSIA

BATER, J. H. *St. Petersburg: Industrialization and Change.* London, 1976.

EGOROV, I. A. *The Architectural Planning of St. Petersburg.* Athens, Ohio, 1969.

HAMILTON, G. H. *The Art and Architecture of Russia.* Baltimore and Harmondsworth, 1954.

HAUTECOEUR, L. *L'architecture classique a Saint-Pétersbourg à la fin du XVIIIᵉ siècle.* Paris, 1912.

ILYIN, M. *Moscow Monuments of Architecture: Eighteenth–the First Third of the Nineteenth Century.* 2 vols. Moscow, 1975.

KIRICHENKO, E. *Moscow Architectural Monuments of the 1830s–1910s.* Moscow, 1977.

SPAIN

CAREDA, J. *Memorias para la historia de la Real Academia de San Fernando y de las Bellas Artes en España.* 2 vols. Madrid, 1867.

GAYA NUÑO, J. A. *Arte del siglo XIX.* Ars Hispaniae, vol. 19. Madrid, 1966.

NAVASCUES PALACIO, P. *Arquitectura y arquitectos Madrileños del siglo XIX.* Madrid, 1973.

PARIS, P. "L'art en Espagne et en Portugal de la fin du XVIIIᵉ siècle à nos jours." In *Histoire de l'art,* by A. Michel, vol. 8. Paris, 1926.

SWITZERLAND

CARL, B. *Die Architektur der Schweiz: Klassizismus 1770–1860.* Zurich, 1963.

CORBOZ, A. *Invention de Carouge, 1772–92.* Lausanne, [1968].

GERMANN, G. *Der protestantische Kirchenbau in der Schweiz.* Zurich, 1963.

UNITED STATES OF AMERICA

HAMLIN, T. *Greek Revival Architecture in America.* New York, 1944.

PIERSON, W. H. *American Buildings and Their Architects.* Vol. 1 (*The Colonial and Neo-Classical Styles*). New York, 1970.

STANTON, P. B. *The Gothic Revival and American Church Architecture.* Baltimore, 1968.

403

Aerofilms, London: 43

Angel, H., Farnham: IV

Andrews, W., Grosse Pointe, Michigan: 563

Archives Municipales, Bordeaux: 176, 177

Archives Photographiques, Paris: 166, 179, 225, 350, 352

Austin, J., London: 119, 130, 149, 150, 214, 215, 363, 392, 397, 401, 412

Balestrini, B., Milan: 1, 9, 10, 11, 13, 15, 19, 20, 21, 27, 104, 113, 114, 116, 120, 127, 128, 129, 132, 133, 134, 135, 136, 155, 156, 157, 158, 161, 167, 169, 178, 180, 182, 183, 184, 185, 189, 198, 202, 206, 208, 211, 219, 236, 237, 295, 299, 300, 301, 303, 308, 312, 346, 347, 348, 349, 351, 356, 359, 360, 361, 362, 364, 365, 368, 370, 371, 372, 374, 375, 378, 379, 380, 381, 382, 383, 384, 390, 391, 393, 394, 395, 399, 400, 402, 403, 404, 408, 409, 410, 411, 413, 414, 415, 416, 418, 419, 425, 426, 428, 429, 430, 432, 433, 434, 478, 502, 503, 504, 505, 506, 509, 510, 511, 512, 516, 517, 518, 519, 520, 521, 522, 523, 524, 526, 527, 528, 530, 531, 532, 533, 534, 535, 538, 543, 544, 545, 546, 547, 549, 550, 551, 552, 610, 611, 612, 613, 614, 615, 616, 617, 619, 620, 621, 622, 623, 624, 625, 629, 630, 631, 632, 633, 634, 635, 636, 637, 646, 649, 650, 654, 655, 656, XXII

Bibliothèque Nationale, Paris: 137, 138, 143, 159, 202, 207, 282, 283, 284, 285, 286, 287, 288, 289, 290, 344, 398, XXXII

Bildarchiv Preussischer Kulturbesitz, Berlin: XXXV

Bulloz, Paris: 151, 304, 405, XI

Cirani, N./Ricciarini, L., Milan: XXXI, XXXIX, XLIII, XLVI, XLVII

Combier, J., Macon: 317

Country Life, London: 33, 34, 35, 41, 42, 48, 50, 51, 54, 55, 56, 68, 93, 96, 97, 98, 101, 103, 105, 106, 111, 153, 238, 239, 240, 241, 244, 247, 251, 252, 253, 254, 255, 256, 257, 258, 260, 262, 264, 265, 268, 269, 271, 272, 274, 275, 280, 281, 328, 437, 454, 455, 458, 459, 460, 463, 464, 465, 573, 575, 577, 587, 588, 595, 598, 599, V

Courtauld Institute of Art, London: 64, 67, 95, 246, 248, 249, 270, 333, 466, 592, 593, 600, 601

Dalton, C., Daventry: 99, 100

Danver, A.G., Bordeaux: X

De Grivel, J., Besançon: 190, 191, 192, 193, 194

Deutsche Fotothek Dresden, Dresden: 59, 60, 61

Fitzwilliam Museum, Cambridge: 152

Fotocielo, Rome: 540

Gibson, J.M., Guildford, Surrey: 69

Giraudon, Paris: 4, 78, 174, 187, 201, 216, 217, 221, 223, 298, 314, 385, 386, 387, 396

Godfrey New Photographics Ltd., Sidcup: XIV, XLV

Greater London Council, Photographic Unit Department of Architecture and Civil Design, London: 435, 451, 467, 469

Irish National Trust Archive, Dublin: 572

Kersting, A.F., London: 263, 462, 604, VI, XV, XVI, XVII, XVIII, XIX, XX, XXI, XLIV

Kupferstich Kabinett und Sammlungen der Zeichnungen, Berlin: XXXVI

Landesbildstelle, Berlin: 109, 110, 470

Lauros-Giraudon, Paris: II, XII, XIII, XXV, XXVI, XXVII, XXVIII, XXX

Leeds Art Galleries, Leeds: 267

Library of Congress, Washington, D.C.: 557, 558, 559, 560, 561, 562, 564, 565, 566, 567

Liot, R., St.-Germain-en-Laye: 197

Mayer, N./Ricciarini, L., Milan: VIII

Mensy, Besançon: 80

Münchner Stadtmuseum, Munich: 477

Musée de Strasbourg, Strasbourg: 186

Musei Vaticani, Archivio Fotografico, Rome: 513, 514, 515

National Monuments Record, London: 336

National Museet, Copenhagen: 497, 498, 499, 500

National Trust, London: 39, 45, 65, 66, 574

Newbert, S.W., London: 342

Novosti Press, Rome: 482, 483, 484, 485, 486, 487, 488, 489, 490, 491, 492, 494, 495, 496

Pagliarani, A., Verona: 507

Perret, F., La Chaux-de-Fonds: 195, 196

Photo Pierrain-Carnavalet, Paris: 79, 125, 131, 165, 204, 205

Pineider, G.B., Florence: 525

Pitkin Pictorials Ltd., London: XLVIII

Studio Pizzi, Milan: XXIX

Reilly and Constantine Commercial, Birmingham: 639

Ricciarini, L., Milan: XL, XLII

H. Roger-Viollet, Paris: 406, 407

Royal Commission on Ancient Monuments (Scotland), Edinburgh: 108, 259, 261, 447, 448

Royal Commission on Historical Monuments (England), London: 329, 335, 336, 338, 438, 439, 440, 441, 443, 444, 446, 459, 461, 576, 578, 580, 581, 582, 583, 584, 585, 590, 591, 594, 596, 597, 607, VII. All rights reserved.

Royal Library, Copenhagen: 498

Scott, T., Edinburgh: 44

Semper-Archiv der ETH, Zurich: 662, 663, 664

Service Photographique des Archives Nationales, Paris: 323

Simion, F./Ricciarini, L., Milan: I, IX, XLI

Smith, E., London: 445

Sir John Soane's Museum, London: 242, 243, 330, 331, 339, 340, 343, XXIII, XXIV

Staatliche Antikesammlungen, Munich: XXXVII, XXXVIII

Staatliche Schlösser und Gärten, Berlin: XXXIV

Stoedtner, F., Düsseldorf: 472

Tate Gallery, London: 115

Thorvaldsen Museum, Copenhagen: 501

Topical Press, London: 341. All rights reserved.

University Library, Warsaw: 154

Verroust, J., Neuilly: 2

Verwaltung der Staatlichen Schlösser, Gärten, und Seen, Munich: 479

Victoria and Albert Museum, London: 30, III, XLIX

Wallace Collection, London: 144. All rights reserved.

Work in Progress/Ricciarini, L., Milan: XXXIII